The Politically Incorrect Guide™ to

the Bible

The **Politically Incorrect Guide**™ to
the Bible

Robert J. Hutchinson

Since 1947
REGNERY
PUBLISHING, INC.
An Eagle Publishing Company • Washington, DC

Library of Congress Cataloging-in-Publication Data
    Hutchinson, Robert, 1957–
    The politically incorrect guide to the Bible / Robert Hutchinson.
    p. cm.
    Includes bibliographical references and index.
    ISBN 978-1-59698-520-9
    1. Bible—Evidences, authority, etc. I. Title.
    BS480.H88 2007
    220.1—dc22

                          2007034533

Published in the United States by
Regnery Publishing, Inc.
One Massachusetts Avenue, NW
Washington, DC 20001
www.regnery.com

Manufactured in the United States of America

10 9 8 7 6 5 4 3 2 1

Books are available in quantity for promotional or premium use. Write to Director of Special Sales, Regnery Publishing, Inc., One Massachusetts Avenue NW, Washington, DC 20001, for information on discounts and terms or call (202) 216-0600.

For Robert, James, Kelly,
Mary, and Jane

CONTENTS

Chapter One

WHY DO THE HEATHENS RAGE?

"We're told that four-fifths of American homes have a Bible, so go get it," bellows Penn Jillette of the controversial comedy/magic act Penn & Teller, on their Showtime TV series, *Penn & Teller: Bullsh*t!*

"Really, no kidding! Go get your g*dda*n Bible! If you don't read along with us tonight, you're going to think we're making this sh*t up."

And so begins the controversial duo's debunking of the holy scriptures of Christianity and Judaism—a twenty-eight-minute foul-mouthed harangue exhibiting all the erudition of a biker bar and just about as much sensitivity.

Penn, a towering lumberjack of a man with a ponytail and Norris Skipper goatee, does all the talking in the show while Teller illustrates his points with little magic tricks.

"Tonight, we're going to take you through the da*n Bible and show you it's full of inaccuracies, inconsistencies, and outright impossibilities... that it's more fiction than fact," he announces solemnly—and then, thumping his black leather Bible, he adds, "You know, being on TV, in a suit, and yelling with this da*n book in my hand.... I look just like one of those evangelical assh*les."

On and on it goes.

Guess what?

- Contrary to what anti-religious secularists assert, far more lives have been snuffed out throughout history by faith-hating fanatics than by religious believers.

- The total number of people murdered by their own anti–Judeo-Christian governments in the twentieth century equals about 170 million.

Anyone who says that Christianity in general, and the Bible in particular, are not mocked in popular culture has not been watching TV in a while.

Penn and Teller trot out a handful of alleged biblical "experts"—such as Michael Shermer, publisher of *Skeptic* magazine—to make their case against the Bible.

"The more we learn about archaeology and history of biblical times," says Shermer excitedly, "the more we realize that most of the stuff in the Bible is fiction."

Want proof?

In the first chapter of Genesis, Shermer points out, Adam and Eve are created at the same time. In the second chapter, Adam is created first.

See? Right off the bat, you know the whole book is a complete fraud. Inconsistencies like that just rattle your faith to the very bone.

"Sometimes the Bible is the word of God," explains Penn, "sometimes it's the word of one man, sometimes it's the word of two men. Sometimes the Bible is literal, and sometimes it's simply symbolic."

Clearly, this makes it unreliable and a waste of time.

All of this might be merely amusing—yet another example of how high you can climb in Hollywood with a high school education—were it not for the fact that such village-atheist assaults on the Bible are now commonplace in public schools, universities, the media, and even some elite seminaries.

It wouldn't be so bad if these attacks on the Bible represented something genuinely *new*—something witty and entertaining on the level of, say, a Nietzsche or a Swinburne—but instead they are merely repetitions of allegations made for about 1,800 years. They are as original as dirt—and about as interesting. The problem is, many of these new champions of enlightened reason, standing on high from the pinnacles of academia, don't appear to be aware that their ideas are *literally* millennia old.

The Bible's enemies

The Bible was not exactly a raging best-seller when it was first "published" in the centuries after Jesus's death. The Romans didn't particularly like the Jews to begin with, considering them barbaric and quite primitive. In the Jewish Wars of 66–70 AD, the Romans put down the Jewish fight for freedom with definitive ferocity: Up to a million Jews were slaughtered and the holy city of Jerusalem (and its world-famous Temple) was razed to the ground.

Scripture Says

"Why do the heathen rage, and the people imagine a vain thing? The kings of the earth set themselves, and the rulers take counsel together, against the Lord, and against his anointed, saying, 'Let us break their bands asunder, and cast away their cords from us.'"

Psalm 2:1–3

When Christianity came on the scene, it was viewed as worse—a bizarre, superstitious cult whose founder, a wild-eyed Jewish fanatic stirring up trouble, was sensibly put to death. His erstwhile followers were said to meet secretly where they ate human flesh and drank human blood. There were rumors of rampant immorality, even incestuous orgies, as the members of the cult referred to one another as "brother" and "sister." Plainly, as "new religions" go, this Eastern superstition had little to recommend it when compared with, say, the elevated mystery rites of Isis or Mithra or the Stoics.

And then there was their holy book!

If there was anything designed to chase an educated Roman away from Christianity, it was the Christian Bible.

The Christian and Jewish scriptures had to be seen to be believed, they said: A ragtag collection of folktales, strange laws, badly written letters, biographies of wonder-working magicians—all written with no regard to literary style, verbal felicity, or the rules of rhetoric.

To educated Romans raised on the polished elegance of Virgil and Cicero, Ennius and Cato, the Christian writings were positively juvenile, filled with vulgar misspellings, absurd grammatical errors, and ridiculous plots. As the second century Latin Christian apologist Tertullian put it, "Men are so far from accepting our Scriptures, no one approaches them unless he is already a Christian." St. Augustine, the greatest theologian of the first millennium of Christianity, was so put off by the Bible he ignored it (and Christianity) for a dozen years.

"It is clear to me that the writings of the Christians are a lie, and that your fables are not well-enough constructed to conceal this monstrous fiction," said the second-century anti-Christian polemicist Celsus. "I have heard that some of your interpreters . . . are on to the inconsistencies and, pen in hand, alter the original writings, three, four, and several more times over in order to be able to deny the contradictions in the face of criticism."[1]

Who Said It?

"The Bible has been the Magna Carta of the poor and oppressed. The human race is not in a position to dispense with it."

Thomas Huxley

As an example of the absurd stories found in the Christian and Jewish scriptures, Celsus cites the account of Noah's ark: "So too their fantastic story—which they take from the Jews—concerning the flood and the building of an enormous ark, and the business about the message being brought back to the survivors of the flood by a dove (or was it an old crow?). This is nothing more than a debased and nonsensical version of the myth of Deucalion, a fact I am sure they would not want to come light."

Nor was Celsus alone in his contempt for Christianity and the Bible. Around the year 280 AD, the Roman philosopher Porphyry wrote a fifteen-volume work entitled *Against the Christians*. It was a runaway bestseller for its time. Sort of a third-century version of Penn & Teller, only with more education, Porphyry wrote a witty, sarcastic refutation of the Bible almost line by line. Modern-day critics insist that science, archaeology, and critical scholarship have all "proven" that Moses did not write one word of the Torah. They then sit back, with a look of triumph on their faces, as though such a declaration will shock anyone.

The trouble is, Porphyry said the same thing—only he said it 1,700 years ago: "'If you believed Moses, you would have believed me, for he wrote concerning me,'" Porphyry begins, quoting Jesus in the Gospel of John. "He said it, but all the same nothing which Moses wrote has been preserved. For all his writings are said to have been burnt along with the temple. All that bears the name of Moses was written 1,180 years afterwards, by Ezra and those of his time. And even if one were to concede that the writing is that of Moses, it cannot be shown that Christ was anywhere called God, or God the Word, or Creator. And pray who has spoken of Christ as crucified?"[2]

Of course, repeating past criticism doesn't make it false, but one might think that real journalists (assuming they exist) might be curious as to whether these criticisms evoked any responses over the millennia. There are literally thousands of books written by Christian apologists attempting to present rational answers to "Bible difficulties"—alleged historical or scientific contradictions, historical inaccuracies, textual variants, apparent misquotations or erroneous citations of biblical texts by later authors, and so on. Some of these explanations are convincing, others less so—often depending upon how you understand the doctrine of biblical inspiration and how the Bible came to be written.

Oftentimes, the "inconsistencies" and "errors" that critics allege are found in the Bible are little more than misunderstandings of what we mean when we say that the Bible is an "inspired" text. Believers do not mean, and never have meant, the Bible was "dictated" by God in the way that Mohammed says the Koran was dictated. Even Christians who affirm that the Bible is "inerrant" also agree that it was written by limited, fallible human beings within a real historical context, speaking a human language (with all its limitations and accommodations), making use of certain literary forms and social conventions, and possessing a certain worldview

Atheist "Wisdom" Versus the Good Book

"Thou goest to Women? Do not forget thy whip!"

Friedrich Nietzsche

"Husbands, love your wives, even as Christ also loved the church, and gave himself for it."

Ephesians 5:25

which they inherited from their time and place. In other words, proper interpretation and understanding of these ancient texts require patient study and analysis—something difficult to sum up during thirty seconds of *Good Morning America*.

Too often, critics of the Bible mistake descriptions of actual human conduct for God's will. "Whenever we read the obscene stories, the voluptuous debaucheries, the cruel and tortuous executions, the unrelenting vindictiveness with which more than half the Bible is filled, it would be more consistent that we call it the word of a demon than the word of God," wrote Thomas Paine in his notorious *The Age of Reason*. "It is a history of wickedness that has served to corrupt and brutalize mankind."

The notion that you can read an encyclopedia of ancient wisdom like the Bible—written over the course of 1,000 years, in three difficult ancient languages, by many different human authors spread across the breadth of the Middle East—the same way you read a newspaper article only reveals an astonishing comic book (for lack of a better word) understanding of the ancient world.

For Christians, therefore, these and similar attacks on the biblical texts often just seem silly, not threatening. It would be as though they heard a TV news anchor on one of the major networks announce:

"This just in. Scholars at the University of Tübingen in Germany have discovered that there is actually more than one Christian gospel written about the life of Jesus. While Christians continually refer to 'the' Gospel, it turns out that there are actually *many* of them—and they do not always agree on all the details of Jesus's life. The inconsistencies in the various accounts of Jesus's life raise new, often troubling questions about the reliability and authority of these foundational Christian texts. . . . "

The news that there is more than one Christian gospel and they do not always agree on all the details of Jesus's life may be shocking and new to members of the elite media (or even to Penn and Teller) but does not, as astonishing as it may seem, really shake the faith of ordinary believers—most of all because Christians have known these facts for two millennia.

The elites against the people

For approximately 1.8 billion people on the planet—roughly 1 billion Roman Catholics, 280 million Orthodox, 473 million Anglicans and Protestants, and 14 million Jews—the Bible is revered, in one way or another, as the word of God.

It's a source of divine inspiration, moral guidance, and the foundation of Western civilization. There are differences among denominations, of course, but a general consensus exists among faithful Christians and Jews worldwide that the biblical texts communicate vital, often shocking and unusual truths central for our self-understanding and the key to our eternal destinies.

But for an influential group of academic, government, and media elites, the Bible, far from being the cornerstone of Western civilization, is actually the source of most of the evil in the world today—a veritable cornucopia of superstition, obscurantism, and "bad taste."

"Long before modern inquiry and painstaking translation and excavation had helped enlighten us, it was well within the compass of a thinking person to see that the 'revelation' at Sinai and the rest of the Pentateuch was an ill-carpentered fiction, bolted into place well after the nonevents that it fails to describe convincingly or even plausibly," asserts the irascible but always entertaining British journalist Christopher Hitchens in his 2007 book, *God Is Not Great: How Religion Poisons*

Everything.[3] "Intelligent schoolchildren have been upsetting their teachers with innocent but unanswerable questions ever since Bible study was instituted."

Village idiots...er...atheists

The term recently coined for these dogmatic, inflexible, increasingly totalitarian ideologues is "secular fundamentalist," those who believe (despite all evidence to the contrary) that the triumph of civilization has been largely accomplished through the systematic debunking and elimination of religious belief, by force if necessary.

Of course, there have always been village atheists and skeptics in the West—some intelligent, others much less so—fulminating against biblical prohibitions that inhibit their lifestyles.

The Marquis de Sade, for example, the eighteenth-century libertine from whom the word "sadism" was coined, insisted that religions are "cradles of despotism" against which enlightened persons must rebel— primarily through lots and lots of extramarital sex. "Sex is as important as eating or drinking and we ought to allow the one appetite to be satisfied with as little restraint or false modesty as the other," he proclaimed.

In the past, the anti-religious rants were more or less confined to isolated individuals, fulminating in tracts against society and Christianity. The 1960s and 1970s changed that as the secular fundamentalists took control of the media and many academic and government institutions.

Thus, in the West and particularly in the United States, we have the increasingly combustible situation in which most people hold fairly traditional views about the Bible and religion, while a minority of privileged elites is not only indifferent, but actually *hostile* toward them.

If you think that judgment is too harsh, consider the case of Robert Reich. According to Reich, former U.S. labor secretary during the Clinton administration, the "greatest danger we face" in the twenty-first century is—not terrorism, not epidemic disease, not poverty or famine or war—but religious belief itself.

Writing in *The American Prospect*, Reich stated the secular fundamentalist viewpoint with admirable frankness:

> The great conflict of the twenty-first century may not be between the West and terrorism. Terrorism is a tactic, not a belief. The underlying battle will be between modern civilization and anti-modernists; between those who believe in the primacy of the individual and those who believe that human beings owe blind allegiance and identity to a higher authority; between those who give priority to life in this world and those who believe that human life is no more than preparation for an existence beyond life; between those who believe truth is revealed solely through scripture and religious dogma, and those who rely primarily on science, reason, and logic. Terrorism will disrupt and destroy lives. But terrorism itself is not the only danger we face.[4]

If the "great conflict of the twenty-first century" is, as Reich says, between secularists and religious believers, that would put the secularists at war with virtually the entire planet. The world's population is estimated at 6.5 billion.[5] The number of people who claim some religious affiliation stands at about 5.8 billion.[6] Reich and his fellow secularists see as their enemy (real or potential) the overwhelming majority of mankind.

And Reich is not unique in his extremism.

American universities and newspapers are literally bursting at the seams with a kaleidoscopic assortment of former '60s "revolutionaries" or neo-Marxists who espouse similar beliefs.

According to Timothy Shortell, a professor of sociology at the City University of New York's Brooklyn College, "religion without fanaticism is a logical impossibility." In a brief essay published online in

2005, Dr. Shortell elaborated on the essential link between religious belief and murder:

> Anyone whose mind is trapped inside such a mental prison [as religion] will be susceptible to extreme forms of hatred and violence. Faith is, by its very nature, obsessive-compulsive. All religions foment their own kind of holy war. (Those whose devotion is moderate are only cowardly fanatics.) . . . It is no wonder, then, that those who are religious are incapable of moral action, just as children are. . . . The immaturity represents a significant social problem, however, because religious adherents fail to recognize their limitations. So, in the name of their faith, these moral retards are running around pointing fingers and doing real harm to others. . . . They discriminate, exclude, and belittle. They make a virtue of close-mindedness and virulent ignorance. They are an ugly, violent lot.[7]

The British champion of neo-Darwinian evolution, Richard Dawkins, likes to use the same sort of language. Opposition to evolutionary dogma, he says, "comes from an exceedingly retarded, primitive version of religion, which unfortunately is at present undergoing an epidemic in the United States." The United States, he adds, is "slipping towards a theocratic Dark Age."[8]

Charming, no? In the early 1990s, media elites believed—as the famous quote from the *Washington Post* had it—that religious people were "largely poor, uneducated, and easy to command."[9] Now, alas, they've become dangerous. The handful of "moderate" Christians and Jews are simply "cowardly fanatics." There it is in a nutshell: the worldview shared in newsrooms and faculty lounges across America and Europe (although, truth be told, newspaper reporters have slightly better manners).

For secular fundamentalists, religion in general, and the Bible in particular, are not just wrongheaded but actually dangerous. That's because religion and the Bible stand in the way of everything they value most in life—primarily unlimited sex, of course, but also the power to reshape society into a kind of secular utopia free from traditional ethical restraint.

The sudden eruption of Islamic terrorism worldwide has given secular fundamentalists the excuse they've long needed to basically draw a circle around all religious belief—from the Taliban to the World Council of Churches to the Dalai Lama—and insist that, well, it's all the same thing. In principle, they imply, Mother Teresa was no different from Osama bin Laden: only her methods differed.

Thus, former *New Republic* editor Andrew Sullivan—a disgruntled Catholic upset that the Vatican won't declare homosexuality just another "lifestyle choice"—now writes routinely of "Christianist" organizations and figures.

Drawing a parallel with "Islamist" figures who advocate mass suicide bombings, these menacing "Christianist" figures, Sullivan says, are now scheming to impose a kind of Christian theocracy on the enlightened secular societies of the West. Those who object to partial birth abortion, for example—or to the creation of animal-human embryos in laboratory experiments—are no different from Islamic terrorist groups. As the anti-religion crusader Sam Harris put it, "Those opposed to therapeutic stem-cell research on religious grounds constitute the biological and ethical equivalent of a flat-earth society."

Atheist "Wisdom" Versus the Good Book

"A single death is a tragedy; a million deaths is a statistic."

Joseph Stalin

"Are not two sparrows sold for a farthing? And one of them shall not fall on the ground without your Father. But the very hairs of your head are all numbered. Fear ye not therefore, ye are of more value than many sparrows."

Matthew 10:29–31

Harris—the author of the 2005 bestseller and National Book Award–winning *The End of Faith* and, most recently, *Letter to a Christian Nation*—is merely one of a number of widely celebrated writers to warn the world about the growing menace of religious convictions.

According to his biography, Harris is a graduate in philosophy from Stanford University who is currently pursuing a doctorate in neuroscience at UCLA. The stated purpose of his book is not to describe an actual social reality (the end of faith), but rather to issue a call to arms to secular fundamentalists everywhere to drive religious persons of all persuasions out of the public sphere altogether.

Harris openly and proudly insists that what the world needs now is *intolerance*, not tolerance. He reminds the educated reader of the old menacing claim by the eighteenth-century *philosophe* Denis Diderot that

The Bible in American History, Part I

"The Bible is worth all other books which have ever been printed."

Patrick Henry

"It is impossible to rightly govern the world without God and Bible."

George Washington

"Our constitution was made only for a moral and religious people . . . so great is my veneration of the Bible that the earlier my children begin to read, the more confident will be my hope that they will prove useful citizens in their country and respectful members of society."

John Adams

"men will never be free until the last king is strangled in the entrails of the last priest." Or in Harris's own words:

> To speak plainly and truthfully about the state of our world—to say, for instance, that the Bible and the Koran both contain mountains of life-destroying gibberish—is antithetical to tolerance as moderates currently conceive it. But we can no longer afford the luxury of such political correctness. We must finally recognize the price we are paying to maintain the iconography of our ignorance.[10]

Harris's solution is to eliminate biblical religion because "the degree to which religious ideas still determine government policies—especially those of the United States—presents a grave danger to everyone."

Religion the greatest danger to world peace? Think again

Harris's basic arguments are hardly original, but they have an unfortunate pedigree. For more than three hundred years, from the French *philosophes* to Marx, Lenin, and the "death of God" theologies of the 1960s, we have been assured that, freed from the superstitions and imbecilities of organized religion, rational secularists could make the world into a utopia. The results have invariably been horrific—from the Terror of the French Revolution to the terrors of Nazism and Communism.

Contrary to what anti-religious zealots such as Harris assert, throughout history far more lives have been snuffed out by faith-hating fanatics than by religious believers.

Historical demographers estimate that, in the 350 years between 1478 and 1834, the Spanish Inquisition was responsible for the execution of between 2,000 (*Encyclopaedia Britannica*) and 32,000 people (Paul Johnson, *A History of the Jews,* 1987).

That works out to about ninety-seven people a year—a ghastly number, to be sure, but a far cry from the "millions" routinely cited by secular fundamentalists.

As for the "witch hunts," another example Harris and others give of irrational religious fanaticism, the British historian Norman Davies estimates 50,000 people, primarily women, were executed as witches over a four-hundred-year period—an average of about 125 a year.

Yet as horrible as these examples of religious intolerance may be, they pale in comparison with the single-minded, bloodthirsty, satanic fury unleashed upon the innocent by secular fundamentalists—those militantly atheistic regimes that sought to expunge religion from society altogether and which, like Harris, claimed that religious belief and "bourgeois" morality represented intolerable obstacles to social progress.

According to research conducted by the political scientist Rudolph Rummel at the University of Hawaii, the officially atheist states of the Communist bloc committed more acts of genocide than any societies in history. The total number of people murdered by their own anti-Christian governments in the twentieth century—communist, socialist, fascist—equals about 170 million:[11]

- USSR: 61 million people murdered 1917–1987
- Communist China: 35.2 million people murdered 1949–present
- Mao's army: 3.4 million people murdered 1923–1949
- Nazi Germany: 20 million people murdered 1932–1945
- Communist Poland: 1.6 million people murdered 1945–1948
- Communist Cambodia: 2 million people murdered 1975–1979
- Communist Vietnam: 1.6 million people murdered 1945–1975

- Communist Yugoslavia: 1 million people murdered 1944–1987
- Anti-Christian Mexican Revolution: 1.4 million people murdered 1900–1920
- Turkey: 1.8 million people murdered 1900–1918
- Pakistan: 1.5 million people murdered 1958–1987
- Japan: 5.9 million people murdered 1936–1945

And these numbers don't even include the people killed in the *wars* initiated by these officially anti-Christian states—such as the estimated 25 million soldiers killed in World War II.[12]

These are the people lined up against brick walls and shot—often for the crime of merely believing in God—by the rational, more "scientific" social planners of Communist Russia and China, or anti-Christian Mexico and Germany.

Rummel's conclusion is as shocking as it is inescapable: War wasn't the most deadly evil to afflict humanity in the twentieth century. Government was! And not just any government, but atheist government.

As a result, ordinary people—whether religious or not—might be forgiven their general skepticism when today's secular fundamentalists talk about the "intolerance" and "violence" of biblical religion or the people who believe in it.

In terms of raw numbers—which is the only kind of evidence that rationalists such as Harris claim to accept—the evidence is incontrovertible: Freed of any moral restraint, believing that the ends justify the means, scoffing at the notion that they will ever answer to a power higher than themselves, the murderous dictators of atheistic regimes feel little hesitation in committing mass murder if they believe it will advance their more "rational," more "scientific" social aims.

Christopher Hitchens in his book *God Is Not Great* lamely tries to deflect atheism's contribution to global genocide by insisting that all

A Book Atheists Want to Burn

The Black Book of Communism, by Stephane Courtois; Cambridge: Harvard University Press, 1999. This "Black Book" of Communism tallies up all of the horrors caused by the atheistic Communist states of the twentieth century.

tyrannies are really theocratic; and, in any event, Christianity, he says, didn't do enough to stop fascism and Stalinism.

As for Richard Dawkins, he is only slightly more candid. In *The God Delusion*, he concedes that Hitler was ferociously anti-Christian, and that Stalin, Mao, and the other Communist tyrants were dogmatic atheists. He agrees that they were among the greatest mass murderers in history. But, he says, the difference between religious people who kill and atheists who kill is that there is "not the smallest evidence" that atheism per se "influences people to do bad things." Dawkins adds, "Individual atheists may do evil things but they don't do evil things in the name of atheism."[13]

But didn't the atheist dictators of the eighteenth, nineteenth, and twentieth centuries kill priests, nuns, monks, and believers? Did they not kill in the name of science, rational state planning, and revolutionary "morality"?

If God is dead...

Indeed, it was their arrogant belief in the absolute power of the State—in direct opposition to the teaching of the Bible—that led to the horrors of their regimes. It was precisely atheism's teachings that there are no "bourgeois" moral limits—no moral limits whatsoever—that allowed atheistic states to commit mass murder in the name of a higher cause. As Dostoevsky's Grand Inquisitor put it, "If God is dead, all things are permitted."

Most Americans—and all believing Jews and Christians—believe that there are moral limits, that all things are *not* permitted. Some are sinful, some are evil; and we should put our trust not in an all-powerful government, but in all-powerful God who is Himself concerned with our morality and has in fact revealed standards of right and wrong.

We can only gasp in wonder at the wholesale historical ignorance displayed by contemporary secular fundamentalists—their utter lack of knowledge about events as recent as the fall of the Berlin Wall—when they start prattling on about how much more "rational" atheists are and how much more "moral" their social policies would be, freed from the superstitious morality of biblical religion.

A century of firsthand, bloody experience with "rational" atheism has proven that it is atheism, not the Bible or religious belief, that is the greatest danger to world peace.

Chapter Two

THE STONES CRY OUT

I t was the most important archaeological find for the study of the Hebrew Bible since the discovery of the Dead Sea Scrolls. In 1979, a team of Israeli archaeologists discovered nine caves on the hillside just west of Jerusalem in the Valley of Hinnom.

The caves were ancient burial sites that date back to the tenth century BC. Inside one of the caves archaeologists discovered two tiny silver scrolls or amulets, each about the size of a cigarette butt, upon which were written lines in Old Hebrew script. This ancient writing, similar to that found on the Samaritan Torah scrolls, is believed by some Jews to be the same script that Exodus 32:16 says God used when writing the tablets of the Ten Commandments ("The tablets were God's work, and the writing was God's writing, incised upon the tablets").

Because of their delicate condition, four years elapsed before archaeologists were able to unroll the scrolls. When they did, they couldn't believe their eyes: In tiny, almost microscopic letters, they saw the mysterious tetragrammaton YHWH [יהוה], the sacred, ineffable name of God in the Hebrew Bible—one of the few times the full name had been found in Israel or anywhere in the world.

Working with scientists at NASA's Jet Propulsion Laboratory in Pasadena in the early 1990s, archaeologists and paleographers used

Guess what?

▣ Compared with other ancient historical works, the Bible has a tremendous amount of archaeological and historical support.

▣ Skeptics' complaints of no archaeological proof of Pontius Pilate were refuted in 1962 in the form of an inscription mentioning Pilate, "prefect of Judea."

infrared imaging technologies and computer image-processing programs to draw out previously invisible writing on the scrolls. The results took their breath away. Both scrolls, dated to the seventh century BC, had inscribed upon them the Priestly Blessing from Numbers 6:24–26: "May the Lord bless you and keep you; may the Lord cause his face to shine upon you and be gracious to you; may the Lord lift up his countenance upon you and give you peace."

The significance of this find was immediately apparent.

In that hillside cave in Jerusalem, the archaeologists had happened upon the oldest extant piece of the Hebrew Bible in existence—one dating four centuries earlier than the Dead Sea Scrolls. But equally important, the discovery called into question recent skeptical theories that postulate that the Torah was written very late—during or even after the Babylonian Exile of 560 BC—by scribes who learned their monotheism from Zoroastrian priests in Babylon. Instead, the writing on the tiny silver amulets suggested that the Hebrew text of the Torah was in existence much earlier than skeptical modern scholars have assumed—and was so revered that portions of it were inscribed in silver and worn around the neck.

The discovery of the Ketef Hinnom amulets, as they are known, is an example of how recent archaeological discoveries are often strengthening more traditional views of the Bible's origins, undermining some scholarly certainties. The Israeli archaeologist Yohanan Aharoni, hardly a conservative, insists that recent archaeological discoveries such as the Ketef Hinnom amulets "have decisively changed the entire approach of Bible critics. . . . No authors or editors could have put together or invented these stories hundreds of years after they happened."[1]

This isn't the first time that archaeological discoveries have undermined the unquestioned certitudes of modern skeptics. Time and again, archaeology has verified the existence of places, people, and events we once knew solely from biblical records. These discoveries by no means prove that the Bible is divinely inspired, or "inerrant," but they do bolster the credibility of the biblical texts as containing real historical records.

A few examples:

The Merneptah Stela

Scripture Says

"Jesus answered, 'It is written: 'Man does not live on bread alone, but on every word that comes from the mouth of God.'"

Matthew 4:4

In the nineteenth century, as in our own, some scholars questioned the reliability of the biblical narratives. Then, as now, some even suggested that the Israelites never really existed at all as a separate people—that is, until a seven-foot slab of black granite was discovered in a temple in Thebes, Egypt, in 1896. Written in hieroglyphics, the stela boasts of the Egyptian pharaoh Merneptah's conquest of Libya and peoples in Palestine, including the Israelites. One line reads, "Israel is laid waste; its seed is not." Archaeologists have precisely dated the stela to "Year 5, 3rd month of Shemu (summer), day 3"—or 1209/1208 BC. This is definitive proof that, not only did a people known as Israel exist in the 1200s BC, but they were known in Egypt. Israel is grouped together with other defeated city-states in Canaan such as Gezer, Yanoam, and Ashkelon.

The House of David Inscription

In our own time, so-called biblical "minimalists," such as Thomas L. Thompson at the University of Copenhagen, have claimed that many central characters of the biblical narratives are completely fictional—that such figures as King David or Solomon never existed. But then, on July 21, 1993, archaeologists working at Tel Dan in northern Israel, near the foot of Mt. Hermon, uncovered a basalt stone, written in Old Aramaic, that explicitly mentions the House of David. Pottery fragments near where the stela was found date it to the end of the ninth or the beginning of the eighth century BC—and certainly not later than the Assyrian destruction of Tiglath Pileser III in 732 BC. The stela refers to events recorded in the Old Testament Book of II Kings and refers to how the writer "killed [Ahaz]iahu son of [Jehoram kin-] of the House of David."

The Moabite Stone (or Mesha Stela)

Compared with other ancient historical works—such as Thucydides' *History of the Peloponnesian War* or Caesar's *Gallic Wars*—the Bible has a tremendous amount of archaeological and historical support. One of the earliest pieces of evidence that the biblical chronicles concerned real persons and events was the so-called Moabite Stone discovered in 1868 by Anglican medical missionary F. A. Klein. Written in Moabite (a language related to Hebrew) around the year 930 BC, the stela is the personal testimony of a Moabite king that mentions numerous places in the Bible. "I am Mesha, son of Kemoshmelek, the king of Moab, the Dibonite," the stela begins. "My father was king over Moab for thirty years, and I became king after my father." The chronicle goes on to mention Israel and its God by name: "And [the god] Chemosh said to me, 'Go take Nebo against Israel,' and I went by night and fought against it. . . . And I took from there the altar-hearths of Yahweh, and I dragged them before Chemosh. And the king of Israel built Jabaz and dwelt in it while he fought with me and Chemosh drove him out from before me."[2] This text was written in 930 BC, yet biblical minimalists claim that Israel didn't even exist as a separate people at that time—and certainly were not ruled by a king. The Moabite text mirrors closely texts in the Bible, such as 2 Kings 3:4–5: "Now Mesha king of Moab was a sheepbreeder, and

The Bible in American History, Part II

"Education is useless without the Bible."

Daniel Webster

he regularly paid the king of Israel one hundred thousand lambs and the wool of one hundred thousand rams. But it happened, when Ahab died, that the king of Moab rebelled against the king of Israel."

Ironically, after the House of David inscription was discovered at Tel Dan in 1993, scholars returned to the Moabite Stone, housed in the Louvre in Paris, and began studying it more closely. French scholar André Lemaire discovered that the same phrase "House of David" appeared in line 31 of the Moabite Stone. It reads "And the House of [Da]vid dwelt in Hauranen.... Chemosh said to me, 'Go down, fight against Hauranen!' I went down ... and Chemosh restored it in my days." The new evidence even led *Time* magazine to conclude in 1995 that "[t]he skeptics' claim that King David never existed is now hard to defend."[3]

Pharaoh Shishak/Shoshenq's Victory Lists

The book of Chronicles relates that the Egyptian pharaoh Shishak (or Shoshenq) came "with twelve hundred chariots and threescore thousand horsemen" and plundered Israel's capital, as well as such towns and fortresses as Rehov, Megiddo, and Hazor. Archaeologists have long known that Shoshenq's exploits, carved on a monument in the temple of Amun at Karnak, have been confirmed by extra-biblical sources. But a discovery in 2003 at Tel Rehov in Israel, using highly sophisticated techniques of radio-carbon dating, provided additional proof that the biblical account is precisely correct. In the process, it also undermined the theories of biblical minimalists or skeptics, such as Israel Finkelstein and Thomas Thompson, who claim David and Solomon never existed. The radio-carbon dating placed Shoshenq's looting at Rehov in the tenth century (925 BC) rather than the ninth. Additionally, it established that the cities Shoshenq mentions conquering—including Beth-Horon (Jo 10:10), Gibeon (Jo 9:3), Megiddo (Jo 12:21), and Gaza, (Jo 10:41)—all existed when the Bible says they did. These discoveries "have now put another nail in the coffin of [skeptic Israel] Finkelstein's theories," concluded Professor Lawrence E. Stager, director of Harvard University's Semitic Museum, in an article in the *San Francisco Chronicle*. "There's no question that Rehov and the other cities that Shoshenq conquered were indeed there at the time of Solomon. We don't need to rely any more only on the Bible or on Shoshenq's inscriptions at Karnak to establish that Solomon and his kingdom really existed, because we now have the superb evidence of the radiocarbon dates."[4]

Samaritan Ostraca

The Bible goes into great detail about the tribes of Israel, even going so far as dividing up the twelve tribes into specific clans or families. Some modern scholars don't take this seriously and doubt that there really were "Twelve Tribes" of Israel at all. That flies in the face of evidence that was discovered in 1910, under the direction of the Harvard archaeologist G. A. Reisner, in Samaria—sixty-three potsherds bearing inscriptions in Old Hebrew script written in ink, called ostraca. Among the oldest samples of ancient Hebrew writing, the ostraca are commercial records of shipments of wine and oil, but they have one characteristic of historic significance: Thirty of them name the clan or district name of seven of the ten sons of Manasseh mentioned in Joshua 17:2–3, including Abiezer, Asriel, Helek, Shechem, and Shemida. Two daughters of Zelophehad are also identified (17:3): Hoglah and Noah. These potsherds are dated to around 784–783 BC.

The Seal of Baruch

In the fourth year of King Jehoiakim's reign (c. 605 BC), God spoke to the prophet Jeremiah and told him to write his prophecies on a scroll. "Perhaps if the house of Judah hears all the disasters I intend to bring upon them, they will turn back from their wicked ways, and I will pardon their iniquity and their sin," God told Jeremiah (Jer 36:3). "So Jeremiah called

Baruch son of Neriah; and Baruch wrote down in the scroll, at Jeremiah's dictation, all the words which the Lord had spoken to him" (Jer 36:4).

In 1975, a bulla, or clay seal, bearing the name of the scribe was discovered in the antiquities market in Israel. Written in Old Hebrew (pre-exilic) script, the bulla was dated to around 600 BC and authenticated by some Israeli archaeologists. The writing on the bulla reads (left to right):

leyberechiah (Blessed of God)

ben neriyah (son of Neriah)

ha-seper (the scribe)

Many scholars and archaeologists believe the seal belonged to Baruch ben Neriah, the scribe who faithfully recorded the visions announced by the prophet Jeremiah and described in Jeremiah 36:4. Even more interesting, in 1996 a second bulla was discovered, presumably stamped with the same seal, and upon which was found a *thumbprint* embedded in the rock-hard clay—perhaps that of Baruch himself.[5] While not all archaeologists are convinced these bullae are genuine, given the sometimes shady character of the Israeli antiquities trade, they are nevertheless further evidence that the people in the Bible were not "mythic" characters but real historical figures.

The Pontius Pilate Inscription

When contemporary skeptics complain that there is "no archaeological proof" that a certain biblical figure existed—such as Moses—what they often don't admit is that there is little or no archaeological evidence for many figures of ancient history that no one seriously doubts existed. This "argument from silence" has been refuted so many times you would think that modern skeptics would stop using it. For example, until 1962 there was no archaeological proof that Pontius Pilate ever existed—and skeptics made much of the fact. But in that year, an Italian archaeologist working at Caesarea Maritima, on the coast of Israel south of Haifa—the center of government for the Roman administration in the time of Christ—found the long-sought proof. It came in the form of an inscription that mentioned *Tiberieum/[Pon]tius Pilatus/[Praef]ectus Iuda[eae]*, "Tiberius [the Roman emperor of the period]/Pontius Pilate/Prefect of Judea."

The Ebla Tablets

Some modern skeptics now concede that there may have been a minor chieftan named David, but nevertheless insist that the patriarchal narratives are entirely fictional—and no figure such as Abraham existed. What's more, they used to say, the places that Abraham visits in Genesis don't actually exist. We have no archaeological evidence for any of them. Then, in 1964, Italian archaeologists from the University of Rome began excavating a palace found at Tell Mardikh, in northern Syria. Inside the palace they found a virtual library of 15,000 well-preserved cuneiform tablets dating from around 2300 BC. Not only do these amazing tablets, written in Sumerian and Akkadian, reveal laws, customs, and events surprisingly in harmony with the account in Genesis, they also mention explicitly the five undiscovered "cities on the plain" mentioned in Genesis 14:8 that modern skeptics insist never existed—Sodom, Gomorrah, Admah, Zeboiim, and Zoar.

The Siloam Tunnel (or Hezekiah's Tunnel)

According to 1 Kings 2 and Chronicles 2, an elaborate tunnel was constructed during the reign of King Hezekiah—between 727 BC and 698 BC—to protect the Jerusalem's water supply against an imminent Assyrian siege. Most biblical scholars have long believed the 1,750-foot-long tunnel, rediscovered in 1838, did indeed date back to the time of Hezekiah; a minority insisted the passage was built centuries later. Some even claimed that an inscription at the outside of the tunnel proved it was built just before the birth of Christ. But once again, archaeology has proven the textual skeptics to be wrong. In 2003, Israeli and British scientists tested organic material within the plaster lining of the tunnel and dated it back to around 700 BC—just as the Bible says.[6] The testing represented the first time that a structure mentioned in the Bible was dated through radio-carbon methods, according to researchers Amos Frumkin, Aryeh Shimron, and Jeff Rosenbaum in their published results in *Nature* (September 2003).

The Nuzi Tablets

A common tactic that critics use when attacking the historicity of the biblical narratives is to point out cultural anomalies—customs that (allegedly) didn't exist in the period in question. For example, skeptics point to a number of customs in the Pentateuch that, they claim, do not correspond to what we "know" about the Middle East in the second millennium. But excavations in 1925 at Nuzi, in northern Iraq, discovered 4,000 tablets written in Akkadian cuneiform script that dated back to 2300 BC. The Nuzi tablets describe customs that parallel those described in Genesis—for example, a barren wife giving a slave (such as Hagar) to her husband to produce an heir or a father chosing a bride (like Rebekah) for his son. Once again, archaeological discoveries have disproven what was once "known."

Archaeological supports for biblical records

These examples show how unique the Bible really is in the context of other religions' holy books. While they do not prove that everything in the Bible is factually accurate—some chronological and historical correlation problems still remain—they certainly do demonstrate that the Bible's records of events do have substantial outside support from archaeology and other historical records. Certainly, the Bible differs in a remarkable way from many other holy texts, such as the Hindu Bhagavad-Gita or the Buddhist Tripitaka, where the connection to proven historical facts is tenuous at best. There should be no more reason to doubt the truth of

Old Testament historical documents than there is to doubt classical Greek historians Herodotus or Thucydides—whose descriptions of ancient events often lack substantial archaeological support.

The Exodus

For centuries, scholars have debated the historical reliability of the biblical account of the Exodus. But until the late 1970s, biblical scholars, historians, and archaeologists took the biblical account of the Exodus, if not at face value, then at least as a broad outline of historical events.

However, beginning in the late 1970s, a small but increasingly influential group of revisionist scholars came up with a novel way to account for all of the conflicting archaeological and textual evidence: None of it happened at all! It was all just made up!

Put another way: The central event of Jewish history—recounted faithfully each year in the Passover seder—was a complete fraud, made up out of whole cloth.

The first scholars to seriously propose this thesis appear to have been a group of Scandinavian and American scholars working at the University of Copenhagen in the late 1970s and 1980s—such as Thomas Thompson, Niels Peter Lemche, and Peter Davies. While different scholars disagree about the details, this school of thought—which is known as biblical "minimalism"—basically holds that the Bible is a work of fiction with little, if any, verifiable basis in historical fact.

The characters in the Hebrew Bible—from Abraham and Moses and David up to and including Jesus Christ—are merely nationalistic mythic constructs, no more historical than Odysseus in the *Odyssey* and Aeneas in the *Aeneid*.

When the anticlerical denizens of the media finally got wind of this story, in the late 1990s, they had a field day.

Despite the fact that the arguments against the historicity of the Exodus are hardly overwhelming—or could at least be considered "debatable"—the media predictably proclaimed that the matter was settled: The Bible had been "proven" false by archaeology—or, not just false, but an actual fraud, a deliberate lie, perpetrated and perpetuated by religious zealots (not unlike the Taliban!) determined to oppress women, perpetuate homophobia, enforce the death penalty, and so on.

Time magazine featured a cover story in 1995 entitled "Is the Bible Fact or Fiction?" that swallowed the arguments of the minimalists without question or even comment: "If they really spent forty years wandering in the desert after fleeing Egypt, the Israelites should have left at least a few traces," the *Time* article asserted. "But though scientists have evidence of human occupation in the Sinai dating to the Stone Age, nothing suggests that the Israelites were ever there."

The March 2002 issue of *Harper's* went even further. It carried an article written by Daniel Lazare entitled "False Testament: Archaeology Refutes the Bible's Claim to History."

"Not long ago, archaeologists could agree that the Old Testament, for all its embellishments and contradictions, contained a kernel of truth," wrote Lazare. "Obviously, Moses had not parted the Red Sea or turned his staff into a snake, but it seemed clear that the Israelites had started out as a nomadic band somewhere in the vicinity of ancient Mesopotamia; that they had migrated first to Palestine and then to Egypt; and that, following some sort of conflict with the authorities, they had fled into the desert under the leadership of a mysterious figure who was

Who Said It?

"I claim to be a historian. My approach to the Classics is historical. And I tell you that the evidence for the life, death, and the resurrection of Christ is better authenticated than most of the facts of ancient history."

E. M. Blaiklock, chair of classics,
Auckland University

either a lapsed Jew or, as Freud maintained, a highborn priest of the royal sun god Aton whose cult had been overthrown in a palace coup."[7]

Recent archaeological "discoveries," Lazare continued, changed all that. "In the last quarter century or so, archaeologists have seen one settled assumption after another concerning who the ancient Israelites were and where they came from proved false."

Eventually, even some clergy started parroting this line. Rabbi David Wolpe of Los Angeles told 2,000 worshippers at the Conservative Sinai Temple that "the way the Bible describes the Exodus is not the way it happened, if it happened at all."[8]

This is an astonishing remark for a rabbi to make. After all, the events of the Exodus have been central to the religious understanding of Jews (and Christians!) for millennia. Every Passover, Jews meet together for the ritual seder meal when the story is retold of the Israelites' liberation from bondage in Egypt.

What is the basis for this new skepticism? After all, for most of the twentieth century, archaeologists and historians generally believed the Exodus, in some fashion, actually occurred—even if they were unclear how all the details fit together.

In 2001, an Israeli archaeologist named Israel Finkelstein and a journalist named Neil Asher Silberman wrote a book that summarized and gave new life to the minimalist cause. It was entitled *The Bible Unearthed: Archaeology's New Vision of Ancient Israel and the Origins of Its Sacred Texts.*

One argument the authors put forth in the book is that the Exodus didn't happen at all because it's difficult to fit all the known historical dates together. Finkelstein and Silberman discuss the Hyksos, the mysterious West Semitic people who overwhelmed Egyptian society in the sixteenth century BC and who were forcibly expelled from the kingdom. The Egyptian historian Manetho (c. 250 BC) describes how the Pharaoh defeated the Hyksos, "killing many of them and pursuing the remainder to the frontiers of Syria." Finkelstein and Silberman concede that "the basic situation described in the Exodus saga—the phenomenon of immigrants coming down to Egypt from Canaan and settling in the eastern border regions of the delta—is abundantly verified in the archaeological finds and historical texts." But, they say, it's impossible to reconcile all these dates with the biblical account. So, what is Finkelstein and Silberman's conclusion? *It must be all made up!*

But as we have seen, as difficult as it is to fit all the pieces of the historical puzzle together, saying the whole story is fiction is hardly the only, or even the most logical, way to account for all the evidence.

The Hyksos, for example, may have merely been the *forerunners* of the Israelites—one of the first of many waves of impoverished Semitic peoples to seek refuge in Egypt over the course of centuries.

We know from the Amarna Letters, a series of cuneiform letters dictated by the Pharaohs Amenhoptep III (c. 1391 BC) and Tutankhamen (c. 1330 BC)[9] and discovered in the late nineteenth century, that there existed groups of foreigners known as the *'apiru* (or *habiru*) who were considered to be brigands or "disenfranchised peoples on the outskirts of society." While the *'apiru* cannot be simply equated with the Hebrews, the Egyptians may well have considered any Israelite tribe "riffraff" who were a threat to Egyptian society. Middle Eastern historian Robert Stieglitz of Rutgers University argues that carvings on a chapel of Egyptian Queen Maakare Hatshepsut refer to the expulsion of the Hyksos, in 1550, but also to a second, later expulsion of a group with "foreigners amongst them"—a reference that closely mirrors Numbers 11:4, which states that the Israelites fleeing Egypt included "a mixed multitude" (*asafsuf*) and not merely the Israelite tribe.

As for the city the Bible calls Rameses, said to have been built by the enslaved Israelites, archaeologists concede that it was indeed built and occupied at the time the Bible gives for the Exodus but may have been called by a different name at that time.

There are many ways to account for the conflicting evidence other than to simply assert that none of it happened.

A second point against the Exodus that Finkelstein and Silberman make is that we have no written records of Israelites in Egypt from Egyptian sources. The authors point out that, after the forced expulsion of the Hyksos around 1570 BC, the Egyptians established a network of forts along their eastern frontier. Some of these forts have been discovered and excavated. Archaeologists have even found a papyrus that shows how closely the Egyptian border guards, like today's customs and immigration officials, monitored movements of tribes and peoples: "We have completed the entry of the tribes of the Edomite Shasu through the fortress of Merneptah-Content-with-Truth, which is in Tjkw, to the pools of Pr-Itm . . . ," reads one entry on the papyrus.

So what does this evidence tell Finkelstein and Silberman? "If a great mass of fleeing Israelites had passed through the border fortifications of the pharaonic regime, a record should exist."

Of course, this assumes that detailed, comprehensive records, written on papyrus scrolls more than 3,200 years ago, still exist and have survived millennia of wars, revolutions, invasions, fires, floods, and other disasters.

Worse, say the authors, there is no record of Israel in Egypt whatsoever—no tomb inscriptions, no monument, no writing on the temple walls. They concede that the famous Merneptah Stela, found in Egypt in 1898 and erected by Pharaoh Merneptah, son of Rameses the Great, does mention Israel by name. Reliably dated to around 1208 BC, the stela clearly identifies a culture of people named "Israel" whom Merneptah battles in Canaan: "Israel is laid waste, its seed is not."

But the absence of the name "Israel" in Egypt inscriptions really proves nothing. The aristocratic, clean-shaven Egyptians no doubt thought of the descendants of Jacob as just another mass of hairy Semitic marauders, like the hated Hyksos. What's more, the Egyptians, like all ancient peoples, weren't in the habit of making monuments to their failures—like mass escapes of slaves.

However, this doesn't stop Finkelstein and Silberman from taking their argument a step further to assert that a mass migration of people was actually "impossible" during the reign of Rameses II. In addition to pointing out the system of forts along the Egyptian border (mainly along the coastal "Ways of Horus"), they point out that Egyptian power at the time of Rameses II was at its peak—and the Egyptians maintained military control over Canaan.

But there are a number of problems with this argument: First, it assumes that the Exodus occurred in the era of Rameses II, when there are textual arguments against that dating; and second, it ignores the fact that the Bible itself specifically insists the fleeing Israelites did *not* take the coastal road lined with forts, the "way of the Philistines' land, though this was the nearest" (Ex 13:17), but that God led them south, toward the open desert, by way of the Red Sea.

And of course, the Bible *does* describe the Egyptian army pursuing the fleeing Israelites—no fewer than "six hundred first-class chariots and all the other chariots of Egypt, with warriors on them all" (Ex 14:7).

The text even names the place where "Pharaoh's whole army" caught up with the Israelites when they were encamped at Pi-hahiroth, in front of Baal-Zephon, two place names that have not been identified. The text then describes one of the greatest miracles of the Bible.

Whether you understand the crossing of the Red Sea as it is described in Exodus 14:22 (with the waters divided like a "wall to their right and their left") or prefer to think of it in more naturalistic terms (as an army in heavy battle armor getting bogged down in swampy marshes of the "Sea of Reeds" and drowning), there is nothing inherently unrealistic in the basic scenario outlined in the Exodus account. Pharaoh's army gave chase to the fleeing, escaped slaves and fell victim to some type of disaster involving water, with the heavy infantry and charioteers drowning in the Red Sea.

But, say Finkelstein and Silberman, then why is there no archaeological evidence of a large group of people wandering in the desert for forty years? The obvious answer to anyone familiar with the Sinai Desert is that though it is a vast, forbidden wasteland of about 24,000 square miles, it has nonetheless been traversed by countless armies over the millennia, from the Roman legions to the armies of Arabia, and has been the scene of ferocious battles fought by the Arabs and Israelis in the 1956, 1967, and 1973 wars.

Finkelstein and Silberman say that despite "repeated archaeological surveys" in "all" regions of the peninsula, not a single piece of evidence has turned up of the Israelites' "generation-long wandering in the Sinai": "not even a single sherd, no structure, not a single house, no trace of an ancient encampment." This is known as an "argument from silence," and you would think that archaeologists would be humble enough to no longer make them. That's because some of the most embarrassing gaffes in the history of archaeology have been the result of such arrogant "arguments from silence."

Finkelstein and Silberman make much of the fact that archaeologists have "identified" many of the specific places mentioned in the account of the Exodus and haven't found any evidence of ancient encampments there. Specifically, they point to Kadesh-barnea, where the Bible says the Israelites encamped for thirty-eight out of the forty years of wandering in the desert. "The general location of this place is clear from the description of the southern border of the land of Israel in Numbers 34," say the authors. "It has been identified by archaeologists with the large and well-watered oasis of Ein el-Qudeirat in eastern Sinai, on the border between modern Israel and Egypt."

Well, there you have it.

Imagine: After three thousand years, not a trace of an Israelite encampment—even one that lasted thirty-eight years—remains.

Of course, the truth is that the identification of Ein el-Qudeirat with the biblical Kadesh-barnea is not universally accepted, but that is a standard tactic of the biblical minimalists who seek to undermine the believability of the biblical narratives, to treat as settled scientific "facts" what are, in truth, merely the opinions of one group of scholars or archaeologists.

A Book Atheists Want to Burn

The Stones Cry Out: What Archaeology Reveals About the Truth of the Bible, by Randall Price; Eugene, OR: Harvest House, 1997.

The authors' final refutation of the Exodus as a historic event is the claim that it is merely a fictional story, told to unite the Israelites during the reign of King Josiah in the seventh century BC. There is only one major problem with this argument: Some of the biblical prophets, such as Amos and Hosea—whom many scholars confidently date living a full century *before* King Josiah—have numerous allusions to the Exodus and the wandering in the desert. "When Israel was a child I loved him," said Hosea, "out of Egypt I called my son" (Hos 11:1). Amos begins one of his prophecies with the words, "Hear this word, O men of Israel, that the Lord pronounces over you, over the whole family that I brought up from the land of Egypt..." (Amos 3:1). If the Exodus was merely a work of fiction, written between 640 and 609 BC, then how could the prophets have made references to it a century earlier?

Finkelstein and Silberman explain this conundrum by agreeing that there was indeed a "shared memory" of a "great event in history that concerned liberation from Egypt and took place in the distant past" but that it had nothing to do, really, with the Israelites per se. Rather, there was a general collective memory of the expulsion of the Hyksos from Egypt and the authors of the biblical texts merely appropriated this collective memory and made it their own.

What Finkelstein and Silberman propose is that when it came time to invent a new "national epic saga," the authors of the Torah chose to fashion a history for themselves first as abject slaves in Egypt and then to imagine themselves invading the land they already occupied, and indeed had always occupied, destroying all their neighbors' cities and engaging in centuries of bloody warfare with . . . their own people.

In New Testament studies, when something is inherently embarrassing—such as the apostles being dim-witted—historians tend to think of it more likely being true as not because people don't tend to make up stories that make them look bad.

When we think of other "national sagas," such as the *Iliad* or the *Aeneid*, we read of heroic exploits. The Greeks, far from being abject slaves freed only by the power of God, venture forth to repair their wounded honor and destroy the Trojans in an epic battle. In the *Aeneid*, the Trojan Aeneas journeys to Italy and helps to found a new people destined to rule the world and establish truth, justice, and the Roman way. Finkelstein and Silberman want us to believe that royal scribes created a national epic for the Israelites that depicted them as impoverished slaves.

Irrefutable?

The five basic arguments against the Exodus in *The Bible Unearthed* may seem "irrefutable" to the authors, but not to many other distinguished archaeologists and scholars.

Egyptologist K. A. Kitchen argued in his 2003 book *On the Reliability of the Old Testament* that the factual details of the Exodus account—salt-tolerant reeds in the Red Sea, the habits of quails, *kewirs* (mudflats south of the Dead Sea), and so on—reflect detailed, precise knowledge of real local conditions, not something a creative novelist could know sitting in Babylon or Jerusalem.

As for the arguments from silence and the lack of Egyptian "records," Kitchen points out that "a handful of wine-vintage dockets from broken jars is the sum total of our administrative texts so far recovered from Pi-Ramesse."[10] In other words: It's not as though we are holding 3,000 years' worth of comprehensive passport and immigration records and can say, "See, there is no 'Jacob' from Canaan listed as passing through the frontier border check."

Concerning the lack of a "single sherd" in the Sinai, Kitchen also points out that terrified, fleeing refugees might be more inclined to take water skins into the desert, not earthenware amphorae that would leave sherds in the first place.

Chapter Three

ALL SCRIPTURE IS GOD-BREATHED

The Bible's account of its own origins reads like something out of a Hollywood movie. According to Exodus, sometime in the latter half of the second millennium, between 1500 and 1200 BC, the Egyptian pharaoh's adopted son named Moses (probably short for the Egyptian name Thutmoses) led a massive uprising of Semitic slaves who fled from Egypt into the desert wastes of the Sinai peninsula. There, at a mountain called Horeb, the people had a terrifying encounter with a mysterious divine power, surrounded by smoke and fire, that shook the mountain (Ex 19:18) like an earthquake.

This power (which the Bible elsewhere calls "El Aylon," or the Most High God) not only communicated with Moses directly and gave him detailed instructions for the people, but told him to write everything down:

> "Then the Lord instructed Moses, 'Write this down as a permanent record.'" (Ex 17:14)

> "Then Moses carefully wrote down all the Lord's instructions." (Ex 24:4)

> "And the Lord said to Moses, 'Write down all these instructions, for they represent the terms of my covenant with you and with Israel.'" (Ex 34:27)

Guess what?

- Most modern skeptics' attacks on the Bible are based on a profound misunderstanding of what most Christians and Jews mean by biblical inspiration.

- Most alleged biblical "inconsistencies" are simply the result of modern people imposing their own standards and values on ancient peoples with radically different lifestyles and outlooks.

What's more, according to Exodus 32:16, this mysterious divine power gave to Moses the laws we know as the Ten Commandments—inscribed on stone tablets. The first set of tablets was destroyed when the Israelite people worshipped the Golden Calf, but Moses received a second set and these were placed in a special, gold-covered chest—the Ark of the Covenant—that the Israelite people carried throughout their sojourn in the Sinai.

Later, the Ark was placed in the Temple built by Solomon and was kept there until it mysteriously disappeared sometime around the Babylonian invasion of the sixth century BC. But before the ark disappeared, 2 Kings 22 and 2 Chronicles 34 relate how, during the reign of King Josiah (c. 640–609 BC) the people of Israel had fallen into apostasy and were practicing the "abominations" of the pagans—such as child sacrifice through burning. King Josiah set about reforming Israel and ordered a massive repair effort of the Temple be undertaken. During repairs on the Temple, the ancient "book of the Torah of YHWH by the hand of Moses" (2 Chr 34:14) was rediscovered somewhere in the Temple precincts. (Most scholars believe that this Book was likely Deuteronomy.) Later, the king gathered all the leaders of the people near the Temple and "read aloud to them the entire text of the book of the covenant that had been found in the house of the Lord" (2 Chr 34:30).

He stopped the practice of child sacrifice, "removed every abominable thing from all the territory belonging to the Israelites," and "made a covenant before the Lord to follow the Lord and to keep his commandments, decrees, and statutes with his whole heart and soul, thus observing the terms of the covenant written in this book" (2 Chr 34:33). Despite the Israelite repentance, however, it was too late: Over the course of several campaigns, the Babylonian king Nebuchadnezzar (c. 605–562 BC) conquered Judah, sacked Jerusalem, despoiled the Temple of its treasures, and dragged a portion of the population into forced exile.

After the Babylonian Exile, the Temple would be rebuilt, albeit on a more modest scale, and then greatly expanded under King Herod the

Great in the decades before the birth of Jesus of Nazareth—but the Ark and the famed Tablets of the Law were lost to history. Many people believe that the Temple priests, aware of the impending Babylonian invasion, would almost certainly have hidden away such a precious treasure of Israel—as the Qumran community hid the Dead Sea

Scripture Says

"I tell you," he replied, "if they keep quiet, the stones will cry out."

Luke 19:40

Scrolls from the advancing Roman legions in 68 AD. The book 2 Maccabees, written in Greek around 124 BC, refers to ancient records that describe how the prophet Jeremiah took the Ark and hid it in a cave on Mt. Nebo (2 Mc 2:4–10)—a remark that most scholars dismiss as legend.

Some Orthodox rabbis believe that the Ark and the Tablets of the Covenant were hidden, not in a distant cave, but in a secret chamber in the very foundation of the Solomonic Temple, below the Muslim Dome of the Rock on the Temple Mount in Jerusalem, and still exist today. Such a belief, while not widely shared, is certainly not outside the realm of possibility. The foundation and retaining walls of the Temple are one of the wonders of history: The largest single block is forty-two feet long, fourteen feet deep, and fifteen feet high and weighs 544 metric tons (in contrast, the largest block in the pyramids of Egypt weighs just ten tons). Adding to the intrigue is the fact that archaeologists have long known that the Temple foundation is crisscrossed with a maze of tunnels hundreds of feet long. One, known as Warren's Gate after its nineteenth-century discoverer, Charles Warren, surfaces just south of where some scholars believe the ancient Holy of Holies stood in the Temple, but was sealed up in 1981 in deference to Muslim sensibilities. Despite the claims of hucksters in recent years, efforts to discover a hidden chamber in which the Ark has been hidden have not been successful.

Of course, many modern scholars (but not all) do not believe there ever were any stone tablets of the law, any Ark of the Covenant, or, for that matter, any Moses. Instead, they believe the Hebrew Bible is a largely composite, sometimes fictionalized work composed very late, perhaps even after the Babylonian Exile. First popularized by the German biblical scholar Julius Wellhausen (c. 1844–1918), this approach—known as "higher criticism" and based on what is called the Documentary Hypothesis—asserts that close textual analysis reveals that the final document we call the Torah was based on a number of different sources and pieced together, over hundreds of years, by many different editors.

These critical scholars claim they can discern at least three, sometimes four or six, major written sources that were woven together in the tapestry that is the Torah—a ninth-century BC source, known as J, that refers to God as YHWH; an eighth-century source that refers to God as Elohim, known as E; a seventh-century source that reflects the teaching of Deuteronomy, known as D; and a postexilic source that reflects the concerns of the priestly class, known as P. As they would do later in New Testament scholarship, these critical scholars would eventually claim they could actually detect *layers* of tradition within the various sources— J_1, J_2, and so on—and often their speculations became more and more esoteric. A lucid popular exposition of the theory can be found in Richard Elliott Friedman's *Who Wrote the Bible?* and *The Bible with Sources Revealed: A New View of the Five Books of Moses.*

Ironically enough, while the assumptions behind the higher criticism are still widely embraced by biblical scholars—such as the notion of prior written sources—the actual *conclusions* that have been drawn from them are far from being universally accepted, even among liberal scholars.

We do have examples of historical works that went through a gradual process of composition over centuries—the Epic of Gilgamesh is one— but we have no actual evidence of that in the case of the Bible, only hypothetical or reconstructed sources. Plus, among some scholars there is a trend to push back the dating of postulated sources to earlier and earlier periods. Put simply, even some critical scholars now believe that at least portions of the Hebrew Bible are much older than scholars originally supposed—perhaps as old as the Exodus itself.

A Book Atheists Want to Burn

On the Reliability of the Old Testament, by K. A. Kitchen; Grand Rapids, MI: Eerdmans, 2006.

Finally, it's by no means clear why the mere existence of written sources or an editing process poses any sort of logical threat to the traditional understanding of the Bible's origins. It has been known for millennia that the Bible itself mentions written sources that various authors presumably consulted in the creation of the biblical texts. Numbers mentions "the Book of the Wars of the Lord" (Numbers 21:14). Joshua talks about "the Book of Jashar" (Jo 10:13). One Kings describes the "Book of the Acts of Solomon (1 Kgs 11:41). Two Chronicles talks about "the Book of the Kings of Israel and Judah" (2 Chr 35:27).

What's more, the Bible itself gives plain evidence of different stages of composition and the existence of a later editor. As the conservative evangelical *Dictionary of the Old Testament* points out, Joshua 6:24–25 mentions the destruction of Jericho from the point of view of an eyewitness who describes the ruins that exist "until this very day" and also contains a note, apparently written centuries later, about how the spoils from the sacked city ended up in the Temple in Jerusalem (which didn't exist when Jericho was sacked).

Thus, at least some of the current controversy between liberal and conservative scholars over "who wrote the Bible" is largely unnecessary. The Bible nowhere says that Moses wrote the *entire* Torah, only that he wrote down "all the Lord's instructions." What's more, the Torah itself contains many lines that do not appear to have been written by Moses—such as when Deuteronomy describes Moses' death and funeral or when, in Deuteronomy 34:10, it is stated that "never has there been another prophet like Moses." While some conservative scholars like to say that Moses was merely prophesying about his own death or accurately describing his own greatness, others concede that it makes more sense that passages like this were written by someone other than Moses and simply put into the text at a later date. The truth is, while many conservative Christians and Jews insist that Moses wrote the entire Pentateuch, there are no overwhelming biblical arguments in support of this; on the other hand, it is just as probable that a highly literate "son of a pharaoh," educated in the Egyptian palace, could indeed have written documents that were preserved and which served as primary sources, along with the "Book of Jashar," when the Bible was edited over the centuries until it is in the form we have it today.

The fact that the final biblical texts in some instances are or could have been collaborative efforts, organized and even edited by professional scribes, in no way undermines the Jewish and Christian belief that they are divinely inspired and contain revelations from God—any more than the fact that the work of a battlefield journalist, whose original manuscript is a hastily written, unpolished effort, could be considered a "fake" if a later editor expands certain passages or reorders and even edits material for greater clarity.

What is meant by biblical inspiration

For millennia, faithful Jews and Christians have believed that the collection of ancient texts that we today call the Bible is divinely inspired—that is, that it contains truths that, in some way, were revealed by God.

The source for this belief arose, not first from a reverence for written texts, but from the *prior* belief in the reality of prophetic inspiration. The ancient Israelites believed that the mysterious, ineffable Creator of the Universe in some way communicated directly to certain chosen men and women, known as *navi'im* (prophets) or *ro'im* (seers)—preeminent among whom was the great prophet and lawgiver Moses. The Book of Leviticus alone has sixty-six instances in which it says, "The Lord spoke unto Moses..." (Lv 1:1, 4:1, 5:14, 6:1, etc.).

When the oracles of these inspired prophets were later written down, either by the prophets themselves or by their disciples and scribes, the written texts came to be revered by the Israelites and then later by the Jews as embodying God's word to human beings. The three major parts of the Hebrew scriptures that form the Tanakh, or Hebrew Bible—the Torah, the Prophets, and the Writings—are all based, in one way or another, upon prophetic utterances. That's the central truth affirmed by 2 Peter 1:19–21: "We have the prophetic word made more sure.... First of all, you must understand this, that no prophecy of scripture is a matter of one's own interpretation, because no prophecy ever came by the impulse of man, but men moved by the Holy Spirit spoke from God."

When we get to the New Testament period, however, prophecy had been absent from the land for hundreds of years. Jewish writers in this period, therefore, as well as the authors of the New Testament books and Jesus himself, routinely refer to the written Hebrew holy books as expressing God's will or even his words. The Jewish historian Josephus, a near-contemporary of Jesus writing in about 90 AD, describes the Hebrew scriptures this way:

> For we have not an innumerable multitude of books among us, disagreeing from and contradicting one another [as the Greeks have], but only twenty-two books, which contain the records of all the past times; which are justly believed to be divine, and of them five belong to Moses, which contain his laws and the traditions of the origin of mankind til his death.... The prophets wrote down what was done in their times in thirteen books. The remaining four books contain hymns to God, and precepts for the conduct of human life.[1]

That was written two thousand years ago and is a pretty good summary of what the Jewish Testament is. He describes the twenty-two books of the Hebrew Bible (as enumerated by the Jews) as containing the "records of all past times," the laws of Moses, and the "traditions of the origins of mankind," as well as material from the prophets, "hymns" (Psalms), and "precepts for the conduct of human life."

Archaeological Discovery: Were Hebrews the "Habiru"?

In 1887, a series of cuneiform clay tablets was discovered in Egypt, written by Canaanite scribes in the Akkadian language. The tablets appeared to be correspondence between vassal kings in Canaan and the Egyptian pharaohs around 1330 BC. These letters mention a people known as the *habiru* attacking cities in Canaan and causing trouble in Egypt itself. When first discovered, scholars were quick to assume that the habiru—also mentioned in Sumerian, Egyptian, Ugaritic, and Hittite sources—must be the same as the Hebrews (*ivri* in Hebrew). That's because some of the letters contain eerie parallels with the biblical account of the Conquest. In one of the letters, for example, the vassal Abdu-Heba of Jerusalem writes to the Egyptian pharaoh that "the Habiru sack the territories of the king" and insists that "if there are archers [sent] this year, all the territories of the king will remain (intact); but if there are no archers, the territories of the king, my Lord, will be lost!"

Today, however, many scholars believe that the *hapiru* or *habiru* was a generic designation for marauding "foreigners" or refugees that attacked settled communities throughout the Middle East.

It is perfectly plausible, however, that the Egyptians would have considered wandering Semites, including those of the tribes of Israel, to be "habiru" and the sort of danger described in the first lines of Exodus: "Then a new king, who knew nothing of Joseph, came to power in Egypt. He said to his subjects, 'Look how numerous and powerful the Israelite people are growing, more so than we ourselves.'"

As for Jesus, in the records we have of his teaching he routinely referred to at least some written Hebrew texts as reflecting God's word to mankind. He condemned the Pharisees who "nullify the word of God for the sake of your tradition," (Mt 15:6), in a reference to the written text of Genesis. Later on, Jesus cites Genesis 2:24, in which the author of the Hebrew text says, "For this reason, a man will leave his father and mother and be joined to his wife, and they will become one flesh." Matthew quotes Jesus as saying, "The Creator 'made them male and female,' and said, 'For this reason, a man will leave his father and mother and be joined to his wife, and the two will become one flesh' "—implying that, for Jesus at least, it was God himself who was speaking through the Hebrew text of Genesis.[2]

It's hardly surprising, then, given the attitude of Jesus toward the written Hebrew holy books, that the early Christians viewed these ancient texts as divinely inspired—without specifying precisely what that entails. The classic proof text for this view is 2 Tim 3:16: "All scripture [*graphe*] is inspired by God [*theopneustos*] and profitable for teaching, for reproof, for correction, and for training in righteousness, that the man of God may be complete, equipped for every good work."

Obviously, the "scripture" that Paul is speaking about here is the Hebrew Bible, since what we call the New Testament was, at that very moment, in the process of being written and didn't yet exist. The word Paul uses, *theopneustos*—which can be translated literally "God-breathed" or, more typically, "inspired"—is rare, used only once in the New Testament and only four other times in existing Greek literature. Scholars debate whether it should be translated as a predicate ("all scripture is inspired") or as an attribute ("all inspired scripture"); but the context of the passage appears to favor the former, because the apostle Paul, writing to his disciple Timothy, is insisting that the "sacred writings" of the Jews "are able to instruct you for salvation through faith in Jesus Christ" (2 Tm 3:15).

This would quickly become a controversial issue when the Jesus movement spread out into the Gentile world and some Greeks and Romans came to believe, as the early heretic Marcion of Sinope (c. 110–160) did, that the Jewish writings should be abandoned in favor of the allegedly more elevated Gospels and writings of Paul. Paul is saying, No, the Jewish scriptures are indeed "God-breathed" (or inspired) and "profitable."

But note: Paul says *nothing* about scripture being "inerrant," or useful for studying astrophysics, or even as a primary source for historical study. These are *later* controversies projected backward onto the Bible. That doesn't mean the Bible isn't inerrant necessarily, only that the primary emphasis for the Pharisee Paul, as a good Jew, is on the *practical use* of the biblical texts for "instruction for salvation." Scripture, he says, is for (1) teaching, (2) reproof, (3) correction, and (4) training in righteousness, not for debating evolution or cosmology.

What biblical inspiration does and does not mean

We are discussing all this background material because at least half of the attacks that modern skeptics make on the Bible are based, one way or another, on a profound misunderstanding of what most Christians and Jews mean by biblical inspiration—or even of what the Bible is actually saying. Many of the attacks by skeptics are downright silly.

Christians and Jews have never claimed that the Bible was "written" by God—except perhaps for the eerie reference in Exodus 31:18 to the two tablets of the law "inscribed with the finger of God" (*ktuvim beet-zbah elohim*). They have always understood that the biblical texts were written by real human beings—in specific times and places—and with all the limitations and difficulties associated with grammar, human knowledge, limited memories, cultural assumptions, mixed metaphors, analogies, and so on. As a result, Christians and Jews have had a wide variety of views as to what the divine inspiration of the Bible actually means concretely.

Mainline or more liberal Protestant denominations believe that God speaks through the biblical texts but that, since he communicates through the medium of human beings, many of the minor "details" can be in error. They accept most of the presuppositions of modern biblical scholarship, view the first chapters of Genesis as largely mythic and not to be taken literally, and believe the Bible is true but not necessarily free from error.

Conservative Protestants and Orthodox Jews, on the other hand, believe that the biblical texts "come from God" (2 Tm 5:16) and that "God does not lie" (Num 23:19) and that therefore the Bible is "inerrant" in everything that it affirms—with a few important provisos about what it means for the Bible to "affirm" something.

The conservative evangelical theologian Norman Geisler—who believes that "even though the Bible was not mechanically dictated by God to man, . . . the result is just as perfect as if it had been"—pointed out that a belief in the divine inspiration of the Bible does *not* guarantee that:

"every part of a parable is conveying a truth (as opposed to the truthfulness of the point the parable is illustrating—Lk 18:2)

"everything recorded in the Bible is true (as opposed to only what is taught or implied—Gn 3:4)

"no exaggerations (hyperboles) can be used (Col 1:23)

"all statements about God and creation are purely literal (Heb 4:13, Job 38:7)

"all factual assertions are technically precise by modern standards (as opposed to accurate by ancient standards—2 Chr 4:2) "all statements about the universe must be from a modern astronomical perspective (as opposed to a common observational standpoint—Jo 10:12)

"all citations of Scripture must be verbatim (as opposed to faithful)

"all citations of Scripture must have the same application as the original (Hos 11:1, Mt 2:15), rather than having the same interpretation (meaning)

"the same truth can be said in only one way (as opposed to many ways, such as in the Gospels)

"whatever a writer personally believed (as opposed to merely what he actually affirmed in Scripture) is true (Mt 15:26)

"truth is exhaustively revealed or treated (as opposed to adequately presented) in the Bible (1 Cor 13:12)

"quotations imply the truth of everything in the source it is citing, rather than only the part cited (Titus 1:12)

"the grammatical construction will always be the customary one (rather than an adequate one to convey the truth)"

With these clarifications, about half of the most common arguments against the Bible fall away—as we will see shortly.

The Roman Catholic and Orthodox Churches represent a third way of approaching the biblical texts. Most people don't know that the Catholic Church also believes in the "inerrancy" of the Bible but, as in the second point listed, only in what is actually being taught or implied. The Second Vatican Council, in its dogmatic constitution *Dei Verbum*, put it this way: "[T]he books of scripture must be acknowledged as teaching, firmly, faithfully *and without error* that truth which God wanted put into the sacred writings for the sake of our salvation." In practice, the Catholic approach is closer to that of mainline Protestant denominations in its use of contemporary biblical scholarship but closer to conservative Protestants in its doctrinal formulations.

Alleged errors in the Bible

There is nothing wrong, of course, in modern people asking pointed questions about the Bible—where it came from, how it was created, who wrote it and why, and whether what it appears to say squares with what we know (or think we know) from other areas of knowledge, such as modern science or history.

Indeed, such a critical spirit, far from being denounced, is actually endorsed by the Bible itself. "Test everything," St. Paul admonishes the Thessalonians, "keep what is good."

But what the village atheists of today fail to realize (in their monumental arrogance and ignorance of history) is that every seeming contradiction found in the Bible—every discrepancy, every apparent historical or scientific error, grammatical mistake, or puzzling fact or comment—has been noted and argued about and debated literally thousands of times, for thousands of years, by the greatest minds in history. Nothing—literally nothing—they say is new.

That doesn't, in and of itself, mean that every question is answered and every problem resolved, but it does suggest just a modicum of modesty when approaching the holy book of one-third of the world's population. Before modern skeptics announce to the world their monumental discovery that there are *two* versions of Creation in Genesis—or, for that matter, *four* canonical Gospels—you'd think that they might consider inquiring whether believing Christians and Jews have noticed these shocking facts and how they have handled these potentially lethal threats to their faith.

So, let's take a brief look at the alleged "inconsistencies" and contradictions in the Bible.

Alleged inconsistencies in the Bible

Genesis 7:4 says the Flood lasted forty days while Genesis 7:11 says it lasted an entire year. Genesis 6:19 says two of each animal went in the ark; Genesis 7:2 says seven. Genesis 11:28 says Abraham came from Ur of the Chaldees (in southern Iraq); Genesis 29:4 says he came from Haran (in northern Iraq). Genesis 22:2 calls Isaac Abraham's "only son," but Genesis 16 says he had Ishmael before that and Genesis 25 says he had other sons as well.

Modern critics rattle these examples off as if they're definitive refutations of everything Christianity and Judaism represent. Hardly. These alleged inconsistencies are known among conservative Christians as "Bible difficulties," and there are entire books dedicated to attempts to resolve them—if you think they need resolving.

Most alleged inconsistencies are easily explained by a more careful reading of the texts themselves. For example, conservative Bible scholars will explain the apparent inconsistency in the length of the Flood by pointing out that the forty days refers to how long the rain fell while the entire year was how long it took for the waters to *subside* so Noah and his family could step upon the ground again. Similarly, Genesis 6:19 says at least two of "all that lives" went into the ark; Genesis 7:2 is more specific and says that seven pairs of every *clean* animal went into the ark and one pair of every *unclean* animal. Abraham's family originally came from Ur but had migrated to Haran before Abraham was called by God. And so on. Most of the time, these alleged "inconsistencies" are simply the result of modern skeptics imposing their own standards and values on ancient peoples with radically different lifestyles and outlooks. For example, Abraham's "other" sons, including Ishmael, were children he fathered with concubines and considered secondary heirs, while Isaac, his son with his chief wife, Sarah, was considered his "only" (or at least primary) heir.

Liberal Christian and Jewish scholars, who accept the documentary hypothesis, dislike these tidy explanations. They prefer to believe that the apparent inconsistencies and contradictions in the Bible result from, in effect, bad editing. In their view, the compilers of the Bible cobbled together different versions of similar stories and then forgot to go back and harmonize the texts. They put two different versions of Creation into Genesis (Chapters 1 and 2) and then *didn't notice* that they tell the story of the creation of mankind in slightly different ways (with both the male and female being created in the first version and the male human created first in the second). While such editorial sloppiness is indeed possible, it's not as persuasive as modern skeptics believe.

The Bible in American History, Part III

"My custom is to read four or five chapters of the Bible every morning immediately after rising.... It seems to me the most suitable manner of beginning the day.... It is an invaluable and inexhaustible mine of knowledge and virtue."

John Quincy Adams

Alleged errors of quotation

The New Testament authors appear to misquote the Hebrew Scriptures frequently—a sure sign, say critics, of error in the Bible. For example, Matthew 4:14–16 quotes Isaiah 9:12, but the quotation does not match our texts of Isaiah, in either the Hebrew or the Greek version. Matthew 2:6 seems to misquote Micah 5:2 and adds words that aren't in the original. And Matthew 2:23 quotes a prophecy—"he shall be called a Nazarene"—that doesn't exist in the Hebrew Bible that we have.

Most of these examples are easily explained by the fact that Jews in the time of Jesus quoted the Bible by memory and rarely verbatim. What's more, they often had recourse to very loose Aramaic paraphrases of the Hebrew, known as *targumim* (Hebrew for translations). (For example, one of these first-century Aramaic paraphrases of Genesis begins, "At the beginning the Lord created the heavens and the earth. And the earth was vacancy and desolation, solitary of the sons of men, and void of every animal; and darkness was upon the face of the abyss, and the Spirit of mercies from before the Lord breathed upon the face of the waters.") Thus, our New Testament texts could well be Greek translations of loose Aramaic paraphrases of Hebrew quotations. It's little wonder that the texts are not word-by-word quotations.

As for the "lost prophecy" in Matthew 2:23, that hardly poses any difficulty. As we've seen, the Bible frequently refers to ancient books we no longer have (such as the Book of Jashar). Furthermore, we know that not all the words of the prophets were written down; some were passed on through oral tradition. Therefore, it's quite possible that there was a lost prophecy that Matthew is quoting that we simply don't know anything about. It's also possible that "Nazarene" refers to Nazareth's poor reputation ("Can anything good come out of Nazareth?" John 1:46), and this is an elliptical reference to Isaiah's prophecies concerning the suffering servant of God (e.g., Isa 53:3).

Alleged historical errors in the Bible

Many of the alleged historical errors or anachronisms in the Bible involve place names—which suggests more the reality of a later editor than actual "error." For example, Genesis 14:14 describes Abram pursuing the surviving kings of Sodom and Gomorrah to the City of Dan—which did not exist in Abram's time as far as we know. There are numerous instances in the Torah, especially, of places being referred to by their later names. But this is hardly "error"—any more than it would be for a modern writer to say that Catherine the Great of Russia built a palace outside of Leningrad—even though, in her time, it was called (and is now again) St. Petersburg. Another example of historical "error" is the reference to the "Philistines" found in Genesis 21 because, it is said, the Philistine people only arrived around the year 1180 BC, long after the events described. However, this is easily resolved, as above, because the text refers to the "*land* of the Philistines," not to the people, and thus would be like Americans saying "the Dutch founded New York" when, technically, they did no such thing: they founded New Amsterdam which was later renamed New York.

A more serious charge of anachronism concerns references to the use of camels in Genesis because camels purportedly were not domesticated until centuries after the period in which Abraham is supposed to have lived. Skeptics cite this as proof that the patriarchal narratives were fabricated at a later date. They insist that there is "no evidence" of the use of camels in the Middle East prior to about 1200 BC.

But the Egyptologist K. A. Kitchen disputes this claim—pointing to such archaeological finds as a figurine of a kneeling camel from Byblos, circa 1900 BC, and mentions of camels in Sumerian texts dating back to the early second millennium. He concludes that camels were used sporadically in the patriarchal age but usually only for long-distance journeys. What's more, excavations at Shajr-i-Sokhta in eastern Iran have uncovered extensive camel remains in human encampments that have led scientists to argue that camel domestication began in Turkmenia as early as 2700 BC. Evidence of early camel domestication has also been found in India around 2300 BC and in southern Arabia. As the *Anchor Bible Dictionary* notes, "we would not be totally amiss in suggesting that domestic camels may have been known to the inhabitants of Syria-Palestine as early as the turn of the third millennium BC"—that is, contemporaneously with the biblical account of Abraham. Once again, the "certitudes" of skeptics—their assertions of what "science says"—are often disproved by archaeological evidence.

Alleged scientific errors in the Bible

Modern naysayers often point to the lowly bat as proof that the Bible is riddled with scientific errors and therefore cannot be divinely inspired. Bats are flying mammals, not birds, they say, so why does Leviticus 11:19 describe them as being numbered among the "birds"? Other examples of alleged scientific errors found in the Bible include:

Leviticus 11:6—where the rabbit is described as "chewing the cud"

Leviticus 11: 21–24—where grasshoppers and beetles "that walk on all fours" are mentioned (insects have six legs, not four)

Leviticus 11:4—where the camel is described as "not having split hoofs" (camels do have split hooves)

Genesis 3:14—where the snake is described as being condemned to crawl on its belly (as though at one time it did not)

2 Kings 6:5–6—where Elisha the prophet is described as making an iron ax head float to the surface of the water (iron doesn't float)

But these "errors" are really just attempts to impose a scientific precision on texts that were never intended to be read in such a way. The Bible uses the casual, imprecise language of everyday life, not that of empirical science. Just as today we wouldn't say someone was "lying" or in "error" if he said that the sun rose at six o'clock in the morning—when, scientifically speaking, the sun actually doesn't move at all relative to the earth—the same is true of biblical descriptions of plants, animals, and the natural world. The Bible is conveying broader moral and philosophical ideas rather than the minutiae of zoology. For example, the Hebrew word used for bird (*ohf*) could just as easily be translated "flying thing." In other passages, the same word is used for birds, bats, and certain insects.

The phrase "walk on all fours" (*ha-holech al arbah*) is just a colloquial expression, not a scientific one—and people in biblical times could count legs just as easily as people today. While the rabbits mentioned in Leviticus 11 appear to chew the cud, we now know that they are not, in fact, ruminants but technically "refectives"—that is, they chew their droppings to better digest their food, not cud like a cow. But again, this was a popular description, not a scientific one.

When modern "debunkers" of the Bible contend that such imprecise descriptions of natural reality undermine the credibility of the text as a whole, they only prove that they are missing the point of what is actually being said. Most of the other examples of scientific "errors" that skeptics cite refer to miracles—such as Jesus walking on water (Mt 14:24) or the burning bush that is not consumed (Ex 3:2–5). (The passage in 2 Kings in which Elisha causes an iron ax head to float to the surface is described as a miraculous event, not a normal phenomenon of nature.) These are scientific errors, the modern critics say, because such things are impossible.

Extra-Biblical Writings: the Didache

Long considered lost, the Didache was rediscovered in the 1870s. Although no date is settled upon for its origin, it is easily one of the earliest important Christian documents outside the New Testament, dating anywhere from 70 to 120 AD. The Didache is presented as a summary of the teachings of the Twelve Apostles, and was quoted extensively by the early Christian theologians. It underscores how Christianity, from the beginning, was defined by certain rituals (like baptism), a defined faith in God the Father, God the Son, and God the Holy Spirit, and a moral worldview that affirmed, among other things, every unborn child's undeniable right to life.

But that is not a refutation, it is only a dogmatic assertion that miracles cannot happen—which is really not an argument at all. In the end, virtually every example of scientific "error" that is alleged to be in the Bible falls into the category of applying the exacting standards of modern science to language that never aspired to this but reflected the language of common people.

Some Christian apologists go to the opposite extreme. They claim that modern scientific theories or discoveries—such as the second law of thermodynamics (entropy), for example—can be discerned in poetic or figurative biblical passages such as Isaiah 51:6 ("the heavens shall vanish away like smoke, and the earth shall wax old like a garment"). But this is to misunderstnd the nature of biblical revelation as well: the Bible is not concerned with the details of science but with the ultimate truths about the world that will make science possible in the first place.

Alleged moral errors in the Bible

If truth be told, the alleged moral errors in the Bible are often the real reason why modern skeptics and atheist crusaders attack the Bible's authority.

"People in general do not know what wickedness there is in this pretended word of God," wrote the American revolutionary leader and freethinker Thomas Paine, in his classic attack on Christianity, *The Age of Reason*. "Brought up in habits of superstition, they take it for granted that the Bible is true, and that it is good; they permit themselves not to doubt of it, and they carry the ideas they form of the benevolence of the Almighty to the book which they have been taught to believe was written by his authority. Good heavens! It is quite another thing; it is a book of lies, wickedness, and blasphemy; for what can be greater blasphemy than to ascribe the wickedness of man to the orders of the Almighty?"

Modern writers, lacking Paine's erudition or eloquence, agree in spirit.

"The God of the Old Testament is arguably the most unpleasant character in all fiction," writes Richard Dawkins in *The God Delusion*. "A petty, unjust, unforgiving control-freak; homophobic, racist, infanticidal, genocidal, filicidal, pestilential, megalomaniacal, sadomasochistic, capriciously malevolent bully. Those of us schooled from infancy in his ways can become desensitized to their horror."

"The Bible is one of the most genocidal books in history," agrees the leftist theoretician Noam Chomsky. "The first thing [governments should] do is ban the Old Testament. There's nothing like it in the literary canon that exalts genocide, to that extent. And it's not a joke, either. Like where I live, New England, the people who liberated it from the native scourge were religious fundamentalist lunatics, who came waving the holy book, declaring themselves to be the children of Israel who are killing the Amalekites, like God told them."

What about the substance of the charge? Does the Bible, in fact, promote genocide and other forms of villainy? It's true that there are a handful of texts in the Old Testament in which God orders the Israelites to drive out entire populations—for example, Exodus 23:32–33 and 34:11–16, Deuteronomy 7:1–2 and 20:16–18, and 1 Samuel 15:18. Attempts to whitewash or ignore these texts are dishonest. The command to place certain peoples under the "curse" or "ban" (Hebrew: *herem*) was strictly limited, in the Old Testament, to just a few specific peoples—the Hittites, the Amorites, the Canaanites, the Perizzites, the Hivites, and the Jebusites (six out of the seven Canaanite nations in Deuteronomy 7:26), as well as the Midianites and the Amalekites.

Deuteronomy 7:2–6 is unambiguous:

"When the Lord your God gives them over to you and you defeat them, then you must utterly destroy them. Make no covenant with them and show them no mercy. Do not intermarry with them, giving your daughters to their sons or taking their daughters for your sons, for that would turn away your children from following me, to serve other gods. . . . But this is how you must deal with them: break down their altars, smash their pillars, hew down their sacred poles, and burn their idols with fire. For you are a people holy to the Lord your God."

What was it that God had against the seven tribes of Canaanites that would justify this apparent call to genocide? Of course, some modern critics deny that the Canaanites ever practiced human sacrifice as described in the Bible—but then again, they also deny that the Israelites waged war against the Canaanite populations. For these critics, neither the genocide, nor the alleged justification for the genocide, ever occurred.

Nevertheless, it's clear that the Bible views the tribes as something akin to the Mesoamerican Aztecs—a corrupt society that sacrificed innocent children to evil idols and practiced bestiality, gang rape, and other evil deeds. "When you come into the land that the Lord your God is giving

Which Bible?

There are more versions of the Bible than there are colors of the rainbow. When picking one, make sure you look for one that has as its prime emphasis being true to the original biblical sources. For Protestants, the King James Bible is still, well, king—at least for the beauty of the language. The New English Bible and the New International Version are among the best of the newer translations. For Catholics, traditionalists prefer the Douay-Rheims Bible as revised by Bishop Challoner (it has the status of being the "Catholic King James"), but the Revised Standard Version (Catholic edition) is also good. Some Catholics also like the original Jerusalem Bible (not the "New" version). The original had J. R. R. Tolkien as one of its translators.

you, you must not learn to imitate the abhorrent practices of those nations," says Deuteronomy 18:9. "There shall not be found among you anyone who makes his son or his daughter pass through the fire, or one who practices witchcraft, or a soothsayer, or one who interprets omens, or a sorcerer. . . . It is because of such abhorrent practices that the Lord your God is driving them out before you." Earlier, Deuteronomy 9:5 made it clear that "it is not because of your righteousness or your integrity that you are going in to take possession of their land, but on account of the wickedness of these nations."

The phrase "pass through the fire" refers to the pagan practice of taking newborn infants and rolling them, while still alive, into an enormous furnace as "food" for the gods. The prophet Jeremiah accused the syncretizing Judahites of setting up a "high place of Tophet" in the Valley of Ben-Hinnom outside Jerusalem (Jer 7:30–32), where they "burn their sons and their daughters in the fire." Plus we know from other historical sources that the Phoenecians, who settled in Palestine, were fond of this practice. According to the Greek historian Diodorus (c. 90–30 BC), "there was in their city a bronze image of Cronus, extending its hands, palms up and sloping toward the ground, so that each of the children when placed thereon rolled down and fell into a sort of gaping pit filled with fire." Archaeological excavations in Carthage, the North African colony founded by the Phoenecians of Tyre in 814 BC, have found 20,000 urns containing the remains of sacrificed children—the largest cemetery of sacrificed humans ever discovered. According to the *Biblical Archaeology Review*, experts believe that child sacrifice took place there "almost continuously for a period of nearly six hundred years."

As we will see in a subsequent chapter, when the Israelites eventually adopt this pagan practice of child sacrifice—as early as the reign of Solomon—the Bible says that God made good on his threat and removed them from the land as punishment. According to 1 Kings 17:17–18, when "they mutilated their sons and daughters by fire . . . the Lord, in his great anger against Israel, put them away out of his sight" (2 Kgs 17:17–18). Two Kings also describes, in detail, how the reforming King Josiah "did away with the Moabite horror" (23:13) and "the Sidonian horror," so that "there would no longer be any immolation of sons or daughters by fire in honor of Moloch."

Theodicy, the effort to "justify the ways of God to men," is a dicey and presumptuous business at best, but given the way in which the Israelite campaign to expel the Canaanite tribes from the land is used as a general indictment against the entire Bible—from Genesis to Revelation—perhaps it can be appropriate in this case. During World War II, Jewish leaders begged—actually *begged*—Allied military leaders to bomb the death camp at Auschwitz. They did so even though they knew it would mean certain death, not only to "innocent" Nazi women and children living nearby, but also to thousands of Jewish and Allied prisoners in the camps. The Jewish leaders felt that the horror of the death camps was so great that it simply had to be stopped—even at the cost of thousands of innocent Jewish lives. At least if the camps were destroyed, they reasoned, the lives of hundreds of thousands of other Jews, not yet at the camps, would be spared in the future. The killing machine would be eliminated.

Right or wrong, it's clear that the Bible views the Canaanites in a similar way—that the "abominations" of the pagan death cults were so great that they justified even attacking entire populations. This is a delicate comparison to make and certainly modern skeptics are correct that we must view any form of indiscriminate killing in war as a great crime against humanity. This is all the more so because modern people are well aware of how the concept of "holy war," like the Muslim jihad, can be used to justify widespread barbarism. But as the case of Auschwitz demonstrates, sometimes human evil can appear so great that even acts like saturation bombing of an entire village (with innocent people present) can seem, if not justified, then at least understandable. This is the context in which the biblical concept of *herem*, or of "banning" the tribes of Canaan, can be understood.

This is all the more true because, with the exception of the Canaanite tribes, the biblical texts enjoin mercy on captured enemies. "When you draw near to a town to fight against it, offer it terms of peace," says Deuteronomy 20:10. "If it accepts your terms of peace and surrenders to you, then all the people in it shall serve you at forced labor." Female captives, however, are not to be treated as sex slaves. They are to be allowed to mourn their lost husbands for a full month and, if an Israelite forcibly marries one and then decides to divorce her, she shall go free and cannot be sold for money. "You must not treat her as a slave," Deuteronomy says, "for you have dishonored her" (21:14).

This may not strike modern people as exactly the Geneva Convention, but compared with the "rules of warfare" in the ancient Near East generally, the commandments are unprecedented in their compassion. We forget that, throughout history, barbarism is the rule rather than the exception: The palace reliefs of the Assyrian king Ashur-nasir-pal II (c. 884–859 BC) depict Assyrian armies cheerfully skinning captured prisoners alive, cutting off hands and feet and ears, pulling out tongues and eyes, and making enormous mounds of decapitated human heads in order to further terrify their victims.

In short, people who attack the Bible on moral grounds usually make the same error of anachronism as those who attack it on scientific ones: They apply contemporary standards of justice or morality—in societies that have had thousands of years of *benefiting* from the biblical injunctions—to a time of lawlessness and murder. The people in Old Testament times were not exactly like members of a contemporary women's book club. They lived in an era of bandits and caravans, ruthless empires and slavery, child sacrifice and gang rape—when might made right and whoever could slaughter the most people became king.

It was a cruel time, and the God of the Bible issued harsh edicts to cruel people. Gradually, however, over literally centuries of war and exile, through the harsh words of his prophets and the even harsher lessons of history, this same God led his people to greater and greater levels of compassion and mercy. "You shall not molest or oppress an alien," He commands the Israelites in Exodus, "for you were once aliens yourselves in the land of Egypt" (Ex 22:20). "Seek peace and pursue it," sang the Psalmist (Ps 34:14). "Love truth and peace," counseled Zechariah (8:19).

No, modern critics who assert that the Bible justifies war and genocide are looking at isolated passages taken out of their historical and textual context. It was only because of their long and bloody history that the Jewish people came to understand just how much the Creator of the universe hates war and killing. "Your hands are full of blood!" God tells the Israelite people through the eighth-century Jerusalem prophet Isaiah. "Wash yourselves clean! Put away your misdeeds from before my eyes; cease doing evil; learn to do good. Make justice your aim: redress the wronged, hear the orphan's plea, defend the widow" (Is 1:15–17).

Indeed, we forget that, for the biblical prophets especially, war is the *punishment* that God metes out for injustice and bloodshed. Isaiah warns the people what will happen if they refuse to listen to God's demands for justice: "He will give a signal to a far-off nation, and whistle to them from the ends of the earth; speedily and promptly will they come.... Their arrows are sharp, and all their bows are bent. The hoofs of their horses seem like flint, and their chariot wheels like the hurricane" (4:26, 28).

But after the long, bloody march of history, the Bible says, mankind will finally turn its back on killing. There will come a messianic age when God's anointed shall destroy war once and for all. As the prophet Zechariah (9:10) put it:

"Rejoice greatly, O Daughter of Zion! Shout, Daughter of Jerusalem! See, your king comes to you, righteous and having salvation, gentle and riding on a donkey, on a colt, the foal of a donkey.

"I will take away the chariots from Ephraim and the war-horses from Jerusalem, and the battle bow will be broken. He will proclaim peace to the nations. His rule will extend from sea to sea and from the River to the ends of the earth."

A time will come, Isaiah agreed, when nations "shall beat their swords into plowshares; and their spears into pruning hooks; nation shall not lift up sword against nation, neither shall they learn war any more" (2:4).

This is hardly a God who loves war, much less genocide.

Who Said It?

"I have been reading poems, romances, vision literature, legends, myths all my life. I know what they are like. I know that none of them is like this [the Gospel according to St. John]. Of this text there are only two possible views. Either this is reportage—though it may no doubt contain errors—pretty close to the facts; nearly as close as Boswell. Or else, some unknown writer in the second century, without known predecessors or successors, suddenly anticipated the whole technique of modern, novelistic, realistic narrative. If it is untrue, it must be narrative of that kind. The reader who doesn't see this simply has not learned to read."

C. S. Lewis

Chapter Four

IN THE BEGINNING

The great Babylonian creation epic known as *Enûma Elish* begins with the mingling of the god of fresh water, Apsu, with the great ocean and mother of all things, Tiamat. The other gods are born of them. But because the young gods were noisy and wild, Apsu decided to destroy them. The young gods, however, learn of their father's plan and kill Apsu. They then turn on their mother Tiamat. Tiamat, in self-defense, unleashes an army of monsters against the young gods. Finally, a god named Marduk challenges his mother to single combat for dominion over all the gods. Tiamat opens her vast mouth to swallow Marduk, but he hurls the winds against her and lets loose a great arrow, which tears her entrails from her body and pierces her heart. Pitiless, he executes his mother and throws her lifeless corpse on the ground. He splits her skull and cuts her corpse in two, one half becoming the firmament of the sky and the other the earth. Eventually, Marduk creates mankind in order to provide the gods some relief from their labors.

Written around the fifteenth century BC in cuneiform Akkadian, *Enûma Elish* was first discovered by modern scholars on a series of seven clay tablets in the ruined library of Ashurbanipal at Nineveh (modern-day Mosul, Iraq).

What is interesting about this ancient mythological account of the creation of the world is how many of its fundamental themes are found in

Guess what?

- The God of the Bible is unlike any other divinity described in the history of mankind.

- The creation account of Genesis is a victim of its own success: its influence is so pervasive that people today don't realize how unusual it is.

other creation myths worldwide: the primordial sexual union (*hier gamos*) of the gods, the overthrow of the "old" gods and their replacement by the new, the suffering of the gods, the rank immorality and scheming of the gods, the need the gods had for human beings as slaves or providers of nourishment, and so forth.

Indeed, it is only when you spend some time studying the mythologies of ancient peoples (or modern ones, for that matter) that you truly grasp that the creation account described in the Bible is unique. The details of ancient mythologies differ; but many of their key concepts, their underlying assumptions about the nature of the world and man's place in it, are identical.

Take the ancient Greeks, for example. Everyone knows something about the Greek gods if only from watching *Xena: Warrior Princess* or *Hercules* on TV.

According to the Greek poet Hesiod, the primordial earth mother, Gaea, first gave birth to Uranus, the sky. She had an incestuous relationship with Uranus and gave birth to the first gods, the twelve Titans. She also gave birth to hundred-armed monsters known as the Centimanes. Gaea's son-husband Uranus was horrified by these deformed offspring and shut them up in the depths of the earth.

But Gaea plotted with her youngest child, Cronus. When evening came and Uranus slept next to Gaea, as he always did, Cronus crept up on the sleeping Uranus and, wielding a large sickle, castrated him and flung his bleeding genitals into the sea. The blood from these bleeding genitals fell to earth and became the Furies.

You can see immediately how similar this all is with the account of creation in Genesis.

Later, Cronus liberated his brothers, the Titans, who eventually mated with one another and gave birth to nymphs and gods. Cronus himself married his sister, Rhea, but each time she gave birth, Cronus, fearing an ancient oracle that he would be overthrown by one of his children, swallowed up each infant as it was born.

Zeus escaped his father Cronus's murderous cruelty, however, and eventually forced his father to vomit up the god-children he had swallowed. Then began a great war between the old gods, the Titans, and their upstart children, the Olympians. For ten years, the earth shook in fury as the gods did battle with one another, with Zeus flinging lightning bolts across the heavens. Eventually, the Titans were defeated, locked and chained in the depths of the earth, and Zeus and the other "young gods" reigned on Olympus.

Scripture Says

"The earth was without form, and void; and darkness was upon the face of the deep. And the Spirit of God moved upon the face of the waters. And God said, "Let there be light." And there was light.

Genesis 1:2–3

And God said: "Let there be light"

For more than two centuries, liberal scholars have pointed to superficial similarities between biblical religion and the religions of the ancient Near East—in an effort to demonstrate either how Israelite religion "evolved" out of Near Eastern mythologies or, alternatively, that "all religions teach the same thing"—while ignoring the vast differences between them.

For example, scholars point to alleged parallels between the *Enûma Elish* and the account of creation in Genesis. In Genesis, creation is accomplished in six days followed by a day of rest. In the *Enûma Elish,* there are six generations of gods followed by rest.

But while modern scholars ponder these minor parallels, they often miss the staggering differences between the two accounts.

The great Israeli biblical scholar Yehezkel Kaufmann divided the religions of the world into two basic groups:

pagan religion, by which he meant all the religions of mankind from the beginning of history until today with the sole exception of...

the religion of ancient Israel and its successors, Christianity and Islam.

For Kaufmann, virtually all religions of the world—up to and including the "high paganism" of Hinduism, Buddhism, and the like—are based upon a very simple, very fundamental idea: the existence of "a realm of being prior to the gods and above them, upon which the gods depend, and whose decrees they must obey."

This "meta-divine" realm—envisioned as a great womb, water, mist, or sky—contains the preexisting "seeds" or eggs from which all things, including the gods and goddesses, are created.

In a sense, Kaufmann agreed with New Age followers who insist that "all religions teach the same thing," although Kaufmann would qualify that by saying, "All religions except the religion of the Bible teach basically the same thing."

What they all teach, in essence, is that the universe is a *closed system* determined by fixed, mechanistic laws, and all things in it—up to and including gods and goddesses—must obey these unchanging, eternal laws.

The religions differ in the details, but the underlying worldview is remarkably consistent. In the words of atheist philosopher Jean-Paul Sartre, there is, quite literally, "No Exit." This is karma or the Tao: the law of cause and effect. And all things, including both gods and men, are subject to it.

That is why the ancient divinities of "the nations" are sexual beings who desire and mate with one another. They are subject to time, to fate, to death and resurrection. They sleep. They suffer. They must do battle to keep chaos at bay.

For example, in the *Rig Veda*, a vast collection of proto-Hindu hymns that dates back to 2000 BC, the central god Indra does battle against Vritra, a monstrous dragon who holds back the waters of the world in a mountain. This is a common motif in ancient mythology: a sky god that does battle against the primordial chaos of the sea or waters. Eventually, Indra uses his thunderbolt (*vajra*) to split open Vritra's head and releases the waters.

The world of paganism is, therefore, one of divine conflict, of cosmic struggle and uncertainty. The forces of nature, while often harmonious,

Were Adam and Eve Real?

What Skeptics Say: The Hebrew word *adam* simply means "man," and therefore the story of Adam and Eve is clearly just a myth. There was no real Adam and Eve.

Reply: The fact that the Bible describes the first human being by the name Man (Adam), or the first woman Eve (from the Hebrew *haya*, for "life"), hardly proves that Adam and Eve are merely mythic figures. In the dawn of creation, there was certainly an original human couple from whom all of humanity is descended—an idea that recent DNA testing has supported. So-called "mitochondrial Eve" is the name given by geneticists for an ancient ancestor from whom all human beings are descended. Ironically, Charles Darwin and biblical conservatives both argued for monogenism, the belief that human beings are all descended from a primeval human couple. The alternative, polygenism, has very little support in scientific circles. The fact that the Bible uses figurative, non-scientific language in describing the original human pair does not detract from the truth of what it affirms.

The Bible in American History, Part IV

"That Book [the Bible] is the rock on which our Republic rests."

Andrew Jackson

can sometimes be fierce and cruel...and paganism has a very simple, very logical explanation for this reality: The gods frequently do battle with one another.

Virtually alone of all the world's religions, the religion of the Bible has no such theogonic myth.

"In the beginning, God created heaven and earth," Genesis 1 says simply. We are so used to hearing it, and so unfamiliar with alternative accounts of creation, that we don't realize what is missing.

There is no story of, or explanation for, the origin of the Divinity. The Bible does not tell us where God comes from.

God simply is.

And not only that: The God of the Bible is utterly unlike any other divinity described in the long history of mankind.

"The basic idea of Israelite religion is that God is supreme over all," Kaufmann says in his magisterial, multivolume history of Israelite religion, *The Religion of Israel*. "There is no realm above or beside him to limit his absolute sovereignty. He is utterly distinct from, and other than, the world; he is subject to no laws, no compulsions, or powers that transcend him."[1]

The God of the Bible does not sleep. He does not mate. He does not suffer any material hardship. His power is limitless.

All it takes for God to create is for Him to will it.

"And God said, 'Let there be light,' and there was light" (Gn 1:3). The great cosmic phenomena of the universe—the sun and the moon, the firmament of the sky—are not rival divinities but his creation. "The main point of Christianity was this," wrote G. K. Chesterton in *Orthodoxy*. "Nature is not our mother; Nature is our sister."

There is no pre-existent realm. There was only a "formless void" (*tohu vevohu*).

There is no inexorable Fate, no Destiny. There is only the will of God.

There are poetic figures of speech, to be sure—God walks "in the garden in the cool of the day"—but he does not eat, does not sleep, does not mate. He draws upon no external source of power. He never tires. He does not need sacrifices for food.

What's more, the God of the Bible is a God of justice and morality. The pagan universe was, according to Kaufmann, one of "amoral magical forces." In contrast, the world of the Bible is one of divine righteousness. The God of the Bible does not lie, cheat, or steal. He keeps all his promises.

And God said: "Let them be misconstrued"

Kaufmann was no fundamentalist, no believer in the inerrancy of scripture.

In fact, he believed that the radicalness of the Bible's conception of God led to actual *errors* in the Bible text. Specifically, Kaufmann believed the Bible's depiction of pagan religion was factually incorrect.

This presented to Kaufmann a vast enigma: Liberal scholars have long presupposed that Israelite religion evolved slowly out of its surrounding pagan milieu with YHWH merely being viewed as the chief or tribal god of Israel among many other gods. Yet Kaufmann says, "The Bible is utterly unaware of the nature and meaning of pagan religion."

Pagan religion, as it actually was, views the gods and goddesses as personified natural forces that are *represented by* statues or idols. Yet the Bible, Kaufmann said, seems to think that the idols are all there is to pagan belief. It refers to "Milcom, the abomination of the Ammonites" or to "Chemosh, the abomination of Moab," but not to the gods' functions in nature or even to their alleged characteristics.

"The myths of the pagans are not even derided as idle tales, as fabrications, nor are they utilized in poetic figures," Kaufmann says. Instead,

A Book Atheists Want to Burn

Anything and everything by G. K. Chesterton—one of the most quoted writers in English—who proves that a Christian apologist can be cleverer, wiser, and funnier than any skeptic. Good places to start: *Orthodoxy* and *The Everlasting Man*.

they are denounced as fetishes, mere "wood and stone."

"Those who have recognized this remarkable peculiarity are too enthralled by the assumption that the biblical writers knew the pagan myths to recognize its significance," Kaufmann says. If the biblical authors "meant to say that idols are vain because the gods they represent are nonexistent, why do they persist in arguing that idols are things of naught because wood and stone are of no avail?... How is the silence of the entire Bible—prophets, narratives, and laws alike—concerning pagan mythology to be explained?"

Kaufmann's answer to this riddle is a controversial repudiation of liberal biblical scholarship of the last two hundred years.

He argues that the radical monotheism of the Bible, far from evolving gradually and only appearing in its full-fledged form during the Babylonian Exile, in fact goes back to "the earliest strata of Israelite religion." This is, in fact, precisely what the biblical account in Genesis insists is the case.

For a variety of complex reasons that we cannot discuss here, Kaufmann rejects the traditional "source" theory of the Hebrew Bible, along with the view that Israelite religion "evolved" gradually out of lower, pagan forms.

He does this, not because of a belief in scriptural inerrancy, but because the evidence of Israel's radical monotheism was so all-pervasive throughout the entire Hebrew Bible that it could only have come through a sudden, society-wide transformation.

Not surprisingly, Kaufmann locates this "society-wide transformation" with Moses and the theophany at Sinai.

It was Moses—whom Kaufmann believes was absolutely a historical figure—who ultimately gave shape to the radical monotheism of the Bible, just as the biblical text says.

Old Testament scholars (liberal or conservative) have not fully embraced or even digested Kaufmann's theories, yet he raises interesting questions about the dominant assumptions that have undergirded critical biblical scholarship.

He is an example of how rigorous, text-critical scholarship frequently turns the pet theories of conservative and liberal scholars on their heads—how a careful reading of the text can actually support a more traditional viewpoint.

The biblical forest

In the end, the creation accounts in Genesis demonstrate how the Bible is the victim of its own success: In Western societies, at least, so all-pervasive is its influence—so universal is its basic cosmological outlook—that people today don't realize just how unusual it really is.

Its ideas, values, and cosmological outlook now so totally dominate the world we live in that we are largely unaware of them. But by shaping Western civilization—including Western law, government, science, media, and education—the Bible has shaped the world.

Indeed, for all the talk of "multiculturalism," the truth is that most modern people in the West are almost entirely ignorant of the sacred texts of other peoples, whether ancient or modern.

To put it simply: living in the midst of the biblical forest, we quite literally can't see the trees.

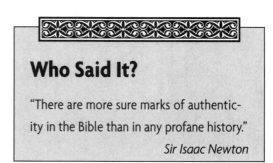

Who Said It?

"There are more sure marks of authenticity in the Bible than in any profane history."

Sir Isaac Newton

A Book Atheists Want to Burn

The Canon of Scripture, by Frederick Fyvie Bruce; Downers Grove, IL: InterVarsity Press, 1988.

It's similar with Western liberal democracy.

Because our world embraced the ideals of democratic self-government, the typical young Westerner has a difficult time realizing just how radical and world-altering these ideals really are—at least until he or she visits a society that utterly rejects them.

People who grew up under Communist dictatorships, or spent time in Islamic countries, have a better appreciation for ideas such as limited government, the separation of powers, free speech, universal human rights, the dignity of women, and the illegitimacy of slavery—ideas, as we'll see, that come from the Bible.

Most fundamental of all, however, is the Bible's view of cosmic origins. It represents a radical, historic break with virtually every religion and philosophy that came before and most of what came after it.

Chapter Five

BE FRUITFUL AND MULTIPLY

In the biblical account of creation, God creates man and woman—and the first thing he tells them to do is to have children.

"Be fruitful and multiply [*pru veh-ravuh*], fill the earth," is the first commandment of the Bible, according to rabbinic tradition.

But for some people today, children are viewed more as a curse than a blessing.

For example, according to Episcopal Bishop John Shelby Spong, author of the 2005 work *The Sins of Scripture: Exposing the Bible's Texts of Hate to Reveal the God of Love*, the Genesis account of the creation of man and woman, and the biblical injunction to "be fruitful and multiply," are "texts of hate" that modern men and women must forcefully repudiate.

"Can anyone seriously argue today that these words are the 'Word of God?'" the bishop asks. "Are they not little more than texts of oppression?"[1]

Spong is particularly agitated about the injunction to have procreative, heterosexual sex.

In his chapter "The Ethics of Overbreeding," Spong writes what is, in effect, a Planned Parenthood brochure, using the same old, now discredited Malthusian arguments from the 1960s about global "overpopulation."

Guess what?

◈ The Bible, unlike secular society, considers children a blessing—not a burden.

◈ Roman legislation, the Law of the Twelve Tables, actually required a father to put deformed children to death.

◈ Jews were almost alone among ancient peoples in their opposition to infanticide.

His example of "overbreeding" is a woman who has five children. He describes a fictional character—clearly modeled after the infamous Andrea Yates—an evangelical Christian who followed the teaching of Genesis, had five children, and became so overwrought that she drowned them all.

From this and similar examples, Spong concludes that the divine commandment to "be fruitful and multiply" is "nothing less than a prescription for human genocide."

Spong's argument is as follows:

   a) We know for a fact that having children is evil. It causes pollution and overpopulation.

   b) The Bible clearly states that we *should* have children, should "be fruitful and multiply."

   c) Therefore, the Bible is obviously wrong, is not to be trusted, and should be ignored whenever we feel like it.

Denouncing the Roman Catholic Church and "fundamentalists" who continue to welcome children into their lives with joy and gratitude, Spong darkly warns about the need to enforce a "limitation on human expansion."

It is hardly surprising to discover, then, that Spong is an enthusiastic proponent of abortion and homosexuality—both of which encourage a "limitation on human expansion."

Yet in the biblical account, heterosexual attraction and procreation are part of the divine plan, ordained from the beginning of creation. "Therefore a man shall leave his father and mother and cling to his wife and they shall become one flesh." "They were both naked, the man and his wife, and they were not ashamed" (Gn 2:24–25).

The Genesis account may be a "text of hate" for the Episcopal Bishop Spong, but no less an authority than Jesus cited it explicitly when asked about the legitimacy of divorce. "From the beginning of creation, 'God made them male and female. For this reason, a man shall leave his father and mother and be joined to his wife, and the two shall become one flesh.' So they are no longer two but one flesh. Therefore, what God has joined together, no man should separate" (Mk 10:5–9).

Scripture Says

"Children are a heritage from the Lord, offspring a reward from him."

Psalm 127

Although Christianity did later develop an openness to celibacy and virginity as religious vocations—accepting Jesus's invitation in Matthew 19 to renounce sex for the sake of God's kingdom—the ancient biblical texts heap praise upon human fertility and view children as an unqualified blessing to be cherished rather than as a curse to be avoided.

Jesus himself appears to have had a singular appreciation for the wondrous spirit of children, which was rare in the ancient world. "Let the children come to me," he told his disciples, who no doubt tried to shoo away some young followers, "for the kingdom of God belongs to such as these. Amen, I say to you, whoever does not accept the kingdom of God like a child will not enter it" (Mk 10:14–15). In this, as in many things, Jesus was merely reflecting and intensifying the insights of the Hebrew Bible.

"Truly children are a gift from the Lord," proclaims Psalm 127. "The fruit of the womb is a reward. Like arrows in the hand of a warrior, so are the children of one's youth. Happy is the man who has his quiver full of them; they shall not be ashamed, but shall speak with their enemies in the gate."

Indeed, procreation and human fertility are so central to the biblical narratives that they form the very basis of God's covenantal (*brit*) promise to Israel. God promises Abram, "This is my covenant with you. You shall be the father of a multitude of nations. . . . I will make you exceedingly fertile" (Gn 17:4, 6).

Ancient Israel's pro-life stance

The Old Testament has such a "pro-child" orientation that "barren-ness"—the inability to conceive children—is widely viewed as a curse from God.

Abraham's wife Sarah, the women of Abimelech's household, Rebekah, Rachel, Manoah's wife, Hannah, the Shunamite woman, and Elizabeth, the cousin of Mary, all were "barren" women whose wombs were "opened" by God. And once their wombs were "opened," they gave thanks:

> "Shout for joy, O barren one, you who have borne no child;
> Break forth into joyful shouting and cry aloud, you who have
> not travailed; For the sons of the desolate one will be more
> numerous than the sons of the married woman," says the Lord
> (Is 54:1).

Plus, it's not as though the biblical authors were unaware of birth control.

The texts may not describe the scientific details, but the gist of the matter was well understood. Even as early as Genesis, there is a plain awareness of human biology.

Genesis 38 relates the strange story of Tamar and Onan. Tamar was married to Judah's son Er, who died. Invoking what was known as the Levirate Law, Judah said to Onan, "Go in to your brother's wife, and perform your duty as a brother-in-law to her, and raise up offspring for your brother," Genesis relates. But "Onan knew that the offspring would not be [considered] his so when he went in to his brother's wife, he wasted his seed on the ground in order not to give offspring to his brother"[2] (Gn 38:8–9).

This act of *coitus interruptus* or contraceptive sex so angered God that he took Onan's life.

But Tamar was not to be deterred in her desire to have children. When Judah reneges on his promise to have his younger son father a child by

Tamar, she tricked him into fathering one himself—by pretending to be a Temple prostitute.

This "pro-child," pro-family orientation set Jews—and later, Christians—apart in ancient times.

"In our time, all Greece was visited by a dearth of children and a general decay of population," lamented the Greek historian Polybius around 140 BC. "This evil grew upon us rapidly, and without attracting attention, by our men becoming perverted to a passion for show and money and the pleasures of an idle life."[3]

Go to your room, or we'll kill you

Many ancient pagan societies believed that parents possessed an unqualified right to kill their own children for any or no reason.

The Law of the Twelve Tables, a Roman legislation circa 450 BC, actually *required* a father to put to death any deformed child (*Cito necatus insignis ad deformitatem puer esto*). (Modern moral philosophers, like Joseph Fletcher and Princeton University's Peter Singer, advocate the same thing.)

The killing of female children was so widespread that, just as in Asia today, the ancient world had a large abortion- or infanticide-caused imbalance in the sexes. (That imbalance today is about 100 million lost female lives.) A letter written in 51 BC from a pagan husband in Egypt to his wife, revealed the casual way pagans viewed killing infants, particularly young girls:

Atheist "Wisdom" Versus the Good Book

"Woman's destiny is to be wanton, like the bitch, the she-wolf; she must belong to all who claim her."

The Marquis de Sade

"My soul doth magnify the Lord.
And my spirit hath rejoiced in God my Saviour.
Because he hath regarded the humility of his handmaid; for behold from henceforth all generations shall call me blessed."

*The Canticle of Mary,
from the Gospel of Luke*

A Book Atheists Want to Burn

What's So Great About Christianity, by Dinesh D'Souza; Washington, DC: Regnery Publishing, 2007. Glad you asked—Dinesh D'Souza has the answers, especially to refute such atheist advocates as Christopher Hitchens, Richard Dawkins, and Sam Harris. Other books that might lie among the ashes of the atheist book-burners are John Stott's *Basic Christianity* and C. S. Lewis's *Mere Christianity*.

Know that I am still in Alexandria.... I ask and beg you to take good care of our baby son, and as soon as I receive payment I shall send it up to you. If you are delivered [before I come home], if it is a boy keep it, if a girl, discard it.[4]

Ritual child sacrifice was also widely practiced.

According to Plutarch, for example, the Carthaginians "offered up their own children, and those who had no children would buy little ones from poor people and cut their throats as if they were so many lambs or young birds; meanwhile the mothers stood by without a tear or moan."[5]

This is the cultural background for the practice of passing children "through fire," which biblical prophets denounced in Ezekiel: "You slaughtered my children and offered them up to idols by causing them to pass through the fire" (16:21).

And in the book of Jeremiah: "They built the high places of Baal that are in the valley of Ben-Hinnom to cause their sons and their daughters to pass through the fire to Molech, which I had not commanded them nor had it entered my mind that they should do this abomination, to cause Judah to sin" (32:35).

The Jews—almost alone among ancient peoples—abhorred killing children. The Roman historian Tacitus actually condemned the Jews for their inexplicable opposition to infanticide. "It is a crime among them to kill any newly born infant," he said, adding that they have a strange "passion for propagating their race"[6] (*Histories* 5.5).

But eventually Israel—in its desire to emulate the practices of "the nations"—began to kill its own children as well.

According to Psalm 106, "They mingled with the nations and learned their works.... They sacrificed their sons and their daughters to demons, and they shed innocent blood, the blood of their sons and their daughters, whom they sacrificed to the idols of Canaan, desecrating the land with bloodshed" (Ps 106:35, 37–38).

In fact, the sin of child sacrifice is understood by the Bible as being one of the major reasons why the northern Kingdom of Israel was destroyed by the Assyrians, in 750 BC, and the people taken into exile.

"They mutilated their sons and daughters by fire ... till the Lord, in his great anger against Israel, put them away out of his sight" (2 Kgs 17:17–18).

Today's "culture wars" rip at our roots

The more things change, the more they remain the same.

At the root of today's so-called "culture wars" there lies a fundamental disagreement about just this issue: Is natural, procreative, heterosexual sex a *good* thing—as it is depicted in the ancient Hebrew Bible? Or something from which men and women need to be "protected"?

Are children a *blessing* to be cherished, as the Bible teaches? Or are they a burden to be avoided or dispensed with as pagan philosophers claim?

For more than two thousand years, the Jewish and Christian communities assumed as a matter of course that procreative, heterosexual sex—and the children produced by it—are good things.

The Jewish sages taught that sex is the *woman's* right (*onah*), not the man's. A man has a positive duty "to give his wife sex regularly and to ensure that sex is pleasurable for her." The Talmud taught that once a man had a son and a daughter, he had fulfilled the commandment (*mitzvah*) of procreation—but in practice, Jewish law (*halakha*) limited when birth control was permitted.

As for Christianity, virtually every Christian ecclesial community viewed the deliberate avoidance of children as a sin. Martin Luther, the Protestant reformer who married a former Catholic nun, believed that "truly in all nature there was no activity more excellent and more admirable than procreation." Luther insisted that each conception of a new child was an act of "wonderment...wholly beyond our understanding," a "faint reminder of life before the Fall."[7]

Luther even denounced birth control and abortion long before they became widely practiced:

> How great, therefore, the wickedness of [fallen] human nature is! How many girls there are who prevent conception and kill and expel tender fetuses, although procreation is the work of God! Indeed, some spouses who marry and live together... have various ends in mind, but rarely children.[8]

Planned Parenthood's dark beginnings

But beginning in the early twentieth century, anti-family crusaders—such as Margaret Sanger, the founder of Planned Parenthood—began to target Christian churches and liberal Jewish organizations in an effort to "convert" them to the anti-child point of view.

While sometimes Sanger appealed to women's health issues, her most powerful arguments were largely social in nature. In the *Birth Control Review*, Sanger wrote frankly about the eugenic agenda behind the "planned parenthood" movement:

> Birth Control is thus the entering wedge for the Eugenic educator...the unbalance between the birth rate of the "unfit" and the "fit" is admittedly the greatest present menace to civiliza-

tion.... The most urgent problem today is how to limit and discourage the overfertility of the mentally and physically defective.[9]

For Sanger, among the most "unfit" of all were minority populations, particularly African Americans, whom she believed exhibited an unfortunate tendency to "breed" excessively.

From the very beginning, Planned Parenthood crusaders deliberately "infiltrated" Christian churches in order to inculcate their ideas. They found useful idiots—such as Planned Parenthood supporter Robert Drinan, a Jesuit priest who ran for Congress and publicly supported the entire birth control agenda, including even partial birth abortion—who could spread the anti-child gospel among the churches and synagogues in ways that they, avowed atheists, could not.

At first, the Christian and Jewish communities were skeptical of the notion that children were something that should be avoided or, at the very least, "planned."

But slowly, step by step, one by one, over about twenty or thirty years, the various Christian denominations and liberal Jewish organizations caved in. With the advent of oral contraceptives in the early 1960s, the sexual nirvana prophesied by Margaret Sanger—which she defined as "unlimited sexual gratification without the burden of unwanted children"—had arrived.[10]

Within a few short years, Ellen Peck would publish *The Baby Trap* in 1971 and proclaim that having a baby is "the biggest mistake of your life" and Paul Ehrlich, author of the 1968 book *The Population*

The Bible in American History, Part V

"It is impossible to enslave mentally or socially a Bible-reading people. The principles of the Bible are the groundwork of human freedom."

Horace Greeley

Who Said It?

"I have always said that a studious perusal of the sacred volume will make better citizens, better fathers, and better husbands."

Thomas Jefferson

Bomb, would convince government and media elites that the greatest problem the world faced was too many children.

Even though virtually every single one of Ehrlich's dire predictions would be proven dead wrong—and the developed countries of Europe now face a disastrous "birth dearth," not a population bomb—his conclusions about "over-population" are still unquestioned dogma among the older, more insensate members of the media, government, the law courts, academia, and the clergy.

Chapter Six

IN THE IMAGE AND LIKENESS OF GOD

Many conservative Christians and Jews believe that the Bible is inerrant in what it proposes to teach. But to understand what the Bible is teaching often requires that we recognize the genre or type of text in a given passage.

For example, there are many cases where the *intent* of a biblical author is not to present objective, scientific history in the modern sense—with fixed dates, correlated sources, eyewitness testimony, and so on—but to present the "big picture" to make a specific theological point. This is particularly true with the creation account in Genesis: most Christians and Jews understand that the intent of the biblical author was not to write a treatise on astrophysics or developmental biology but to convey a much bigger, more important, even more startling truth:

"Then God said, 'Let us make man in our image, after our likeness. Let them have dominion over the fish of the sea, the birds of the air, and the cattle, and over all the wild animals and all the creatures that crawl on the ground.' God created man in his image; in the divine image he created him; male and female he created them" (Gn 1:26–27).

As such, for most Jews and Christians, controversies over "evolution" and "creation" create a false dichotomy. The real issue isn't whether evolution is a valid theory, it's how that theory is applied or understood.

Guess what?

- Polls show that religiously observant individuals account for two-thirds of all charitable donations made annually in the United States.

- The so-called "social Darwinism" of the nineteenth century ultimately led to the anti-humanitarian degradations of the Nazis.

87

For instance, in his "Message to the Pontifical Academy of Sciences on Evolution," delivered on October 22, 1996, the late Pope John Paul II pointed out earlier popes' insistence that "there is no conflict between evolution and the doctrine of the faith regarding man and his vocation, provided that we do not lose sight of certain fixed points."

Calling evolution "more than just a hypothesis," the pope said that it was proper to speak of "theories" of evolution rather than a single "theory."

"The use of the plural is required here—in part because of the diversity of explanations regarding the mechanism of evolution, and in part because of the diversity of philosophies involved," he said. "There are materialist and reductionist theories, as well as spiritualist theories. Here the final judgment is within the competence of philosophy and, beyond that, of theology."

Pope John Paul II didn't endorse a particular theory of evolution, and certainly not a materialist theory advocated by neo-Darwinists. He merely pointed out the same thing that Pope Pius XII did nearly fifty years earlier in his encyclical *Humani generis*: that, in and of itself, "the doctrine of evolution, insofar as it inquires into the origin of the human body as coming from pre-existent and living matter," is not incompatible with Christian faith as revealed in the biblical texts.

Nor was Pius XII alone in this opinion.

One of the most prominent writers in the classic four-volume collection of articles, published in 1917, called *The Fundamentals*—from which the term "fundamentalist" derives—insisted that religious believers don't object to evolution as such

Who Said It?

"So great is my veneration for the Bible that the earlier my children begin to read it the more confident will be my hope that they will prove useful citizens of their country and respectable members of society. I have for many years made it a practice to read through the Bible once every year."

John Quincy Adams

but rather to a theory of evolution that is atheistic and mechanistic.

"The Bible, indeed, teaches a system of evolution," explained George Frederick Wright, in an article entitled "The Passing of Evolution." "The world was not made in an instant, or even in one day (whatever period day may signify), but in six days. Throughout the whole process there was an orderly progress from lower to higher forms of matter and life."[1]

Scripture Says

"What is man that you are mindful of him, and the son of man that you visit him? For you have made him a little lower than God, and you have crowned him with glory and majesty."

Psalm 8:4–5

Wright went on to say that what conservative Christians in his day objected to was a doctrine of evolution that "practically eliminates God from the whole creative process, and relegates mankind to the tender mercies of a mechanical universe, the wheels of whose machinery are left to move on without any immediate divine direction."

Most Christian denominations and Jewish organizations today take the view that their members are free to debate the relative merits of evolution, creationism, or intelligent design based on the evidence.

And while the scientific evidence for evolution *of some type* seems compelling to many, there are religious groups and thinkers who have pointed to numerous inconsistencies and "holes" in the naturalistic theories of evolution, based on the principle of natural selection, presented in many textbooks. Many biological scientists now concede that the available scientific evidence (in the form of the fossil record) does not wholly support Darwin's theory of gradual change based on natural selection, because species seem to appear quite suddenly without any intermediate steps.

Indeed, even Richard Dawkins, the atheist popularizer of evolution and author of *The Blind Watchmaker* and *The God Delusion*, concedes that "some biologists . . . have had doubts about Darwin's particular theory of *how* evolution happened."[2]

But these debates are scientific in nature, not theological.

"For theology, both the creationist and evolutionary hypotheses are permissible, in principle," explains Professor Alexey I. Osipov, a leading Orthodox theologian at the Moscow Theological Academy. "That is with

How Could a Flood Cover "All" the Earth?

What Skeptics Say: Genesis 8:9 says that the flood covered the "whole earth." But we know that is scientifically impossible: If the entire earth was covered by 30,000 feet of water, enough to cover the highest mountains, there would be no place for the water to recede and it would still cover the earth. The notion of a flood covering the entire earth is scientifically impossible.

Reply: Given the recent obsession with global warming, the possible melting of the polar ice caps and rising ocean waters covering entire landmasses, the knee-jerk opposition to the historicity of the flood narratives in Genesis is ironic. Nevertheless, biblical Hebrew frequently uses absolute terms that are not meant to be taken literally. The Hebrew phrase translated in English as "the whole earth" (*kol eretz*) literally means "all the land," and is used frequently to refer to people, not geography, and to local regions, not the entire planet. For example, 2 Samuel 18:8 says that "the battle was spread over the whole [*kol*] earth [*erets*]," meaning the entire region around Mahanaim, not the entire planet. 1 Chronicles 14:17 says that King David's fame extended to the "whole earth" (*kol erets)*, although it's doubtful the Bible is speaking of people in ancient China or Australia. For those who accept that the flood was an actual historical event and not a mere legend, the best way to understand it that does justice to the biblical texts is as a cataclysmic regional catastrophe such as those mentioned in numerous ancient Near Eastern records, including those of Sumer, Babylonia, Egypt, and Greece. While geologists insist there is no evidence of a universal flood covering the entire planet, there were numerous prehistoric deluges of catastrophic proportions, such as when the lower Tigris-Euphrates Valley was flooded 12,000 years ago and the Black Sea region was flooded 7,600 years ago.

In the Image and Likeness of God

the condition that in both cases the Lawgiver and the Creator of the world is God. All existing species He could create either by 'days,' at once and in final form, or gradually, in the course of 'days' to 'bring them forth' from water and earth, from lower forms to the highest by way of laws that He built into nature."

"Created" means we are endowed with dignity and rights

Where people of faith disagree most with secularists is not over the *mechanics* of creation but over a central point of Genesis that human beings are precious in the eyes of the Creator—or, as Jesus put it, "even the hairs on your head are numbered" by God (Lk 12:7).

If you're an atheist or pagan, it is hard to believe in the inherent dignity and worth of human beings. "Miserable creatures thrown for a moment on the surface of this little pile of mud," is how the modern pagan and atheist philosopher known as the Marquis de Sade characterized the human situation.

If human beings are merely "miserable creatures thrown for a moment on the surface of this little pile of mud," their lives are not worth much. For that reason the marquis was one of the first modern writers to champion abortion and infanticide.

"Dread not infanticide," he had one of his female characters say. "The crime is imaginary: we are always mistress of what we carry in our womb, and we do no more harm in destroying this kind of matter than in evacuating another, by medicines, when we feel the need."

If you believe that human beings are nothing more than chemical accidents—random, effervescent bubbles of consciousness in a cold, indifferent universe—it's difficult to believe that human life is inherently sacred or that human beings have rights that are anything more than mere social convention.

That is precisely why the early champions of scientific evolution quickly extended their theories into social and political realms.

The so-called "social Darwinism" of such nineteenth-century theoreticians as Herbert Spencer led to eugenics, to the belief in the "survival of the fittest," and, ultimately, to the anti-humanitarian degradations of the Nazis.

The dangers of anti-creationist thought

Charles Darwin's own half-cousin, Francis Galton, argued that charitable institutions such as orphanages allowed "inferior" human beings to survive and reproduce faster than "superior" ones.

The biblical belief that human beings, male and female, were created in the "image and likeness" of God necessarily carries with it certain logical corollaries—namely, that we have an obligation to our fellow man.

God says through the prophet Isaiah, "Woe to those who enact unjust decrees, who compose oppressive legislation, to deny justice to the weak and to cheat the humblest of my people of fair judgment, to make widows their prey and to rob the orphan (Is 10: 1–3)."

Christians, for their part, must confront such chilling texts as Matthew 25, which appear to make their very salvation dependent upon how they treat their fellow human creatures:

> When the Son of Man comes in his glory...he will separate the people one from another as a shepherd separates the sheep from the goats. He will put the sheep on his right and the goats on his left.
>
> Then the King will say to those on his right, "Come, you who are blessed by my Father; take your inheritance, the kingdom prepared for you since the creation of the world. For I was hungry and you gave me something to eat, I was thirsty and you

gave me something to drink, I was a stranger and you invited me in, I needed clothes and you clothed me, I was sick and you looked after me, I was in prison and you came to visit me."

Then the righteous will answer him, "Lord, when did we see you hungry and feed you, or thirsty and give you something to drink? When did we see you a stranger and invite you in, or needing clothes and clothe you? When did we see you sick or in prison and go to visit you?"

The King will reply, "I tell you the truth, whatever you did for one of the least of these brothers of mine, you did for me."

Then he will say to those on his left, "Depart from me, you who are cursed, into the eternal fire prepared for the devil and his angels. For I was hungry and you gave me nothing to eat, I was thirsty and you gave me nothing to drink, I was a stranger and you did not invite me in, I needed clothes and you did not clothe me, I was sick and in prison and you did not look after me" (Mt 25:31–43).

The Bible in American History, Part VI

"I am profitably engaged in reading the Bible. Take all of this Book upon reason that you can, and the balance by faith, and you will live and die a better man."

Abraham Lincoln

Faith and charity

Given biblical texts such as these, it's not surprising that, according to the Social Capital Community Benchmark Survey (SCCBS), undertaken in 2000 by researchers at the Roper Center for Public Opinion Research, participation in worship services is *by far* the most accurate predictor for charitable giving.

According to the Gallup Organization, religiously *observant* individuals (only 38 percent of all Americans) donate fully *two-thirds* of the $280

A Book Atheists Want to Burn

When Critics Ask: A Popular Handbook on Bible Difficulties, by Norman Geisler & Thomas Howe; Grand Rapids, MI: Baker Books, 1992.

billion donated in the United States annually—or $184 billion.[3] Foundations donate $25 billion and American corporations another $9 billion.

Among those who attend worship services regularly, 92 percent of Protestants give charitably compared with 91 percent of Catholics, 91 percent of Jews, and 89 percent of other religions.[4]

What's more, religious belief is more important that political ideology. The SCCBS study found that "religious liberals are 19 points more likely than secular liberals to give to charity, while religious conservatives are 28 points more likely than secular conservatives to do so."

This doesn't mean, of course, that religious persons are necessarily more ethical than their secular counterparts. Atheist crusaders such as Richard Dawkins, Christopher Hitchens, and Sam Harris angrily insist that you don't have to believe in God to be a good person—and indeed you don't. There are and have been many heroic "secular saints"—such as people who volunteer with Médecins Sans Frontières (Doctors Without Borders), Amnesty International, and other humanitarian groups—who sacrifice much to serve their fellow human beings through medical missions and many philanthropic enterprises.

But certainly we can say that that the biblical idea of man being created in the image and likeness of God has been and continues to be the most powerful motive for philanthropy in the world.

Chapter Seven

KEEP MY COMMANDMENTS

One of the wittiest attempts to undermine the authority of the Bible in recent years—and which was, perhaps inadvertently, a fairly vicious attack on the very foundations of Judaism—was the infamous "Open Letter to Dr. Laura" that made the rounds on the Internet around the year 2000.

At the time, Dr. Laura Schlessinger, the popular U.S. radio talk show host and a convert to Orthodox Judaism, was under fire by activist groups for her very public opposition to the "gay lifestyle," particularly as it relates to the parenting of children. She had just launched a TV version of her radio show, and activists in Hollywood pulled out all the stops in an ultimately successful effort to get the show canceled. According to the Web site StopDrLaura.com, 170 advertisers were pressured into abandoning Dr. Laura's TV show—which was canceled on March 30, 2001, almost a year after it began.

It was about this time that the "Open Letter to Dr. Laura" appeared—a letter that raises interesting questions about the relevance of Old Testament commandments to modern society:

> Dear Dr. Laura,
>
> Thank you for doing so much to educate people regarding God's Law. I have learned a great deal from your show, and I try to share that knowledge with as many people as I can.

Guess what?

- The principles of justice, mercy, concern for the poor, and equality before the law are the foundation of the biblical commandments.

- Unlike the Code of Hammurabi, the Torah places great importance on caring for those less fortunate in society.

- The laws of the Torah apply to all people equally, regardless of social or political status.

When someone tries to defend the homosexual lifestyle, for example, I simply remind him that Leviticus 18:22 clearly states it to be an abomination. End of debate.

I do need some advice from you, however, regarding some of the specific laws and how to best follow them.

a) When I burn a bull on the altar as a sacrifice, I know it creates a pleasing odor for the Lord (Lv 1:9). The problem is my neighbors. They claim the odor is not pleasing to them. Should I smite them?

b) I would like to sell my daughter into slavery, as sanctioned in Exodus 21:7. In this day and age, what do you think would be a fair price for her?

c) I know that I am allowed no contact with a woman while she is in her period of menstrual uncleanliness (Lv 15:19–24). The problem is, how do I tell? I have tried asking, but most women take offense.

d) Leviticus 25:44 states that I may indeed possess slaves, both male and female, provided they are purchased from neighboring nations. A friend of mine claims that this applies to Mexicans, but not Canadians. Can you clarify? Why can't I own Canadians?

The letter continues to touch on several more points, and even many devout Christians and Jews couldn't help chuckling at this creative piece of satire.

A number of writers took credit for the letter, but according to the producers of the TV series *The West Wing*, it was written in May 2000 by a freelance guitarist from Bowie, Maryland, named J. Kent Ashcraft. A version of the letter was incorporated into an episode of the show in October 2000 and the producers compensated Ashcraft for his contribution.

The episode, "The Midterms," portrays the fictional (and liberal) President Bartlet (played by actor Martin Sheen) demonstrating his allegedly superior knowledge of the Bible in ridiculing a conservative character named Dr. Jenna Jacobs, modeled on Dr. Laura Schlessinger.

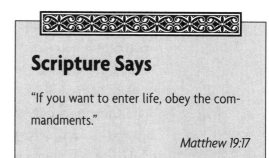

Scripture Says

"If you want to enter life, obey the commandments."

Matthew 19:17

BARTLET: You're Dr. Jenna Jacobs, right?

JACOBS (obviously pleased to be recognized): Yes, sir!

BARTLET: It's good to have you here.

JACOBS: Thank you!

BARTLET: . . . Forgive me, Dr. Jacobs. Are you an M.D.?

JACOBS: A Ph.D.

BARTLET: A Ph.D.?

JACOBS: Yes, sir.

BARTLET: In psychology?

JACOBS: No, sir.

BARTLET: Theology?

JACOBS: No.

BARTLET: Social work?

JACOBS: I have a Ph.D. in English Literature.

BARTLET: I'm asking 'cause on your show people call in for advice—and you go by the name Dr. Jacobs on your show—and I didn't know if maybe your listeners were confused by that and assumed you had advanced training in psychology, theology, or health care.

JACOBS: I don't believe they are confused, no, sir.

Just as an aside, the producers of the show were attempting, with this exchange, to make the millions of viewers of *The West Wing* believe that Dr. Laura Schlessinger has no qualifications to dispense parenting advice—

and therefore, by extension, that her views on the psychological healthiness of the homosexual lifestyle are unfounded. The truth, however, is that Dr. Laura is eminently qualified to do what she does, whatever you may think of her opinions. She received a BS in biological sciences from the State University of New York–Stonybrook, as well as her M.S., M. Phil., and Ph.D. in physiology from Columbia University. She also has postdoctoral certification in marriage, family, and child counseling from the University of Southern California–Los Angeles. She later worked as a member of the biological sciences faculty at USC for five years, as well as on the graduate psychology faculty at Pepperdine University for eight years. Dr. Laura is licensed in marriage, family, and child counseling in California, and had a private practice for twelve years.

BARTLET: I like your show. I like how you call homosexuality an "abomination!"

JACOBS: I don't say homosexuality is an abomination, Mr. President. The Bible does.

BARTLET: Yes it does. Leviticus!

JACOBS: 18:22.

BARTLET: Chapter and verse. I wanted to ask you a couple of questions while I had you here. I wanted to sell my youngest daughter into slavery, as sanctioned in Exodus 21:7. She's a Georgetown sophomore, speaks fluent Italian, always cleared the table when it was her turn. What would a good price for her be? (Bartlet only waits a second for a response, then plunges on.)

BARTLET: While thinking about that, can I ask another? My chief of staff, Leo McGary, insists on working on the Sabbath. Exodus 35:2 clearly says he should be put to death. Am I morally obligated to kill him myself? Or is it okay to call the police? (Bartlet barely pauses to take a breath.)

BARTLET: Here's one that's really important, because we've got a lot of sports fans in this town. Touching the skin of a dead pig makes one unclean. Leviticus 11:7. If they promise to wear gloves, can the Washington Redskins still play football? Can Notre Dame? Can West Point? Does the whole town really have to be together to stone my brother John for planting different crops side by side? Can I burn my mother in a small family gathering for wearing garments made from two different threads? Think about those questions, would you? (The camera pushes in on the president.) One last thing. While you may be mistaking this for your monthly meeting of the Ignorant Tight-Ass Club, in this building when the president stands, nobody sits.

For the Deep Thinkers in Hollywood, this little exchange represents a fatal, unanswerable blow to the Bible and all it represents (even though it deliberately misrepresents what the Bible actually says regarding these laws).

But what about the *substance* of this assault?

Does the Bible *really* teach that President Bartlet should "burn his mother in a small family gathering" for wearing garments made from two different threads?

Or that he should stone his brother for planting different crops side by side?

Or sell his daughter into slavery?

And, if so, how could the most brilliant minds in history—from Augustine, Aquinas, and Maimonides to John Locke and Sir William Blackstone—insist that the biblical law is the foundation upon which the great innovations of Western law and civilization, including the recognition of basic human rights, was based?

Let's look a little closer.

Two of the laws referred to in the episode of *The West Wing* are the law of *sha'atnez* (the wearing of combined fibers, *sha'atnez,* of wool and linen together, Dt 22:11, Lv 19:19) and the law of *kilayim* (the mixing of seeds, Lv 19:19).

A Book Atheists Want to Burn

Hard Sayings of the Bible, by Walter C. Kaiser, Jr., Peter H. Davis, F. F. Bruce, and Manfred T. Brauch; Downers Grove, IL: Inter-Varisty Press, 1996.

In typical Hollywood fashion, however, the writer—series creator Aaron Sorkin, who is himself Jewish—deliberately misrepresented what the Torah actually says in both instances just to take a cheap shot at Dr. Laura and strike a blow for homosexuality.

So what if he had to misrepresent the texts in the process and malign the Jewish people and religion to do it?

Here are the actual biblical laws word for word:

Leviticus 19:19: "Keep my statutes: do not breed any of your domestic animals with others of a different species; do not sow a field of yours with two different kinds of seeds; and do not put on a garment woven with two different kinds of thread."

Deuteronomy 22:11: "You shall not wear cloth of two different kinds of thread, wool and linen, woven together."

As you can see, while the Torah indeed forbids the mixing of the fibers or seeds, there is no specific penalty stated for the failure to do so—and certainly not, as *The West Wing* producers have President Bartlet say, *"burning my mother* in a small family gathering" or the whole town *"ston[ing] my brother* John for planting different crops side by side."

In other words: The TV producers and writer just *made that part up out of whole cloth*—to make the biblical laws seem more harsh than they actually are.

Like Dan Brown in *The Da Vinci Code*, writer/producer Aaron Sorkin used specific biblical citations a couple of times to give the appearance of authenticity to other material he just made up. (Predictably, there wasn't a peep of complaint heard about this slander from leading media critics.)

The Mosaic Law: To amend or not to amend?

In Judaism, these incomprehensible biblical laws are known as *hukim*, "commandments for which there is no convincing explanation, but which loyal Jews simply obey to demonstrate their obedience to the Divine will."[1] These include the laws of *kashrut* (or kosher eating), although many Jewish thinkers in the nineteenth century tried to find scientific rationales for many of the kosher laws (for example, the ban on eating pork might be related to avoiding the disease trichinosis).

The truth is, of the 613 commandments that the rabbis find in the Torah, the overwhelming majority fall into one of three categories:

a) still in force today in most civilized societies, although usually not with the same penalties

b) ceremonial and cultic regulations for the Ark of the Covenant and the Temple (both of which no longer exist) or

c) practical regulations related to life in a nomadic desert setting, which most people today do not share

Does the fact that most modern people no longer observe various regulations relating to the Jewish Temple and dietary laws mean that we should ignore *all* of the laws in the Torah, including the prohibitions against incest, bestiality, and child sacrifice?

In some ways, this is a more delicate question for observant Jews than it is for Christians, because Christianity has always believed that the Mosaic Law was, in some ways, only a partial and temporary dispensation meant to prepare a cruel world for the teachings of Christ. Orthodox Jews don't look at it this way, of course, and find such an attitude more than a little condescending.

In the Gospel of Mark, probably the earliest of the Gospels to be written, Jesus is asked by the Pharisees if it is "lawful" for a husband to divorce his wife.

Jesus replies, "What did Moses command you?"

The Pharisees say, "Moses permitted him to write a bill of divorce and dismiss her"—a reference to Deuteronomy 24:1.

But Jesus says, "Because of the hardness of your hearts he wrote this commandment. But from the beginning of creation, 'God made them male and female. For this reason, a man shall leave his father and mother, and the two shall become one flesh.' So they are no longer two but one flesh. Therefore, what God has joined together, let no man separate."

The clear implication of this passage is that some parts of the Mosaic Law, at least, were promulgated because of "the hardness of your hearts" and were not intended by God to be universally valid for all time.

This willingness of Jesus to amend the written Law of Moses rattled and scandalized pious Jews of his time—as it, quite understandably, still

The Bible in American History, Part VII

"In all my perplexities and distresses, the Bible has never failed to give me light and strength."

Robert E. Lee

"My advice to Sunday Schools no matter what their denomination is: Hold fast to the Bible as the sheet anchor of your liberties; write its precepts in your heart, and practice them in your lives. To the influence of this Book we are indebted for the progress made in true civilization and to this we must look as our guide in the future. 'Righteousness exalteth a nation, but sin is a reproach to any people' (Proverbs 14:34)."

Ulysses S. Grant

does today. In Matthew's version, Jesus says, "It was also said, 'Whoever divorces his wife must give her a bill of divorce.' But I say to you..."

I say to you? The Jewish Talmud scholar Jacob Neusner, in his little book *A Rabbi Talks with Jesus*, claims that a pious Jew would have replied, "Who do you think you are? God?"

Little wonder that the Gospels report the crowds were "astonished" by Jesus's teaching—because he taught with "authority" and "not like the scribes."

At that same time, however, it doesn't follow that Christians are supposed to *ignore* the biblical commandments, either.

Jesus told his followers that he did not come to abolish the law and the prophets but to fulfill them—and added that "whoever breaks one of the least of these commandments and teaches others to do so will be called least in the kingdom of heaven and whoever obeys and teaches these commandments will be called greatest in the kingdom of heaven" (Mt 5: 19).

It was clear that Jesus's message was not a rejection of the Mosaic Law but a radicalizing of it: "You have heard that it was said, 'You shall not commit adultery.' But I say to you, everyone who looks at a woman with lust has already committed adultery with her in his heart" (Mt 5:27–28).

So, why are these biblical commandments so blithely ridiculed on American television and through the Internet?

Are they really a harsh regime of cruelty, comparable to the Islamic shariah of the Taliban, as the secular media pretend?

A closer look at the Old Testament laws

On the one hand, some of the penalties (death!) given for specific acts (bestiality, incest, homosexuality, striking one's parents) seem harsh by contemporary standards—although in most cases there is little evidence that such penalties were ever actually enforced. "In practice...these [physical] punishments were almost never invoked, and existed mainly as a deterrent and to indicate the seriousness of the sins for which they were prescribed," said the late biblical scholar Rabbi Aryeh Kaplan. "The rules of evidence and other safeguards that the Torah provides to protect the accused made it all but impossible to actually invoke these penalties."

The biblical commandments also contain concepts of justice, mercy, concern for the poor, and equality before the law that were unprecedented in their own time and that did indeed lay the foundation of Western law and civilization.

Scholars point out that most of the biblical "rules" (*mishpatim*) and "commands" (*devarim*) are found in three collections in the Torah:

> The Book of the Covenant (Ex 21:1–23:19), which contains rules about ceremonies and rituals that follow from the covenant between God and Israel
>
> The Holiness Code (Lv 17–26), known in German as *Heiligkeitsgeserts* and abbreviated H, considered by many scholars to be very ancient and dating back to the dawn of Israelite existence
>
> The Deuteronomic Collection (Dt 12–28), which Deuteronomy itself calls The Book of Instruction (*sefer ha-Torah*), and is the only book in the Bible actually ascribed to Moses himself (31:9).

But because the various legal decrees are scattered throughout the entire Torah—mixed together with long naratives—rabbinic tradition has organized all this legal material inanother way.

As is well known, the rabbis have enumerated 613 individual commandments (*mitzvot*) in the Torah—265 positive commandments ("do this!") and 348 negative ones ("don't do this").

Just so we're clear about what is actually in these laws, here are a few of the things that the Torah forbids:

Committing murder ("You shall not murder," Ex 20:13)

Doing nothing when someone's life is in danger ("You shall not stand idly by the blood of your neighbor," Lv 19:16)

Committing adultery ("You shall not lie carnally with your neighbor's wife," Lv 18:20)

Homosexual sex ("You shall not lie with a man as one lies with a woman; it is an abomination," Lv 18:22)

Incest ("You shall not approach any close relative to uncover their nakedness," Lv 18:6)

Bestiality ("Do not lie with an animal," Lv 18:23)

Castration of man or beast ("One whose testicles are squeezed, crushed, torn or cut, you shall not offer to the Lord nor shall you have such practices in your Land," Lv 22:24)

Forcing a newlywed man to join the army or perform government service ("When a man marries a new wife, he shall not go out with the army, nor shall he be responsible for any service," Dt 24:5)

Ill-treating widows and orphans ("You shall not ill-treat any widow or orphan," Ex 22:21)

Cheating people in business ("When you sell anything to your neighbor, or make a purchase from the hand of your fellow, you shall not wrong one another," Lv 25:14)

Committing robbery ("You shall not commit robbery," Lv 19: 13)

Drinking blood ("You shall eat no blood," Lv 3:17)

Bodily mutilation ("You shall not make gashes in your flesh for the dead," Lv 19:28)

Selling your daughter into prostitution ("You shall not degrade your daughter by making a prostitute of her, else the land will become corrupt and full of lewdness," Lv 19:29)

There are other laws, of course, that we find strange or irrelevant today—which are the basis for the satire in the "Open Letter to Dr. Laura" and in the episode of *The West Wing*.

For example, there are five commandments requiring farmers to leave "gleanings" in the fields for the poor (e.g., Lv 19:9) that are difficult to obey in downtown Manhattan or London.

The command to help a tired donkey that is overburdened, even if it belongs to someone who hates you (Ex 23:5), cannot be followed literally today but reveals a principle that is still relevant to today and that actually prefigures Christ's teaching on the love of enemies.

For more than two thousand years, the Jewish people have pondered, prayed about, debated, and commented upon these ordinances.

Indeed, for observant Jews it is through the contemplation and living out of these myriad laws—whether understood or not—that God's will is known on earth.

"Take to heart these commands [*devarim*] which I enjoin on you today," God says to the Israelites in Deuteronomy. "Drill them into your children. Speak of them at home and abroad, whether you are busy or at rest. Bind them at your wrist as a sign and let them be as a pendant on your forehead. Write them on the doorposts of your houses and on your gates" (Dt 7:6–9).

This is precisely what Orthodox Jews do—through the wearing of *tefillin* (phylacteries—leather cords with attached prayer boxes), for example, and the placement of a *mezuzah* (an ornament bearing a scriptural inscription) on the doorway of a house.

Biblical law was originally word-of-mouth

The original delivery of these laws complicates the matter for both Orthodox Jews and Christian scholars. Most of the Mosaic Law was oral, with a small written portion, and it wasn't until much later that the law became fully written.

The oral law, which helped to explain and expand upon the written law, was handed down from generation to generation. For example, the biblical law forbids "work" on the Sabbath but nowhere defines what "work" actually means—a quite necessary requirement if you are to use this law in real life.

As a result, the rabbis, drawing upon oral tradition, formulated thirty-nine categories of activities that constitute "work," such as kindling a fire, sowing and ploughing, kneading, baking, shearing, writing more than two letters, carrying an object more than a certain distance, and so on. These rabbinic laws constitute the famous "fence around the Torah" that ensure that none of the written Torah commands is broken.

It was only following the catastrophe that occurred in 70 AD, when Roman legions besieged Jerusalem, destroyed the Temple, and dragged Jewish leaders off to captivity in Rome, that the Jewish sages decided to write down the oral law for posterity. Their debates about the law and how it is to be understood and applied became what is known as the Mishnah, an encyclopedia of legal commentary written about 200 AD in Jamnia, on the coast of Palestine. Further debates and commentaries about the Mishnah became the Talmud—one of the most complex and comprehensive bodies of legal knowledge ever created.

Modern atheist crusaders, such as Richard Dawkins and Christopher Hitchens, are largely ignorant of the influence of biblical law on the development of both Western morality generally and the law specifically.

Dawkins, in particular, goes to great lengths to argue that "modern morality, wherever else it comes from, does not come from the Bible"—and by "modern morality" he means our modern sense of right and wrong, our legal outlook.

"My purpose has been to demonstrate that we (and that includes most religious people) as a matter of fact don't get our morals from scripture," he writes in *The God Delusion*. "If we did, we would strictly observe the Sabbath and think it just and proper to execute anybody who chose not to. We

Atheist "Wisdom" Versus the Good Book

"The heaviest blow that ever struck humanity was the coming of Christianity. Bolshevism is Christianity's illegitimate child. Both are inventions of the Jew. The deliberate lie in the matter of religion was introduced into the world by Christianity."

Adolf Hitler

"And ye shall know the truth, and the truth shall make you free."

John 8:32

would stone to death any new bride who couldn't prove she was a virgin, if her husband pronounced himself unsatisfied with her."

Dawkins realizes that Christians, at least, do not believe the edicts of the Torah were universally valid for all time and for all people—although he can't help displaying a hint of traditional British upper-class anti-Semitism when he concedes this point. "Well, there's no denying that, from a moral point of view, Jesus is a huge improvement over the cruel ogre of the Old Testament," he sneers. "But the moral superiority of Jesus precisely bears out my point. Jesus was not content to derive his ethics from the scriptures of his upbringing. He explicitly departed from them, for example when he deflated the dire warnings about breaking the Sabbath.... Since a principal thesis of this chapter is that we do not, and should not, derive our morals from scripture, Jesus has to be honoured as a model for that very thesis."

But what Dawkins ignores is that, if Jesus did in any way depart from the "ethics" of the Torah—and, as we've seen, he himself said that he "came not to abolish the law and the prophets but to fulfill them"—it was only to radicalize and extend them, not repudiate them. Christian moral teaching grew out of, and mirrored, the fundamental principles found in the Torah and throughout the Jewish testament. What Dawkins, Hitchens, and other atheist ideologues are blind to is the dramatic ways in which biblical law shaped the development of Western legal codes and moral standards. The way we know this is by comparing the biblical law with other legal codes of the ancient Near East and with later legal systems.

In the authoritative collection of texts found in James B. Pritchard's *Ancient Near Eastern Texts Relating to the Old Testament*, we can find enormous chunks from the law codes of the ancient Near East—including the Code of Hammurabi (c. 1728–1686 BC), the Laws of Eshunna (c. 1850 BC), the collection of Sumarian laws of King Lipit-Ishtar (c. 1870 BC), a collection of ancient Assyrian laws found at Qal'at Sharqat in Iraq, and at least 200 Hittite laws (c. 1500 BC) discovered at Boghazköy in Turkey.

Eight great differences

Once again, when scholars compare the laws in the Bible with other legal codes in the ancient Near East, what's truly surprising is not the superficial similarities (such as the famous *lex talionis*, or law of an "eye for an eye") but the vast differences between them.

According to the great Jewish scholar Nahum Sarna, former professor of biblical studies at Brandeis University, there are at least eight major differences between the laws in the Torah and all other law codes in the ancient Near East.

Difference #1: Many of the laws in the Hebrew Bible concern matters of individual morality not enforceable by the state

The Code of Hammurabi is concerned solely with public acts; the Torah looks to private conscience. The Torah commands the Israelites to "honor" your father and mother, not to "covet," to "fear" the Lord. Leviticus 19:17–18 commands that "you shall not hate your kinsman in your heart" or "bear a grudge." These are largely interior acts that are completely off the radar of other ancient legal codes—and many modern ones as well.

Difference #2: Obedience to the law is the primary way to maintain a relationship with the Divinity

As Sarna notes, Israel's entire destiny is tied to whether it does, or does not, follow the divine decrees. This is a striking difference from the laws of surrounding peoples for whom the laws of the state reflect the will of the *king,* not the divinity. The legislation in the Torah, Sarna says, is inextricably linked to, and can only be understood in the context of, the vast narrative sweep of Israel's history.

"Be careful not to forget the Lord, your God, by neglecting his commandments and decrees and statutes which I enjoin on you today," Moses tells the Israelites in Deuteronomy. "Lest when you have eaten your fill, and have built fine houses and lived in them, and have increased your herds and flocks, your silver and gold, and all your property, you then become haughty of heart and unmindful of the Lord, your God, who brought you out of the Land of Egypt, that place of slavery" (Dt 8:11–14).

What's more, the law in the Bible mixes up religious and civil matters in a way quite unlike other law codes in the ancient Near East. According to Sarna, for most Near Eastern societies, the law was something imposed or declared by the king. For Israel, in contrast, the law was something decreed by God, as part of his covenant with the entire people.

Difference #3: The Torah places heavy emphasis on caring for the unfortunates of society, including the widow, the orphan, and even the alien

As Sarna puts it, the Code of Hammurabi "exhibit[s] almost no concern for the disadvantaged of society." In fact, quite the opposite: the general tendency of the laws in the ancient Near Eastern kingdoms was "to safeguard the interests of the upper class, and to preserve and promote its rights." In the Torah, in contrast, God commands special attention be paid to the downtrodden: "You shall not molest or oppress an alien, for you were once aliens yourselves in the land of Egypt. You shall not wrong any widow or orphan (Ex 22:21–22)." The text actually goes further than that, and God issues a stern warning to the rich and powerful: "If ever you wrong them and they cry out to me, I will surely hear their cry. My wrath will flare up, and I will kill you with the sword; then your own wives will be widows, and your children orphans" (Ex 22:23–24). In fact, the prohibition against oppressing a stranger—"for you were strangers in the Land of Egypt"—is repeated thirty-six times in the Torah.

There is nothing like this emphasis on the poor and alien in any Near Eastern legal system. It is a theme repeated throughout the Torah: "If you lend money to one of your poor neighbors among my people, you shall not act like an extortioner toward him by demanding interest from him. If you take your neighbor's cloak as a pledge, you shall return it to him before sunset; for this cloak of his is the only covering he has for his body. What else has he to sleep in? If he cries out to me, I will hear him, for I am compassionate" (Ex 22:25–27).

Difference #4: The laws of the Torah apply equally to all regardless of social status

Uniquely among ancient law codes, the Torah is no respecter of rank. "You shall have one standard for stranger and citizen alike: for I the Lord am your God" (Lv 24:22). King or peasant, mighty general or common foot soldier, all must obey God's commands. The Old Testament soap opera of King David and Bathsheba, the wife of Uriah the Hittite, found in 2 Samuel 11, illustrated this equality under the law.

Having seen Bathsheba bathing from the roof of his palace, King David sent for her and seduced her; she became pregnant. Attempting to cover up his sin, David sent for her husband, who was serving in the battle-fields, and offered him a furlough home with Bathsheba. Being of noble character, Uriah refused to take time off while his unit fought, even to see his wife, so David sent him to the front lines, where he was killed.

David then married the widowed Bathsheba. But God sent the prophet Nathan to David, who told David one of the first parables (outside of the New Testament) in the Bible. He told David the story of a rich man who had many flocks and herds, but insisted on taking a poor man's only lamb to feed a visitor instead of one from his vast flocks. When David became outraged that such a vile person lived in his kingdom, Nathan replied, "You are that man!"

Then Nathan delivered the judgment of God Almighty against King David: "Thus says the Lord: 'I will bring evil upon you out of your own house. I will take your wives while you live to see it, and will give them to your neighbor. He shall lie with your wives in broad daylight. You have done this deed in secret, but I will bring it about in the presence of all Israel, and with the sun looking down" (2 Sm 11, 12).

This notion that all men (and women) stand equally before the law is quite foreign to other Near Eastern societies—which had graduated penalties for offenses depending upon the social status of the offender and/or the victim.

Difference #5: The laws of the Torah forbid vicarious punishment by human magistrates

It is common in Near Eastern law codes for the law courts to punish people other than the perpetrator of the crime—usually a relative. Sarna cites the example in the Code of Hammurabi in which, if a man strikes a pregnant woman and causes her to lose her unborn child, then the *daughter* of the assailant, and not the assailant himself, shall be put to death. This is, Sarna says, unthinkable in the Torah, which explicitly rejects vicarious punishment in Deuteronomy 24:16. "Parents shall not be put to death for children, nor children be put to death for parents: A person shall be put to death only for his own crime."

Difference #6: The laws of the Torah avoid the brutal punishments typical of the ancient Near East

Some punishments in the Torah could be viewed by our modern minds as harsh, yet they are nothing compared with what the kingdoms of the ancient Near East routinely meted out, where mutilation and castration were common. According to Sarna, under the Code of Hammurabi, a slave who challenged his master would have his ear cut off. In Assyria, a man who stole a sheep would earn one hundred stripes with a lash, have his hair torn out, suffer a month of hard labor—and make restitution of the sheep.

Difference #7: Human life is more precious than property

Despite the stereotypes, the death penalty is actually quite rare in the Torah—and, in comparison with other ancient law codes, is reserved for more serious crimes. The Torah prescribes the death by stoning for apostasy (Lv 20:2), blasphemy (Lv 24:14), sorcery (Lv 20:27), violating the Sabbath (Num 15:35–36), disobeying one's parents (Dt 21:21), or cursing them (Dt 27:16), adultery by a wife (Dt 22:21), and rape of a married woman (Dt 22:25). In contrast, the Code of Hammurabi, Sarna points out, ordered that a barmaid who cheats her customer on the price of a drink must be killed by drowning. Human life was cheap in the ancient Near East. "The legislation of the Torah deals with crimes of theft and never imposes the death penalty for the violation of property rights, although it is more severe . . . in matters of sexual offenses and in certain violations of religious norms," Sarna says.

Difference #8: The laws of the Torah take into account voluntary versus involuntary acts

It has been noted many times that the ancient Greek vision of tragedy was due to their fundamentally fatalistic outlook. For the Greeks, what counted was what you *did,* your deeds, and your motives were secondary or even irrelevant. That meant that, if you accidentally killed a blood relative, your fate was sealed: you were quite literally doomed. The view inherent in the biblical legal texts is quite different. There is a clear distinction made between what we would call premeditated murder and involuntary manslaughter—with different penalties for each.

The whole purpose of the Cities of Refuge—to which someone who accidentally killed another could flee to escape the blood vengeance of relatives—was to reinforce this distinction.

The law in the writings of St. Paul

For the apostle Paul, many of the requirements of the Mosaic Law, while a good and necessary thing, were only temporary—and have been superseded by the work and teachings of Christ.

Gentiles, for example, are under no obligation to observe the ritual requirements of the Mosaic Law—as indeed the Jewish sages of the Talmud taught.

Out of the 613 commandments, the Jewish sages decided that only seven were binding on all human beings. These are the so-called Noahide laws, from the covenant that God established with Noah in Genesis 9: (1) the establishment of courts of justice and the prohibition against (2) idolatry (3) blasphemy (4) murder (5) incest and adultery (6) robbery (7) eating the flesh cut from a living animal.

In his letter to the Galatians, Paul makes explicit a distinction that is not found in the Torah itself, namely between (a) those moral precepts that remain universally valid and (b) the temporary social and ritual statutes—including the key covenantal practice of circumcision—that were given as a "disciplinarian" for a cruel age.

"Before faith came, we were held in custody under law, confined for the faith that was to be revealed," Paul writes. "Consequently, the law was our disciplinarian for Christ, that we might be justified by faith. But now that faith has come, we are no longer under a disciplinarian" (3:23–24).

For Paul, the Jewish ceremonial laws actually endanger the spiritual health of Gentiles. "It is I, Paul, who am telling you that if you have yourselves circumcised, Christ will be of no benefit to you," he says. "Once again I declare to every man who has himself circumcised that he is bound to observe the entire law. You are separated from Christ, you who are trying to be justified by law; you have fallen from grace" (Gal 5:2–3).

Does this mean, therefore, that Christians can do anything they please—as apparently the freewheeling citizens of Corinth (and later the Gnostics) taught?

Who Said It?

"You are not educated if you don't know the Bible. You can't read Shakespeare or Milton without it.... And with the schools now, they don't even teach it as a document. They stay out of the whole thing to avoid controversy. So kids can't quote the King James Bible. That's terrible."

Christopher Hitchens

No. For Paul, there is a moral law—that existed *prior to* the commandments of Moses—that is written on the human heart. These moral laws, which are also contained in the Torah, are universally valid. Gentiles who ignore this "natural law" end up degrading themselves.

"For when the Gentiles who do not have the law by nature observe the prescriptions of the law, they are a law for themselves even though they do not have the law. They show that the demands of the law are written in their hearts, while their conscience also bears witness and their conflicting thoughts accuse or even defend them on the day when, according to my gospel, God will judge people's hidden works through Christ Jesus" (Rom 2:14–16).

This Pauline distinction—between a natural (universal) moral law written on the human heart and the biblical commandments found in the Torah—found its way into early English legal commentaries.

"The doctrines thus delivered we call the revealed or divine law, and they are to be found only in the holy scriptures," explained Sir William Blackstone (c. 1723–1780) in his influential commentary on English common law. "These precepts, when revealed, are found upon comparison to be really a part of the original law of nature, as they tend in all their consequences to man's felicity.... Upon these two foundations, the law of nature and the law of revelation, depend all human laws; that is to say, no human laws should be suffered to contradict these."[2]

In conclusion, the biblical law mocked in the "Open Letter to Dr. Laura" and in episodes of *The West Wing*—however harsh some of its penalties may seem today—represented a radical break from the general barbarism and social indifference that was typical of the ancient world.

It introduced unprecedented concepts of individual morality, equality before the law, the preciousness of human life, and the illegitimacy of vicarious or brutal punishments that stood in stark contrast to the legal codes of the time.

There is also little doubt that biblical law had an enormous impact on the development of both church (canon) and later English common law—that vast body of unwritten law that developed based on the customs "common" to all of England and on the usages and rulings by courts in various jurisdictions. According to John Warwick Montgomery, professor of law and humanities at the University of Luton in England, "[I]t is an empirical fact that biblical morality has been well enough understood and effectively enough applied to constitute perhaps the most important single influence on modern Western legal systems."

Unlike civil (statutory) law, which is created by legislatures, common law is the result of the practical rulings of judges over the ages—and, because most judges in the West (at least until recently) were Christians, common law incorporated the moral values and judicial outlook of the Bible.

If parts of the biblical law seem harsh to us, we are only able to recognize that harshness because we live in a society that has been shaped by 2,000 years of reflection upon, and experience with, the principles of justice and mercy found in that very same law.

Chapter Eight

SODOM AND GOMORRAH

Quite apart from the current legal controversy over same-sex civil marriage—and whether secular society should legalize marital unions among same-sex couples or (for that matter) incestuous or polygamous unions—there lies a prior, even more heated religious dispute over the morality of homosexual conduct generally.

For more than 2,500 years, first the Jews and then the Christians have taught that homosexual relations are forbidden by God. Later, Christian theologians would claim that the reason for this prohibition is that homosexuality is intrinsically harmful both to the individuals involved and to society as a whole.

It goes without saying, of course, that the traditional position taken by Christian and Jewish organizations on homosexuality is under relentless attack today—often from vocal minorities within the denominations and religious organizations themselves. Some Christian denominations, most notably the Episcopal Church in America (ECUSA)—which consecrated the first actively homosexual bishop, the Reverand Gene Robinson, in 2003—are coming close to fracturing over the issue.

What's more, since the 1970s, liberal scholars (both Christians and Jews) have been waging a direct, often very scholarly assault on those passages in the Bible that have traditionally been seen as unambiguous condemnations of homosexuality.

Guess what?

- According to the Gospels, Jesus sees God's will expressed in the indissoluble bond of marriage.

- The purpose of sexuality as revealed in the Bible is the propagation of children in a loving, intimate, heterosexual relationship that endures for life.

- The re-definition of marriage to include same-sex couples will ultimately devalue and eventually eliminate the institution altogether.

In fact, academic religious studies departments and seminaries all over the world now frequently assert that the Bible is actually "silent" on the issue of homosexuality.

"The New Testament takes no demonstrable position on homosexuality," explains John Boswell, in his classic defense of homosexuality, *Christianity, Social Tolerance, and Homosexuality*. "To suggest that Paul's references to excesses of sexual indulgence involving homosexual behavior are indicative of a general position in opposition to same-sex eroticism is as unfounded as arguing that his condemnation of drunkenness implies opposition to the drinking of wine."

Progressive theologians often dismiss biblical condemnations of homosexuality by saying that these condemnations are about something else—primarily pedophilia or male prostitution.

"The homosexuality Paul would have known and to which he makes reference in his letters, particularly to the Romans, has to do with pederasty [sex between an adult male and a prepubescent youth] and male prostitution, and he particularly condemns those heterosexual men and women who assume homosexual practices," says the Reverend Peter J. Gomes in his thoughtful *The Good Book: Reading the Bible with Mind and Heart*. "All Paul knew of homosexuality was the debauched pagan expressions of it. He cannot be condemned for that ignorance, but neither should his ignorance be an excuse for our own."[1] Gomes, by the way, has been the minister in the Memorial Church at Harvard University since 1974.

Exhibit A: Getting to know you

The story of the destruction of Sodom and Gomorrah comes in Genesis 19, between the birth of Ishmael to Abraham's concubine Hagar and the birth of Isaac to his wife Sarah. The immediate context is God's establishment of his covenant with the "wandering Aramean" Abram, whom he renames Abraham and promises to make the father of "a host of nations" (Gn 17:4). Three "men" (*anashim*) approach Abraham near his tent. Abraham walks with them for a while and they all look down toward the city of Sodom. Then the Lord reveals to Abraham his plan to destroy the cities of Sodom and Gomorrah because "their sin is so grave"—whereupon Abraham begins to negotiate with God to save the inhabitants of the cities.

Scripture Says

"The Lord said, 'If I find fifty righteous people in the city of Sodom, I will spare the whole place for their sake.'"

Genesis 18:26

"Will you sweep away the innocent with the guilty?" he asks God. "Suppose there were fifty innocent people in the city. Would you wipe out the place, rather than spare it for the sake of the fifty innocent people?" The Lord replies that, if he finds fifty innocent people in the city of Sodom, he will spare the whole place for the sake of the fifty—and then Abraham presses his same argument for "five less than fifty," and then for forty, and then thirty, all the way down to ten.

The other two "men," whom the text now refers to as *malachim* (translated as "messengers" or "angels") proceed to Sodom itself, presumably to investigate the extent of the city's wickedness. They are met at the gate of the city by Lot, Abraham's nephew, who takes them into his house and prepares a meal for them.

But before the visitors are able to go to bed, all the inhabitants of Sodom, young and old alike—"all the people to the last man"—assemble about the house. They call out to Lot and say to him, "Where are the men who came to your house tonight? Bring them out to us that we may know [*yada*] them."

Traditionally, this demand to "know" the men has been interpreted to mean, as it does in a few other places in the Hebrew Bible, "to have sexual

Who Said It?

"Odd, the way the less the Bible is read the more it is translated."

C. S. Lewis

relations with," "be intimate with" or, as it's called, "know in the biblical sense."

In other words, both Jewish and Christian interpreters have understood this passage to mean that the inhabitants of Sodom were demanding to have sex with the male visitors—to rape them, in effect.

But beginning in the 1970s, advocates for homosexuality—including Derrick Bailey, John Boswell, and the Jesuit priest John J. McNeill—have insisted that, quite the contrary, all the text is saying is that the inhabitants of Sodom want to "get to know" the visitors, not commit homosexual rape.

It is merely "homophobia" and prejudice that imposes this meaning on the plain sense of the text, they say.

McNeill quotes the biblical scholar G. A. Barton who concludes that "there is no actual necessity to interpret 'know' in Gen. 19, 5, as equivalent with 'to have coitus with.' It may mean no more than 'get acquainted with.'"[2]

After all, these liberal scholars say, out of the 943 instances in the Hebrew Bible in which the verb *yada* (to know) is used, only fifteen of them are unambiguously in a sexual sense.

What's more, there is another Hebrew verb in the Jewish scriptures (used fifty times) to describe sexual relations per se, *shakav*, to "lie with."

In biblical studies, however, context is everything, and it is difficult to reconcile this revisionist interpretation of the text with what immediately follows it.

That's because the very next thing the text describes is Lot leaving his house, closing the door behind him, and imploring his neighbors not to do this "wicked thing."

Indeed, he even goes so far as to offer his own two daughters to the mob—who have not, he says, yet "known" (*yada*) a man. "Let me bring them out to you, and you may do to them as you please," Lot says. "But don't do anything [*lo ta'asu devar*] to these men, for you know they have come under the shelter of my roof."

The obvious question is: If all the men of Sodom wanted to do was to "get to know" the visitors—find out more about these aliens—why would Lot describe such an endeavor as a "wicked thing" and offer his virgin daughters as a substitute?

Exhibit B: The Levite in Gibeah

And if *yada* merely means "get acquainted with" in this context, why use that same word of the virgin daughters . . . who presumably *have* known, in a non-sexual sense, other men?

That the men of Sodom had homosexual rape on their mind is strengthened by the parallel story in Judges 19: 22–25, which describes a nearly identical event in which a Levite from the hill country of Ephraim stops off with his concubine at Gibeah, in Benjamin, to spend the night. An old man takes them in, but immediately the house is surrounded by "worthless men."

"Bring out the man who has come to your house so that we may know [*yada*] him," the unruly crowd screams. The old man refuses and pleads with the mob not to do this "disgrace" [*nevala*].

Instead, he offers the mob his virgin daughter and his guest's concubine. "Let me bring them out," the old man pleads. "Violate [*anu*] them and do [*asu*] to them what is good in your eyes; but to this man you must not do this disgraceful thing [*devar ha-nevala*]."

But the men were unwilling to listen to him, so the man seizes his concubine and thrusts her outside to them. The men know (*yada*) her and they "wantonly rape" (NRSV) or "abuse" (NAB, NIV, BDB, REB) her (*vay-italluba*) all night long, until the morning.

The Levite finds his concubine on the doorstep of the house in the morning, dead, so he cut her body up into twelve pieces and send one to each of the twelve tribes of Israel.

Quite apart from the appalling cowardice and misogyny shown by the Levite and the old man, clearly the men of Gibeah had other things on their minds than merely "getting acquainted with" the Levite or his concubine—and, therefore, the same can probably be said of the men of Sodom.

In any event, the angelic messengers to Abraham are displeased. They strike the mob outside the door with a blinding light and then tell Lot to take his family and friends and flee the city of Sodom immediately for God himself plans to destroy it. The next sunrise, the Lord rains down "sulfurous fire" from out of the heaven, annihilating the cities of Sodom and Gomorrah and the entire plain, and all the inhabitants of the cities and the vegetation of the ground. Whatever happened at Sodom, it made an enormous impression on later generations of Israelites because it is mentioned by numerous prophets and in the New Testament.

Homosexuality in the ancient world

Both defenders of homosexuality and scholars of ancient Near Eastern Studies insist that archaic civilizations had a much more permissive attitude toward view of homosexual practice than is the case today. In fact, the ancient, particularly the Hellenistic, world had a much more casual view of *most* sexual practices than we do today—including public nudity (*gymnasia*), public orgies (the Dionysian "mysteries"), ritual sex with religious prostitutes, sexual relationships among non-married persons, and pederasty.

The last was quite common in the Hellenistic world—with an older man, an *erastes*, taking on a young boy, an *eromanos*, as a kind of apprentice.

The older man would teach the boy adult male customs—and would expect, in return, to indulge in anal intercourse with the young boy as a purely passive partner. This type of relationship was sometimes praised by Plato, among others, as morally superior to heterosexual relationships because of the allegedly higher intelligence of males and because it taught the manly virtue of domination.

David Greenberg, in his work *The Construction of Homosexuality*,[3] argues (a bit too broadly) that "none of the archaic civilizations prohibited homosexuality per se" and that "with only a few exceptions, male homosexuality was not stigmatized or repressed so long as it conformed to norms regarding gender and the relative ages and statuses of the partners."

He cites Polybius (second century BC, Rome) as proof that, as Polybius reports, "*most* young men had male lovers" and "many of the Roman emperors had homosexual tastes"—a fact that any reader of Suetonius can verify.

The classics scholar Martha Nussbaum, herself a partisan in the current culture wars, sums up what she sees as the more tolerant and laissez-faire attitude of the ancient world toward extramarital sex generally and homosexual practices in particular:

> Ancient categories of sexual experience differed considerably from our own.... The central distinction in sexual morality was the distinction between active and passive roles. The gender of the object... is not in itself morally problematic. Boys and women are very often treated interchangeably as objects of [male] desire.... Sex is understood fundamentally not as interaction, but as a doing of something to someone.

The Jewish context

As the Jewish writer and radio commentator Dennis Prager puts it, Judaism changed all that. Sex was one of the many areas in which "Judaism differed."

In Jewish culture, sex was definitively not to be "a doing of something to someone."

Homosexuality was one of the "abominations" of the pagan world—along with the practice of parents killing their own children (infanticide). Alone of all the ancient civilizations of the Greco-Roman world, Judaism discouraged sexual relations outside of committed heterosexual relationships, and, as a result, homosexual acts. Prager writes:

> The revolutionary nature of Judaism's prohibiting all forms of non-marital sex was nowhere more radical, more challenging to the prevailing assumptions of mankind, than with regard to homosexuality. Indeed, Judaism may be said to have invented the notion of homosexuality, for in the ancient world sexuality was not divided between heterosexuality and homosexuality. That division was the Bible's doing. Before the Bible, the world divided sexuality between penetrator (active partner) and penetrated (passive partner).[4]

The Torah (Lv 18:22) states the principle in quite uncompromising terms: "You shall not lie [masculine, *tishkav*] with a male as with a woman; it is an abomination [*toevah*]." The penalty is added two verses later: "If a man lies with a male as a woman, both of them have committed an abomination; they shall be put to death, their blood is upon them."

Old Testament scholars make several points about this passage.

First, the use of the word for "male" (*zakar*) rather than "youth" (*na'ar*) shows that pederasty was *not* the crime being addressed but rather homosexual sex itself.

Plus the equal punishment of the parties involved suggests that *both* are consenting adults. "Their blood will be on their own heads" (Lv 20:13) shows that both are also aware of what they are doing and of the consequences. The seriousness of the offense is indicated by the penalty (namely, death) and by the term "abomination" (Hebrew *toeva*—

A Book Atheists Want to Burn

The Religion of Israel: From Its Beginnings to the Babylonian Exile, by Yehezkel Kaufmann; New York: Schocken Books, 1960.

a term used of offenses deemed particularly heinous in God's sight, such as blasphemy).

There are two ways this text is rejected out of hand today.

Some liberal scholars say it is based on a primitive, pre-scientific understanding of human procreation, one in which any spilling of male "seed" (semen)—in homosexual sex, masturbation, or *coitus interruptus*—was considered tantamount to abortion and murder.

Other contend that with the text is a scholarly version of the Internet joke that was circulated against radio personality Dr. Laura Schlessinger that we discussed in the previous chapter—namely, that the Holiness Code in Leviticus condemns many things that modern society (both Jewish and Gentile) now finds quite harmless, such as shaving, cross-breeding livestock, blending textile materials, and eating non-kosher food (such as shrimp) as well as requiring the death penalty for such acts as adultery (Lv 20:10) or taking the Lord's name in vain (Lv 24:16).

Regardless of how these texts are to be applied today, it is clear that homosexual conduct was strongly denounced in Israelite and then later Jewish culture, including during the Second Temple period.

As early as the second century BC, Jewish writers were noting the differences between Jewish sexual and family mores and those of their non-Jewish neighbors. In the *Syballine Oracles*, written by an Egyptian Jew probably between 163 and 45 BC, the author compared Jews to the other nations: The Jews "are mindful of holy wedlock," he said, "and they do not engage in impious intercourse with male children, as do Phoenicians, Egyptians, and Romans, specious Greece and many nations of others, Persians and Galatians and all Asia."

The first-century Jewish historian Josephus stated that "our laws own no other mixture of the sexes but that which nature has appointed (*kata physin*) of a man with his wife . . . and it abhors the mixture of a male with a male (*ten de pros arrenas arrenon hestygeken*)."[5]

Homosexuality in the New Testament

Given the creative way that religious defenders of homosexuality try to explain away or re-interpret traditional Jewish condemnations of homosexual conduct, it should not be surprising that they do the same thing with the New Testament.

Most of the exegetical attack is focused on St. Paul because he explicitly discusses the subject—and on two passages in particular.

In 1 Corinthians 6:9–10, Paul writes:

> Do not be deceived; neither fornicators, nor idolaters, nor adulterers, nor the effeminate [*malakoi*], nor homosexuals [*arsenokoitai*], nor thieves, nor the covetous, nor drunkards, nor revilers, nor swindlers, shall inherit the kingdom of God. And such were some of you; but you were washed, sanctified, and justified in the name of the Lord Jesus Christ, and in the Spirit of our God.

In Romans 1, Paul writes:

> For the wrath of God is revealed from heaven against all ungodliness and unrighteousness of men, who suppress the truth in unrighteousness . . . . Professing to be wise, they became

fools, and exchanged the glory of the incorruptible God for an image in the form of corruptible man and of birds and four-footed animals and crawling creatures. Therefore God gave them over in the lusts of their hearts to impurity, that their bodies might be dishonored among them. For they exchanged the truth of God for a lie, and worshiped and served the creature rather than the Creator, who is blessed forever. Amen.

For this reason God gave them over to degrading passions; for their women exchanged the natural function for that which is unnatural, and in the same way also the men abandoned the natural function of the woman and burned in their desire toward one another, men with men committing indecent acts and receiving in their own persons the due penalty of their error.

It is not at all shocking, given the widespread abhorrence that Jews expressed of the homosexual practices of the Greeks, that St. Paul, in his letters, should condemn homosexuality as well. But Paul's attitude towards homosexuality is clarified slightly by examining 1 Corinthians 6:9–10 in the overall context of his letter to the Corinthian community.

That is because one of the occasions for the letter was, in fact, a report of an act of sexual misconduct so reprehensible that, Paul says, it is "of a kind not found even among pagans—a man living with his father's wife" (1 Cor 5:1).

As this makes clear, Paul shares in the Second Temple Jewish attitude that the sexual practices of the pagans stood in marked contrast to those of Judaism. The Romanized Corinthians, of course, had a historic reputation for loose living—Corinth was viewed rather like Las Vegas is in the United States, as a kind of "sin city"—and the newly baptized believed that the freedom they had in Christ meant that, as many liberal believers today insist, sexual issues simply "no longer mattered."

Paul makes it quite clear that this is not the case: "The one who did this deed should be expelled from your midst" (1 Cor 5:2), advocating what appears to be a kind of early excommunication.

What is the reason for this seemingly harsh attitude?

In chapter 6, Paul explains that it is of the nature of sexual sin to involve the entire person, body and soul. "Do you not know that anyone who joins himself to a prostitute becomes one body with her? For 'the two,' it says, 'will become one flesh.' . . . Every other sin a person commits is outside the body, but the immoral person [*pornos*] sins against his own body." And that body, Paul concludes, is not your own to do with as you will. Rather, it is "from God," a "temple of the Holy Spirit." For the same reason, "because of cases of immorality [*porneia*], every man should have his own wife and every woman her own husband" (1 Cor 7:2).

The Greek word *porneia*—from which we get the word "pornography"—can indeed mean prostitution but also merely casual sex or, as we might say, "living together" or concubinage.

Paul is asserting that Christians should marry in the *Jewish* sense—in a formally committed, vowed relationship—rather than indulge in casual fornication.

The traditional translation of *malakoi* and *arsenokoitai* as "effeminate" and "homosexuals," respectively, has been challenged by religious defenders of homosexuality. According to the two standard Greek lexicons (Bauer and Liddell & Scott), the two basic meanings of *malakos* are "soft" and "effeminate." According to Bauer, in the New Testament period the word means "soft, effeminate, especially of catamites, men and boys who allow themselves to be misused homosexually," citing such authors as Dionysius Halicarnassus, Dio Chrysostom, and Dionysius Laertius as examples.[6]

Some defenders of homosexuality within the Christian church, however, stand firmly against this conventional understanding of *malakos*. According to John Boswell, in his influential 1980 work, *Christianity, Social Tol-*

erance and Homosexuality, the word *malakos* should be translated as either "unrestrained" or "wanton," arguing that "to assume that either of these concepts necessarily applies to gay people is wholly gratuitous."[7]

Others ask why Paul would use a word such as *malakos* when condemning homosexuality—a word that has such ambiguous meanings—when there are many other words in Greek that apply specifically to homosexual acts. Nevertheless, many biblical scholars remain unconvinced by the arguments of Boswell and others. Scholars point out that part of Bowell's case for understanding *malakos* as "wanton" is the citing of passages such as Matthew 4:23, 9:35, and 10:1 in which *malakos* allegedly signifies sickness. But the word used in these cases is not *malakos* but *malakia,* which does mean sickness.

The other key word, *arsenokoitai*, is even more puzzling.

In its noun form, it is found in no Greek literature before Paul and may well have been coined by him. According to the *Liddell and Scott Lexicon, arsenokoitai* occurs twice in Greek literature. Bauer's *Greek-English Lexicon of the New Testament and Other Early Christian Literature* lists only six citations for *arsenokoitai*, two from the New Testament and four in the later Church fathers.

The word itself is a compound of two Greek roots, *arseno*, which means simply male, and *koitai*, from which we get the word *coitus*, a somewhat vulgar Greek word for "bedding" or "lying," usually in a sexual sense.

Most scholars believe Paul coined the noun from the Septuagint translation of Leviticus 20:13, which speaks of *meta arsenos koiten gynaikos* (literally: "with a man lying as with a woman").

Again, Boswell argues that the proper meaning of this word, in both this passage and in 1 Timothy 1:10, is "male prostitute" because of its proximity to the word *pornoi*, which can have the connotation of prostitution as well as sexual intercourse outside of marriage generally (fornication). He thus argues that Paul is condemning, not homosexuality itself, but exploitative homosexual prostitution.

The Bible in American History, Part VIII

"A thorough knowledge of the Bible is worth more than a college education."

Theodore Roosevelt

"Moreover, prostitution is manifestly of greater concern to Saint Paul than any sort of homosexual behaviour: excluding the words in question, there is only a single reference to homosexual acts in Paul's writing, whereas the word *pornos* and its derivatives are mentioned almost thirty times."[8]

It's not surprising, therefore—in what seems to some as a shameless kowtowing to political correctness—that the New Revised Standard Version translates *aresenokotai* as ... yes ... "male prostitutes."

Conservative scholars counter that Paul continues firmly in the Levitical tradition here, and that to say that Paul had in mind male prostitution alone (as translated by the NRSV) is simply special pleading, especially when contrasted to what Paul says in Romans and in other letters.

That Paul's attitude toward homosexual conduct is distinctly negative can also be seen by examining a few other key texts in his letters.

The text of 1 Timothy 1:10, which may have been written by an associate of Paul and not Paul himself, is structurally similar to the passage in 1 Corinthians. It is a catalog of examples of the "impious [*asebesi*] and sinful [*amartolois*]," including "those who kill their fathers or mothers, murderers, fornicators [*pornois*], 'male-bedders' or 'sodomites' [*arsenokoitais*], kidnappers, liars, perjurers, and whatever else is opposed to unhealthful teaching...."

As we can see, the same word is used here as in 1 Corinthians 6:10, *arsenokoitais,* which means literally "male-bedders." That Paul numbers the "male-bedders" with murderers, parricides, kidnappers, and liars certainly shows that his attitude toward them—whatever they are—is not exactly positive.

The other key text in Paul—and indeed the only other major text in the New Testament that concerns homosexuality—is Romans 1:26–27.

"Therefore, God gave them up in the lusts of their hearts to impurity [*akatharsian*], to the dishonoring of their bodies among themselves.... Their women exchanged natural relations for unnatural [*para physin*], and the men likewise gave up natural relations with women and were consumed with passion for one another, men committing shameless acts with men and receiving in their own persons the due penalty for their error (Rom 1:24–27)."

There are two ways that defenders of homosexuality deal with this passage: One, the least persuasive, is to say that this text refers, not to homosexuality generally—the sincere love between people of the same sex—but to homosexual temple prostitution. Because Paul is linking homosexuality in this passage to idolatry, the argument goes, he clearly has in mind the ancient goddess cults, such as the Cybelean/Attic mystery cult, in which male castrati, called *galli*, would serve sexually "as women" to male worshipers in the temple.

Old Testament scholars such as Fr. Joseph Fitzmyer, S.J., have a simpler explanation for the text: "Paul is clearly referring here to the conduct of active male homosexual persons and is merely echoing the OT abomination of such homosexual activity."[9]

The second argument, quite creatively put forth by John Boswell, is that what Paul is condemning is not homosexual sex between homosexual persons, but rather homosexual sex between *heterosexual* persons. In other words: Homosexual sex is okay when homosexuals do it, but immoral when heterosexuals (drunk or inflamed with lust) do.

The third, more persuasive argument is that this text is a difficult anomaly—an example of an idiosyncratic teaching not found anywhere else in the New Testament and therefore similar to other strange prohibitions of Paul, such as his forbidding women to speak in church or his insistence that women wear veils, simply ignored by most Christian denominations.

This "argument from silence" is much stronger when you consider that Jesus mentions homosexuality not at all in our records and that the Bible actually mentions it very rarely—only ten times in the Hebrew Bible (Gn 13:13, Lv 18:22 and 20:13, Dt 22:5, Jgs 19 and 2 Kgs 23:27, 1 Kgs 14:24, 15:12 and 22:46 and Ws 14:26), three times in the letters of St. Paul, all of which we have discussed, and once in Jude 7: ("Just as Sodom and Gomorrah and the surrounding cities, which likewise acted immorally and indulged in unnatural lust [lit. 'different flesh,' *sarkos eteras*], serve as an example by undergoing a punishment of eternal fire)."

"Go, and sin no more"

The notion of an easygoing, sexually tolerant Jesus is prevalent among defenders of homosexual practice.

After all, one of the most striking and consistent aspects of the portrait of Jesus received from the Gospels was his willingness to befriend and even make close disciples of social outcasts, including prostitutes, tax-collectors, hated Roman soldiers, Samaritans, and lepers.

However, as Robert A. J. Gagnon argues in his precise exegetical work, *The Bible and Homosexual Practice*, a close examination of the Gospels belies the portrait of the easygoing, sexually broadminded Jesus.

Jesus may have been forgiving of the woman taken in adultery, but his actual attitude toward adultery itself went far beyond what any sage of Judaism, then or since, taught.

In Matthew 5:27, Jesus says: "You have heard that it was said, 'You shall not commit adultery.' But I say to you, everyone who looks at a woman with lust has already committed adultery with her in his heart!"

According to the Gospels, for Jesus the will of God is expressed in the indissoluble marriage bond, which, echoing Genesis, he ties to the very fabric of creation. In Mark, Jesus notes that "from the beginning of creation, God made them male and female," and therefore "a man shall leave his father and mother and be joined to his wife, and the two shall become one flesh. So they are no longer two but one flesh."

It is because of this total physical and spiritual union, Jesus says, that divorce is simply not permissible: "What God has joined together, no man may separate."

Comments Gagnon: "The whole point of Jesus's stance in Mark 10:1–12 is not to broaden the Torah's openness to alternative forms of sexuality but rather to narrow or constrain the Torah's sexual ethic to disallow any sexual union other than a monogamous, lifelong marriage to a person of the opposite sex."[10]

Jesus did indeed forgive the woman taken in adultery, but he said, "Go, and sin no more" and not, "Go ahead and do what feels right to you . . . since whom you sleep with doesn't matter anyway."

Conclusion

The defenders of homosexual practice certainly have one very valid point: The biblical data on homosexuality are few and far between—just a handful of texts, although all uniformly negative. The difficulty for those who advocate a fundamental change in the teaching of Judaism and Christianity on homosexuality is that there is little evidence that these handful of texts (specifically Leviticus and Romans) were meant to apply their negative condemnations of homosexuality merely to exploitative sex acts, such as pederasty or prostitution.

When in Romans 1, Paul says that the men were "consumed with passion for one another," he implies a mutual sexual attraction and not simply the exploitative relationship found in temple prostitution or pederasty.

Clearly, Paul held a general abhorrence of pagan sexual practices— homosexuality in particular—a view typical of Judaism in that period.

This condemnation of homosexuality, then—like the biblical condemnation of adultery or incest—rejects the argument that the parties involved might feel a sincere love for one another. The act is simply forbidden.

Moreover, the isolated but quite firm biblical condemnations of homosexual conduct must be put into the wider context of Second Temple Judaism and the early church. The extra-biblical witnesses—from the pseudepigrapha to the Mishnah and early church fathers—make clear that the biblical condemnations of homosexual conduct make much more sense when put into the more positive context of human sexual love generally and its revealed purpose in nature: It is within the holistic vision of what human sexuality is *for*, revealed initially in the Hebrew Bible, radicalized by the teaching of Christ, and thought through more carefully by the early Christian theologians, that Christianity argues what is wrong about homosexual practice.

Modern exponents of homosexuality are correct: Judaism represented a dramatic break with pagan culture by insisting God intended sex to be confined within the bounds of committed heterosexual relationships. (Strictly speaking, Jewish law prohibited married women from having sex with men who are not their husbands . . . but it was not until 1000 AD that Rabbi Gershom ben Judah (c. 960–1028) wrote a religious responsa, called a *takanah* or "fix," that also prohibited men from having multiple wives or having sex with unmarried women.)

In the Torah, the woman is not a man's property or mere breeding stock but his "help-mate" (*ezer*). Jesus accepted this radical teaching of Judaism and made it even more radical: He declared that not only should married men not divorce their wives—trade in their aging partners for younger, more sexually attractive women—they should not even look with lust on another woman.

He thereby revealed and confirmed the original meaning of the union of man and woman as the Creator willed it from the beginning: permission given by Moses to divorce one's wife, Jesus said, was a concession to the hardness of hearts. Instead, man and woman are to live in a state of such radical intimacy and mutual giving that they do not even have "rights" (that most modern of imperatives) over their own bodies ("A wife does not have authority over her own body, but rather her husband; and similarly a husband does not have authority over his own body, but rather his wife," as Paul put it in 1 Corinthians 7:4).

Thus, the Christian Church traditionally rejected homosexual practice for the same reason it rejected divorce, adultery, and fornication: Because the purpose of sexuality, revealed in the very structure and dynamism of the human body, as well as in the teaching of Christ and the overall vision of the Bible, is clearly the propagation of children in loving, intimate heterosexual relationships that endure for life. Homosexuality is clearly a direct attempt to frustrate and block this fundamental purpose...and therefore contrary to God's will for humanity.

Of course the biblical argument doesn't really settle the dispute for civil society. Just as civil society tolerates divorce even though Jesus himself opposed it, citizens in a free nation may decide that, while homosexual conduct may be immoral or not in the best interests of those who engage in it, nevertheless it should be tolerated just as divorce is tolerated.

This is the position taken by some conservative Jewish rabbis: They equate the biblical ban on homosexuality with the biblical ban on eating pork. Both are forbidden to Jews, of course—the biblical texts are clear—but if the *goyim* want to indulge in such things, who are we to say something against it? Gentiles are only bound by the seven Noahide laws, and homosexuality—while admittedly an "abomination"—is not covered by any of them. This position allows some conservative rabbis to be both very traditional (they won't perform Jewish marriages for same-sex couples) but very progressive at the same time (they are for civil union statutes and commitment ceremonies).

The problem posed by marriage, however, is especially complex because it pits the equal protection concerns of civil law against the historic cornerstone of human society, which is heterosexual marriage and the family. Marriage and the nuclear family have secular, civil purposes over and beyond their religious character—and, for that reason, many conservative Christians and Jews believe that a "re-definition" of marriage to include same-sex couples will ultimately devalue and eventually eliminate the institution altogether.

This can already be seen in the increasingly common custom of referring to male and female couples, whether married or not, as "partners," not husband and wife—with all the casual transitoriness that such a euphemism implies ("Allow me to introduce my temporary sexual partner, Jill..." seems somewhat different from, "Allow me to introduce my wife, Jill"). It is also clear that, once the precedent of same-sex civil marriage is accepted, there is no logical reason to forbid legal recognition of other sexual arrangements that have historically been viewed as harmful to society and the individuals involved—including incest and polygamy.

Who Said It?

"In most parts of the Bible, everything is implicitly or explicitly introduced with 'Thus saith the Lord.' It is...not merely a sacred book but a book so remorselessly and continuously sacred that it does not invite—it excludes or repels—the merely aesthetic approach. You can read it as literature only by a tour de force.... It demands incessantly to be taken on its own terms: it will not continue to give literary delight very long, except to those who go to it for something quite different. I predict that it will in the future be read, as it always has been read, almost exclusively by Christians."

C. S. Lewis

Chapter Nine

THE HEAVENS DECLARE
THE GLORY OF GOD

When it comes to the development of modern science, the ene-mies of the Bible—from Voltaire and David Hume to Penn and Teller and Richard Dawkins—tell the same tale.

For millennia, Christianity in general, and the Roman Catholic Church in particular, attempted to keep mankind locked in a dark prison of superstition and irrational dogma—and it was only when mankind threw off the shackles of revealed religion during the Renaissance and Enlightenment that modern science was able to develop.

As long as mankind looked to the Bible for the truth about the world and man's place within it, these critics say, science was prevented from being born.

"The Bible, it seems, was the work of sand-strewn men and women who thought the earth was flat and for whom a wheelbarrow would have been a breathtaking example of emerging technology," sneers Sam Harris in his 2005 polemic against religion, *The End of Faith*. "We will see that the greatest problem confronting civilization is not merely religious extremism: rather, it is the larger set of cultural and intellectual accom-modations we have made to faith itself."

This has been the conventional view of atheist intellectuals through-out most of the twentieth century.

Guess what?

- Only in Christian Europe, full of churchgoing believ-ers, did mankind begin the systematic study of nature.

- The rational theology of the Catholic Mid-dle Ages and the Protestant Reforma-tion led directly to the discoveries of modern science.

- The scientists who founded entire disci-plines or made land-mark scientific discoveries were primarily devout Christians.

After the flourishing of Greek and Roman civilization, mankind entered a prolonged and terrible Dark Age, an age of blind faith instead of reason, in which "millions" of women were put to death as witches, Crusaders attacked the peace-loving Muslims for no reason, and everyone believed the world was flat.

The Catholic Church did everything in its power to keep people ignorant and illiterate. But despite its best efforts, a few courageous intellectuals arose in the sixteenth century and began to seek out the lost knowledge of classical antiquity. This "Renaissance"—or "rebirth" of knowledge—taught men to think for themselves and led to the development of modern science.

Once freed of the dogmas of biblical Christianity and its taboos against learning and experimentation, mankind was able to realize such useful things as physics, chemistry, and medicine—but only after battling the churches, which fought science each step of the way.

"Throughout the last 400 years, during which the growth of science had gradually shown men how to acquire knowledge of the ways of nature and mastery over natural forces, the clergy have fought a losing battle against science, in astronomy and geology, in anatomy and physiology, in biology and psychology and sociology," explained the militant atheist philosopher Bertrand Russell, in his book *The Faith of a Rationalist*.[1] "Ousted from one position, they have taken up another. After being worsted in astronomy, they did their best to prevent the rise of geology; they fought against Darwin in biology, and at the present time they fight against scientific theories of psychology and education. At each stage, they try to make the public forget their earlier obscurantism, in order that their present obscurantism may not be recognized for what it is."

This conventional view of the development of science, taught as absolute truth in most American universities, from Berkeley to Boston, has one flaw: It is 100 percent demonstrably false—and anyone with even a passing familiarity with the history of early modern science knows that.

As a new generation of historians, sociologists, and philosophers of science has proven, biblical religion was not the enemy of science but rather the intellectual matrix that made it possible in the first place.

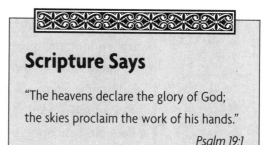

Scripture Says

"The heavens declare the glory of God; the skies proclaim the work of his hands."

Psalm 19:1

Without the key insights that Christianity found celebrated in the Bible and spread throughout Europe, science would never have developed. That is why, as sociologist Rodney Stark points out, the scientific enterprise as such developed in *only one place* and at *only one time* in history: in Christian Europe.

What we know as empirical science and the scientific method did not develop in *any* other of the advanced civilizations on earth—not in China (with its sophisticated society), not in India (with its philosophical schools), not in Arabia (with its advanced mathematics), not in Japan (with its dedicated craftsmen and technologies), not in Mesoamerica, not even in ancient Greece or Rome.

Only in Christian Europe, among millions of pious, churchgoing believers, did mankind begin the systematic study of nature—quantified by precise measurement and experimentation—which led to a whole new way of understanding.

The evidence is incontrovertible: It was the rational theology of both the Catholic Middle Ages and the Protestant Reformation—inspired by the explicit and implicit truths revealed in the Jewish Bible—that led to the discoveries of modern science.

The biblical origins of modern science

If what we know as modern scientific research—with its emphasis on direct observation and experiment, precise measurement, and the formulation of laws of nature—developed only in the context of Western Christendom, the question that naturally arises is: Why?

What is it in Western culture—which key ideas—that led to the development of modern science?

Sociologists such as Rodney Stark have hinted at some of the key scholastic concepts that were the necessary precursors to the development of the scientific method, but many scholars point directly to the ideas found in the Bible that permeated Western society and prepared the way for such geniuses as Galileo, Newton, Gregor Mendel, and Max Planck. Most of these insights are not stated as philosophical assertions explicitly in the biblical texts, of course. They are, rather, the operating assumptions that undergird the entire worldview of the biblical writers—

Who Said It?

"Any number of people assume that the Bible says that Eve ate an apple, or that Jonah was swallowed by a whale. Yet the Bible never says a word about whales or apples. In the former case it refers to a fish, which might imply any sort of sea-monster; and in the second, to the essential experience of fruition, or tasting the fruit of the tree, which is obviously more general and even more mystical....The things that look silly now are the first rationalistic explanations rather than the first religious or primitive outlines. If those original images had been left in their own natural mystery of dark fruition or dim monsters of the deep, nobody would have quarrelled with them half so much....But it is unfair to turn round and blame the Bible because of all these legends and jokes and journalistic allusions, which are read into the Bible by people who have not read the Bible."

G. K. Chesterton

and which can often be seen more clearly when contrasted with the assumptions operating in other ancient religions.

One recent attempt to identify these key biblical insights was made by Dr. Charles B. Thaxton (a chemist), and Nancy R. Pearcey (who writes often on religion and science), in their 1994 book, *The Soul of Science: Christian Faith and Natural Philosophy*. Among the biblical concepts that gave birth to modern science, Thaxton and Pearcey identified:

Biblical Insight #1: The world is real, not an illusion

"To begin with, the Bible teaches that nature is real," the authors say. "If this seems too obvious to mention, recall that many belief systems regard nature as unreal. Various forms of pantheism and idealism teach that finite, particular things are merely 'appearances' of the One, the Absolute, the Infinite. Individuality and separateness are illusions. Hinduism, for instance, teaches that the everyday world of material objects is maya, illusion. It is doubtful whether a philosophy that so denigrates the material world would be capable of inspiring the careful attention to it that is necessary for science."

Biblical Insight #2: God made the world good

Once again, modern Westerners so take for granted the biblical worldview—one part of which is that a Creator made the world and "saw that it was good"—that they are blind to the very real alternatives found throughout history and in many parts of the world.

One of those alternative worldviews is that the world is *not* good but evil—not something they should investigate, but something from which spiritual seekers should seek to escape. This was, in fact, the worldview of the now-famous and "politically correct" Gnostic cults that arose in the first centuries after Christ. It was also the worldview of the Manichees, the followers of the third-century Persian prophet Mani, who was greatly influenced by contact with Buddhism. They believed the material world is a place of darkness and pain. St. Augustine, the greatest Christian theologian of the first millennium of Christianity, was converted to Christianity from Manicheeism: "Behold God, and behold what God has created!" Augustine wrote in his *Confessions*. "God is good. Most mightily and most immeasurably does he surpass these things. But being good, he has created good things."[2] This definitive reaffirmation of the biblical notion of the inherent goodness of the world, Thaxton and Pearcey say, was a profound impetus to the development of science. The idiosyncratic Christian view was that the world, created by a loving God, was good, inherently interesting and therefore worthy of systematic and careful study. Thaxton and Pearcey quote the great astronomer Johannes Kepler, who wrote, "I give you thanks, Creator and God, that you have given me this joy in thy creation, and I rejoice in the works of your hands."

Biblical Insight #3: The world is a garden, not a god

This is the same insight that G. K. Chesterton was pointing to when he said in *Orthodoxy* that nature is not our mother but our *sister*. In virtually all pagan religions, including Buddhism, an animistic substratum runs throughout the various worldviews, so that pagan culture saw all of nature imbued with spirit or mind. But the Bible changed all that in Western culture. "God does not inhabit the world the way a dryad inhabits a tree," say Pearcey and Thaxton. "He is not the personalization of natural forces. He is not the world's 'soul'"—which is precisely what Newton said in his *General Scholium*—"He is its creator."

The Bible makes clear that natural phenomena—the sun and moon, the trees—were created by God according to his purposes, not divinities to be worshipped. Modern atheists like to claim that it was Enlightenment thinkers like René Descartes who pioneered the "disenchantment" (die Enntzauberung der Welt) or "disgodding" (Entgötterung) of nature, but in fact the process began at Sinai: "I, the Lord, am your God, who brought you forth out of the land of Egypt, that place of slavery: You shall have no other gods besides me" (Ex 20:2–3). As we saw in an earlier chapter, the Bible views pagan religion as madness, the worshipping of inanimate wood and stone.

The biblical rejection of nature worship was commented upon explicitly by the author of The Book of Wisdom, a deutero-canonical book written in Greek about a century before Christ:

> For all people who were ignorant of God were foolish by nature . . . they supposed that either fire or wind or swift air, or the circle of the stars, or turbulent water, or the luminaries of heaven were the gods that rule the world . . . . If through delight in the beauty of these things people assumed them to be gods, let them know how much better than these is their Lord, for the author of beauty created them. And if people were amazed at their power and working, let them perceive from them how much more powerful is the One who formed them (13:1–4).

That is precisely why science never arose in such sophisticated, highly philosophical societies like India or China where everyone "knew" that the natural world was imbued with spirit and mind.

"The de-deification of nature was a crucial precondition for science," conclude Pearcey and Thaxton, and this "de-deification" was made possible only by centuries of reflection on the truths revealed in the Bible.

Biblical Insight #4: A rational God created an orderly, dependable world

If you believe that all of nature is imbued with spirit, then any natural phenomenon—a tree or a river, the ocean or the moon—could quite literally have a mind of its own. There is little point to searching for a systematic pattern in the movement of the wind or the stars because the deities or nature-spirits that control them could easily just change their minds tomorrow.

What's more, polytheism usually implies that the various gods of nature can be in conflict, whereas monotheism tends to result in a belief in a unified, coherent universe. "Thy word, O God, stands fast in heaven," the psalmist sang (Ps 119:89).

In contrast, the ancient Greeks—just to take one example—did not think of the world as an orderly, dependable place. For Greek thinkers such as Plato, the world was but a pale shadow of the "really real" world of Ideas. Truth was to be found in the philosophical contemplation of abstract Ideas, not in the inherently flawed and messy material world.

Biblical Insight #5: God created the world according to fixed laws

In the Hebrew Bible, God is *melech ha-olam*, king of the universe, whose decrees alone make the world the way it is. In a remarkable essay entitled "The Biblical Basis for Western Science," the famous philosopher of science, Fr. Stanley Jaki (a priest and professor of physics), argues that science suffered a series of "stillbirths" in all ancient cultures precisely because of the absence of a belief in natural laws. Because of the Bible's overwhelming conviction that "the earth is the Lord's," there naturally arose a corollary belief in the underlying unity of the cosmos—the belief, as Jaki puts it, that "the heavens and the earth are ruled by the same laws."

Thaxton and Pearcey emphasize the crucial importance of this truth. "The biblical god is the Divine Legislator who governs nature by decrees set down in the beginning," they say. "The order of the reasoning here is important. The early scientists did not argue that the world was lawfully ordered, and therefore there must be a rational God. Instead, they argued that there was a rational God, and therefore the world must be lawfully ordered." In other words, it was their profound faith in a good and rational God that made the early Christian scientists seek out a rational order before they even knew what it was. Christian theology taught the early scientists the principle of heuristics: that there is a "known unknown" that can be searched for, described, and ultimately discovered.

Biblical Insight #6: The world was created according to a precise plan

This insight is related to the belief in laws of nature but added an element only found in Western culture: the notion of precision.

A Book Atheists Want to Burn

Scientists of Faith: 48 Biographies of Historic Scientists and Their Christian Faith, by Dan Graves; Grand Rapids, MI: Kregel Publications, 1999.

In the Book of Job, God asks the questioning Hebrew, "Where were you when I founded the earth? Tell me, if you have understanding! Who determined its size; do you know? Who stretched out the measuring line for it? . . . Have you grasped the celestial laws? Could you make their writ run on the earth?" (Job 38:4–5).

The prophet Isaiah describes the God of the Bible as:

[one] who has measured the waters in the hollow of his hand

and marked off the heavens with a span,

enclosed the dust of the earth in a measure,

and weighed the mountains in scales

and the hills in a balance . . . .

This vision of a Creator who "measured the waters in the hollow of his hand" and "weighed the mountains in scales" led the early scientists to expect precision in nature. It was because of this biblical concept—that God "measured" the waters and "weighed" the mountains—that the early scientists began, *in imitatio Dei*, to also measure things.

It seems like common sense, after all, that a cannonball would fall faster than a feather. This was, in fact, what the Greek philosopher

Aristotle taught. But the early scientists of western Europe, inspired by the biblical notion of precise measurement, decided to observe and measure to find out if this common sense idea was, in fact, true. The famous (but probably apocryphal) story of Galileo dropping two different size balls from the Leaning Tower of Pisa—one a small wooden ball, the other a large cannonball—illustrates this experiment. The early scientists embraced the truth that, by precise measurement, it's possible to discover the way the world *actually* works—and this is sometimes not the way human beings *think* it works. As a psalmist said, "Your ways, O Lord, are not our ways."

Biblical Insight #7: Human beings, being made in the image of God, can discover the truth

The belief in a rational order in the world that was created by God, but which is not always what human beings initially expect, led the early scientists of Christian Europe to struggle long and hard with problems and perplexities that pagan societies simply dismissed as being beyond human comprehension. Thus, today's atheist polemicists, such as Sam Harris, have it precisely backwards: The Bible did not keep Western man in darkness; it was biblical religion that gave the early scientists the faith and tenacity to keep looking for answers when they seemed beyond human reach.

This can be quickly seen when comparing Western culture with other sophisticated, ancient societies. Thaxton and Pearcey quote the cultural historian Joseph Needham on why the Chinese, for example, never developed empirical science. The Chinese did believe in an order in nature, after all—the Tao. But a belief in an orderly universe wasn't enough: For science to develop, it was also necessary for men and women to believe that human beings could also discover what that order actually is—and this faith the ancient Chinese did not possess. Nature, while orderly, was simply an inscrutable mystery.

"The Tao is forever undefined," says the *Tao Te Ching* by Lao Tsu (c. 570–490 BC). "Small though it is in the unformed state, it cannot be grasped."[3]

Concludes Needham: "There was no confidence [among the Chinese] that the code of Nature's laws could be unveiled and read because there was no assurance that a divine being, even more rational than ourselves, had ever formulated such a code capable of being read."

But the Christian and Jewish scientists of Western Europe had such confidence. Thaxton and Pearcey point to the example of Johannes Kepler (c. 1571–1630), who struggled for years to understand the "slight difference of eight minutes observation and calculation of the orbit of the planet Mars." This stubbornness led Kepler to abandon the idea, held for more than 2,000 years among astronomers, that the planets orbited in perfect circles rather than in ellipses.

Atheists try to take credit for science

So, if biblical religion was the necessary intellectual precondition for the gradual development of scientific method, how did the myth of the "scientific revolution" come about?

One reason: For the past 400 years, the partisans of irreligion—from the Marquis de Sade to Sam Harris and Richard Dawkins—have deliberately misrepresented the way science actually developed in the West as part of their ideological crusade against Judaism and Christianity.

What's worse, the partisans of atheism have been intellectually dishonest in the extreme: They have tried to take credit for the development of science when, in fact, they had little if anything to do with it.

Many of the most ideological and dogmatic of atheist crusaders, although continually referring to science, and seeking to *use* science to justify their own philosophical assumptions and declarations, were not scientists themselves.

In fact, many of the most famous anti-Christian polemicists of the last 200 years—who sought to use science to justify their unbelief—never themselves set foot in a laboratory or conducted a single field observation.

That includes the Marquis de Sade (a writer), Percy Bysshe Shelley (a poet), Friedrich Nietzsche (a philologist by training), Algernon Swinburne (a poet), Bertrand Russell (a philosopher), Karl Marx (a philosopher), Robert Ingersoll (a lecturer), George Bernard Shaw (a playwright), Vladimir Lenin (a communist revolutionary), Joseph Stalin (a communist dictator), H. L. Mencken (a newspaper columnist), Jean-Paul Sartre (a philosopher), Benito Mussolini (a fascist dictator), Luis Buñuel (Spanish filmmaker), Clarence Darrow (a lawyer), Ayn Rand (a novelist), Christopher Hitchens (a journalist), Larry Flynt (a pornographer), George Soros and Warren Buffett (investors), and Penn and Teller (magicians).

In dramatic contrast, most of the true *giants* of empirical science—the people who founded entire scientific disciplines or who made landmark scientific discoveries—were primarily devout Christians who believed that their scientific studies, far from being in conflict with their religious faith, ultimately were dependent upon it.

Here is just a sampling:

The Bible in American History, Part IX

"The study of the Bible is a post-graduate course in the richest library of human experience."

Herbert Hoover

Nicolaus Copernicus (1473–1543), pioneer of modern astronomy, a canon in the Catholic church; he did not see his system in conflict with the Bible and often referred to God in his works: "When a man is occupied with things which he sees established in the finest order and directed by divine management, will not the unremitting contemplation of them and a certain familiarity with them stimulate him to the best and to admiration for the Maker of everything, in whom are all happiness and every good?"

Galileo Galilei (1564–1642), pioneer physicist, who squabbled with the church, but remained a loyal Catholic: "The Bible shows the way to go to heaven, not the way the heavens go."

Johannes Kepler (1571–1630), astronomer and physicist, a pious Lutheran: "I had the intention of becoming a theologian . . . but now I see how God is, by my endeavors, also glorified in astronomy, for 'the heavens declare the glory of God.' I am a Christian . . . I believe . . . only and alone in the service of Jesus Christ. . . . In Him is all refuge, all solace."

Sir Isaac Newton (1642–1727), founder of modern physics and devout Christian: "This most beautiful system of the sun, planets, and comets could only proceed from the counsel and dominion of an intelligent and powerful Being. This Being governs all things, not as the soul of the world, but as Lord of all; and on account of his dominion he is wont to be called Lord God, or Universal Ruler."[4]

Sir Francis Bacon (1561–1627), philosopher and devout Anglican: "It is true, that a little philosophy inclineth man's mind to atheism, but depth in philosophy bringeth men's minds about to religion; for while the mind of man looketh upon second causes scattered, it may sometimes rest in them, and go no further; but when it beholdeth the chain of them confederate, and linked together, it must needs fly to Providence and Deity."

René Descartes (1596–1650), mathematician, scientist, and faithful Catholic: "I am convinced that those who examine carefully my arguments about God's existence will find that, the more trouble they take to look for mistakes in them, the more demonstrative they will find them, and I claim that, in themselves, they are clearer than any geometrical demonstrations. Thus it seems to me they are obscure only to those who do not know how to lead their minds away from the senses."

Robert Boyle (1627–1691), the founder of modern chemistry and devout Christian with a special interest in promoting Christianity abroad: "Christ's passion, His death, His resurrection and ascension, and all of those wonderful works which He did during His stay upon earth, in order to confirm mankind in the belief of His being God as well as man."

Michael Faraday (1791–1867), inventor of the electric generator and the transformer, a Christian who believed nature substantiated the existence of God as creator: "A Christian finds his guide in the Word of God, and commits the keeping of his soul into the hands of God. He looks for no assurance beyond what the Word can give him, and if his mind is troubled by the cares and fears which assail him, he can go nowhere but in prayer to the throne of grace and to Scripture."

Matthew Maury (1806–1873), the father of modern oceanography followed the Psalms expression "paths of the sea" and found warm and cold continental currents: "The Bible is true and science is true, and therefore each, if truly read, but proves the truth of the other."

James Prescott Joule (1818–1889), a Bible-believing Christian, authored the first law of thermodynamics: "It is evident that an acquaintance with natural laws means no less than an acquaintance with the mind of God therein expressed."

James Clerk Maxwell (1831–1879), physicist credited with pioneering statistical thermodynamics, field equations of electricity, magnetism and light; devout Christian: "Almighty

God, Who has created man in Thine own image, and made him a living soul that he might seek after Thee, and have dominion over Thy creatures, teach us to study the works of Thy hands, that we may subdue the earth to our use, and strengthen the reason for Thy service."

Lord William Kelvin (1824–1907), physicist, inventor of absolute temperature scale in his name; committed Christian who diligently studied the Bible: "Overwhelmingly strong proofs of intelligent and benevolent design lie around us...the atheistic idea is so non-sensical that I cannot put it into words."

Werner Karl Heisenberg (1901–1976), Nobel Prize winner in physics for the creation of quantum mechanics and the Uncertainty Principle and a devout Lutheran: "At this point we also recognize the characteristic difference between genuine religions, in which the spiritual realm, the central spiritual order of things, plays a decisive part, and the narrower forms of thought, especially in our own day, which relate only to the strictly experiencable pattern of a human community....Religion proper speaks not of norms, however, but of guiding ideals, by which we should govern our conduct and which we can at best only approximate. These ideals to not spring from inspection of the immediately visible world but from the region of the structures lying behind it, which Plato spoke of as the world of Ideas, and concerning which we are told in the Bible, 'God is a spirit.'"

Wernher Von Braun (1912–1977), first director of NASA, pioneer of space exploration; Lutheran: "Scientific concepts exist only in the minds of men. Behind these concepts lies the reality which is being revealed to us, but only by the grace of God."

> Albert Einstein (1879–1955), physicist who developed the The-
> ory of Relativity that governs modern physics: "I want to
> know how God created this world. I am not interested in
> this or that phenomenon, in the spectrum of this or that ele-
> ment. I want to know His thoughts, the rest are details."

Sir Isaac Newton and Einstein are both interesting cases.

For centuries, anti-Christian intellectuals, from Voltaire onward, pretended that Newton's theological vision was either irrelevant to his scientific research or, alternatively, merely an insincere and cynical
concession made to the religious authorities of his time.

Indeed, there was even a deliberate effort to suppress Newton's vast
theological writings. The Royal Society of London actually ordered that
his theological works—more than a million words on everything from
biblical prophesy to the Second Coming of Christ—not be printed.

Incredibly, it wasn't until 1935—more than 200 years after his death—
that scholars were able to evaluate just how thoroughly Newton's religious vision shaped his scientific research.[5] That's when the Cambridge
economist and avid Newtonia collector, John Maynard Keynes, bought a
collection of Newton's manuscripts offered by Sotheby's and made them
available, for the first time, to the academic world.

If the founder of modern physics was a devout Christian and a believer
in God, what about the man many people believe was a "second Newton," the great Jewish physicist Albert Einstein?

Obviously, Einstein was an original thinker of profound depth and precision. Rather than merely accept the received opinions of the past, he
sought to take a new look at the conundrums that had plagued physics
for generations. It's hardly surprising, then, that Einstein thought for himself when it came to religious questions.

Although he was born Jewish, it has been a matter of controversy for
years whether he believed in God or not. That's because Einstein wasn't

entirely sure himself. He spoke frequently about God—such as his famous maxim, uttered about the theory of quantum mechanics, that "God does not play dice"— yet plainly he was not an orthodox believer in any sense of the term. Atheists routinely claim him as one of their own, yet Einstein repeatedly and explicitly repudiated atheism as an accurate characterization of his beliefs.

In his book *The God Delusion*, atheist crusader Richard Dawkins once again tries to reclaim Einstein for atheism, citing quotations at length in which Einstein denied belief in a personal God, but the truth is that Einstein was struggling to enunciate a middle position between atheism and classic theism and couldn't seem to make up his mind how to describe it. "There is every reason to think that famous Einsteinisms like 'God is subtle but he is not malicious' or 'He does not play dice' or 'Did God have a choice in creating the Universe?' are pantheistic, not deistic, and certainly not theistic," Dawkins writes. "'God does not play dice' should be translated as 'Randomness does not lie at the heart of all things.' 'Did God have a choice in creating the Universe?' means 'Could the universe have begun in any other way?' Einstein was using 'God' in a purely metaphorical, poetic sense."

Perhaps. Yet when Einstein was explicitly asked whether he believed in "Spinoza's God"—meaning an impersonal Deistic God—this is what he said:

> I can't answer with a simple yes or no. I'm not an atheist and I
> don't think I can call myself a pantheist. We are in the position
> of a little child entering a huge library filled with books in

A Book Atheists Want to Burn

Religion of Peace? Why Christianity Is and Islam Isn't, by Robert Spencer; Washington, DC: Regnery Publishing, 2007. Part of the atheist attack today is to lump all religions together, as if they were all the same— which only shows how primitive, ignorant, and bigoted the modern atheist assault on Judaism and Christianity is.

many different languages. The child knows someone must have written those books. It does not know how. The child dimly suspects a mysterious order in the arrangement of the books but doesn't know what it is. That, it seems to me, is the attitude of even the most intelligent human being toward God. We see a universe marvelously arranged and obeying certain laws, but only dimly understand these laws. Our limited minds cannot grasp the mysterious force that moves the constellations.[6]

Not an orthodox Jew, certainly, but hardly a snide atheist ideologue along the lines of Dawkins, Chistopher Hitchens, or Sam Harris, either.

What Einstein was quite clear about, however, was the origin of the scientific quest in biblical religion. "To the sphere of religion belongs the faith in the possibility that the regulations valid for the world of existence are rational, that is, comprehensible to reason," he said. "I cannot conceive of a genuine scientist without that profound faith. The situation may be expressed by an image: science without religion is lame, religion without science is blind."

Nor is Einstein alone in his belief that the faith in an orderly universe was the legacy of biblical religion.

The great Max Planck (c. 1858–1947), the inventor of quantum theory, perhaps the most influential physicist in the twentieth century after Einstein, was a churchwarden from 1920 until he died.

Again, like Einstein, Planck could hardly be called an orthodox believer—but he was not an atheist, either. Like Einstein, Planck sought the divine through the medium of advanced theoretical physics—which left him with more questions than answers but full of awe.

In his famous essay "On Science and Religion," Planck argued that, at the very least, science and religion are compatible, not opposed as scientifically illiterate atheists like to claim. What's more, both science and religion agree on the existence of a rational world order:

The religion and science meet, on the contrary, in the question about the existence and essence of the supreme power governing the world, and here the answers they both furnish, are *at least to a certain extent* mutually *comparable*. They are in no way, as we have seen, in contradiction, but they agree in that firstly, there exists a reasonable world order (*vernünftiger Weltordnung*) independent from man and secondly, the essence of this order is never knowable directly, but only indirectly, or it can be only intuitively guessed.

To sum up: We have two rival claims.

On the one hand, we have scientific (let's be charitable) amateurs—from Nietzsche and Ingersoll to Chrisopher Hitchens and Sam Harris—insisting that science and biblical religion are fundamentally incompatible.

On the other hand, we have the greatest minds in the history of science, the people who actually made most of the discoveries that created modern science to begin with—luminaries like Galileo, Sir Isaac Newton, Gregor Mendel, Max Planck, Louis Pasteur, Werner Heisenberg, and even Albert Einstein—who insist that, not only is religion not at odds with science, but biblical religion is *what made science possible in the first place.*

Whom should we believe?

Should we believe the attorney Clarence Darrow, who said, "I don't believe in God because I don't believe in Mother Goose" or should we believe Albert Einstein, who said, "My religion consists of a humble admiration of the illimitable superior spirit who reveals himself in the slight details we are able to perceive with our frail and feeble mind"?

Frankly, in the great debate over religion and science, faithful Christians and Jews stand with the more enlightened half—those who make the actual discoveries in science.

Chapter Ten

YOU WERE CALLED TO FREEDOM

Of the many lies told about the Bible and Christianity, perhaps the most egregious concerns the global institution of slavery.

Some pretend that slavery was virtually mandated in the Bible or was a creation of the Christian Church. Others insist that the Christian churches, and the Roman Catholic Church in particular, gave their blessing to the slave trade of the seventeenth and eighteenth centuries—and it was only the pagan "freethinkers" of the French Enlightenment who led the abolitionist cause.

Still others, such as Ninth Circuit justice John Noonan, claim that the Roman popes only condemned slavery very late, in the 1890s, long after secular society had denounced it; and therefore, since the Catholic Church allegedly "changed" its teaching on slavery, it can and perhaps should change its teaching on other controversial issues, such as contraception, abortion, homosexuality, and divorce. All of these contentions are demonstrably false and don't even pass the "desk reference test"— meaning anyone willing to open a one-volume desk reference can discover their falsity.

The truth is that the savage cruelty of slavery has existed on a massive scale all over the world for most of human history—and *still exists today* in parts of the Islamic world and Asia—and yet it was first officially

Guess what?

- ▣ Slavery was first officially banned in Christian Europe.

- ▣ Pagan Greece and Rome were built almost entirely by slave labor.

- ▣ Anti-Christian writers of the Enlightenment categorized slavery as a necessary price to be paid for civilization.

- ▣ The Old Testament is unquestionably anti-slavery.

157

banned, by force of law, only in Christian Europe. No culture on earth questioned the morality of slavery until Christians did the questioning.

The golden age of ancient Greece and Rome, celebrated by the "enlightened" pagans of the eighteenth century, was built almost entirely by slave labor: By some estimates, fully one-third of Roman society was made up of slaves who could be killed at will by Roman householders.

Socrates and Plato could sit around in symposia, drinking wine and discussing the essence of justice, largely because their civilization was maintained by an unimaginable number of slaves.

When the tyrant Demetrius Phalereus ordered a census of Attica, circa 317 BC, he found that there were 21,000 citizens, 10,000 *metics* (resident aliens) and 400,000 slaves. That means there were nineteen slaves supporting every philosophizing Greek citizen in Attica. Herodotus, writing 150 years earlier, estimated that *helots* (Spartan slaves) outnumbered citizens in Sparta by seven to one.[1]

Far from condemning such cruelty, many of the anti-Christian writers of the Enlightenment, such as Edward Gibbon (c. 1737–1794) and David Hume (c. 1711–1776), justified it as a regrettable but necessary price to be paid for civilization.

Slavery was, Gibbon said, "almost justified by the great law of self-preservation." According to the atheist hero David Hume, "the negroes and in general all the other species of men (for there are four or five different kinds) [are] naturally inferior to the whites"[2]—a sentiment that the Enlightenment's great moral philosopher, Immanuel Kant, cited approvingly.

"The Negroes of Africa have by nature no feeling that rises above the trifling," Kant declared, in his 1764 essay, *Observations on the Feeling of the Beautiful and Sublime.* "Mr. Hume challenges anyone to cite a single example in which a Negro has shown talents, and asserts that among the hundreds of thousands of blacks who are transported elsewhere from their countries . . . not a single one was ever found who presented anything great in art or science or any other praiseworthy quality. . . . So fundamental is the difference between these two races of man, and it appears to be as great in regard to mental capacities as in color."[3]

Today, secular liberals continue to lie to themselves that it was the atheist "free thinkers" of the Enlightenment who created the abolitionist movement, but better-informed historians know the truth: That while a few Enlightenment writers like

Scripture Says

"Were you a slave when you were called? Don't let it trouble you—although if you can gain your freedom, do so."

1 Corinthians 7:21

Rousseau and Thomas Paine wrote abolitionist pamphlets, the people who actually risked life and limb to *end* slavery were almost all, without exception, devout Christians. They included Dr. Beilby Porteus (the Anglican bishop of London), classicist and biblical scholar Granville Sharp, deacon Thomas Clarkson, and Tory member of Parliament William Wilberforce, Irish political leader Daniel O'Connell, and the U.S. Baptist journalist William Lloyd Garrison.

Compare what David Hume and Kant said about black slaves to what prominent Christians in this period said:

The Catholic Abbé (Guillaume Thomas François) Raynal (1713–1796): "He who supports slavery is the enemy of the human race."

Quaker leader George Fox (1624–1691): "Consider with your-selves, if you were in the same condition as the poor Africans are, who came strangers to you, and were sold to you as slaves; I say, if this should be the condition of you or yours, you would think it a hard measure; yea, and very great bondage and cruelty."

Founder of Methodism John Wesley (1703–1791), who wit-nessed slavery firsthand in the West Indies: "Slavery is the sum of all villainies and the vilest that ever saw the sun."

American Quakers such as Levi Coffin risked their lives and those of their children running the Underground Railroad that helped more than 100,000 slaves escape their plight. When asked why he did it, Coffin replied, "The Bible, in bidding us to feed the hungry and clothe the naked, said nothing about color, and I should try to follow out the teachings of that good book."

Another abolitionist and Underground Railroad "conductor," the Methodist minister Calvin Fairbank, was caught helping slaves escape and sentenced to fifteen years in prison, which included numerous floggings.

"Secular elites of our day, or for that matter their counterparts of a century or two centuries ago, like to think that all human progress is due to secular reason," is how political writer Michael Barone of *U.S. News & World Report* sums up the politically correct delusions of the academy vis à vis slavery, commenting on David Brion Davis's *Inhuman Bondage: The Rise and Fall of Slavery in the New World.* "But Christian belief in the moral equality of every person played a key role in inspiring the Britons and then the Americans who led the fight to abolish the slave trade and then slavery."

Who Said It?

"To read in the Bible, as the word of God himself that, 'In the sweat of thy face shalt thou eat bread,' and to preach therefrom that, 'in the sweat of other man's faces shalt thou eat bread,' to my mind, can scarcely be reconciled with honest sincerity."

Abraham Lincoln

Slavery in the Hebrew Bible

Ironically enough, modern atheist critics who would indict the Bible as supporting or tolerating slavery actually make common cause with Southern racists who tried to do the same thing—and were easily and roundly refuted by nineteenth century biblical scholars and theologians.

As noted above, what we today call slavery was practiced on a massive scale throughout most of human history—including during the periods in which the Old and New Testaments were written. The word "slave," however—meaning a person who is considered to be the personal property of another human being, without any legal rights—can be understood in a variety of ways.

For example, we talk about "wage slaves" today without really meaning that a salaried employee of a large corporation is a true slave. Most modern people think of slavery in terms of the African slave trade, in which innocent people were essentially kidnapped and sold as servants or field workers. This is slavery in the true meaning of the word.

But in the ancient world, the most common source of slaves was prisoners of war or criminals. Slavery was actually seen as a more humane way to treat conquered populations or criminals than the popular alternative—which was wholesale slaughter.

One of the reasons Rome evolved into a slave society was because of its conquests. Many slaves were prisoners of war. Others were criminals for whom slavery was an alternative to harsh, debilitating, or even fatal punishment.

It was also common for poor people to sell themselves into slavery as a way to survive starvation, to pay off a debt, or even, in New Testament times, to advance their careers. To become a slave of a prominent person, in the late Roman Empire, was more a kind of apprenticeship than what we think of today as slavery.

Those who blame the Bible for all of society's ills like to say that the Old Testament law's regulation of servitude (whether voluntary or involuntary) was tantamount to approving it. But just as the Mosaic Law's regulation of divorce did not signify the Bible's overall approval of the practice—"'I hate divorce', says the Lord, the God of Israel" (Mal 2:16)—so, too, the biblical law's regulation of various forms of servitude did not signify approval but merely the recognition of slavery as a worldly reality.

Just as Jesus proclaimed that it was due to "the hardness of their hearts" that Moses permitted divorce, so, too, the Mosaic Law on servitude can been seen as a concession to the hardness of human hearts in the brutal world of the ancient Near East.

Many societies, rightly or wrongly, attempt to regulate commonly perceived evils, from prostitution to drug abuse, without thereby endorsing or approving what is regulated. The biblical law regulates what should happen when two Israelites fight and one is injured but does not die (Ex 21:18–19)—without thereby approving of, or giving sanction to, assault and battery. It merely recognizes that, when people fight, as they do, certain legal sanctions and consequences should apply.

In actual fact, the biblical law's treatment of involuntary servitude (or slavery) was almost always to moderate it—and differs substantially from other Near Eastern law codes. In the ancient Near East, as in Rome and Greece, slaves had few, if any, rights. A master could buy or sell his slave at will. He could maltreat, beat, or even kill him.

If the slave was a woman, girl, or young boy, the master could use the slave for his sexual pleasure at will—and if a slave girl became pregnant, the master could kill her child without giving her a second thought.

In the Bible, however, such cruelty was not tolerated.

For example, while in the Code of Hammurabi anyone who harbors a runaway slave is to be put to death (16), the Old Testament law actually *commands* that such slaves be given refuge: "You shall not turn over a slave [who has escaped] to his master. He shall dwell with you in your midst . . . you must not ill-treat him" (Dt 23:16–17).

Not only that, but anyone who abducts someone and sells him or her into slavery—as the brothers of Joseph did in Genesis or the slave traders of the eighteenth century did—was to be put to death (Ex 21:16).

The Hebrew word commonly translated as slave, *eved* (plural: *avadim*), comes from the root *avad*, which means "to work." Some Jewish translations of the Hebrew Bible, therefore, prefer the term "bondservant" or "bondsman" because, as we shall see, a Hebrew *eved* was not really a slave in the modern understanding of the term.

"Great confusion is made, and false impressions given, even by anti-slavery men, in calling the bond-service of the Mosaic economy slavery, when in reality it was something else," wrote the abolitionist clergyman, the Reverend John Fee, in his 1851 classic *The Anti-Slavery Manual.* "It was simple bond-service, in which children were bound [apprenticed] by parents until they should be 'of age,' and in the case of adult servants, *they bound themselves* for a term of years, as we shall show. And if it is insisted that these servants were placed in the hands of the Jew without their wills being consulted, we shall show that the Jew might not hold the servant so—in involuntary servitude. Mere bond-service is not slavery."

The anti-slavery clergy of the nineteenth century pointed out that, if any form of involuntary servitude can be justifiably called "slavery," then almost every society on earth practices slavery—for a man conscripted into military service in a draft or forced to perform jury duty should be called a "slave."

In fact, a Hebrew could become a bondsman or slave by order of a court (Ex 22:2) or as payment of a debt (Lv 25:29), but he or she must be freed at the end of six years (Dt 15:12) or at the Jubilee Year (Lv 25:40):

> And if a countryman of yours becomes so poor with regard to you that he sells himself to you, you shall not subject him to a slave's service. He shall be with you as a hired man, as if he were a sojourner; he shall serve with you until the year of jubilee. He shall then go out from you, he and his sons with him, and shall go back to his family, that he may return to the property of his forefathers. For they are My servants whom I brought out from the land of Egypt; they are not to be sold in a slave sale. You shall not rule over him with severity, but are to revere your God (Lv 25:39–42).

What's more, when a Hebrew "slave" was freed, the Bible says, "you shall not send him away empty-handed, but shall weight him down with gifts from your flock and threshing floor and wine press, in proportion to the blessings the Lord, your God, has bestowed upon you. For remember that you too were once slaves in the land of Egypt, and the Lord, your God, ransomed you" (Dt 15:13–15).

You have to have a real ax to grind against the Bible to think that the Old Testament takes a benign view of slavery.

Alien slaves—almost certainly prisoners of war—were indeed slaves for life as were their children (Lv 25:46)—although they, too, had the option of purchasing their freedom or being redeemed by a relative at any time before Jubilee (Lv 25:47–55). However, the Mosaic Law makes clear that, while such slaves were the personal property of their masters, they were regarded as human beings, not mere chattels, and were not to be mistreated.

For one thing, the punishment for killing a slave was the same as that for killing a free person—death (Ex 21:20). This differed dramatically from the practice throughout the ancient world.

In the Hebrew Bible slaves were also expected to participate in all the religious duties of a master's household, including observing the Sabbath rest (Ex 20:10) and all holy days (Dt 11:16). Fee, the author of *The Anti-Slavery Manual*, calculated that this meant Hebrew "slaves" had fully one-third of all their time free—far more than a modern worker!

Not only that, but a slave could inherit a master's entire estate if there was no heir, as Abraham lamented in Genesis 15: 3; could buy his or her own freedom (Lv 25:29); and could own property (2 Sm 9:10). In 1 Chronicles 2:34, the Hebrew Sheshan, in order to continue his family line, married his daughter to his Egyptian slave Jarha.

There are special regulations in the Mosaic Law for female slaves. Whereas sex slaves were common throughout the ancient Near East and in the Islamic world—with all the degradation and cruelty that this implies—this was forbidden under the Mosaic Law.

If an Israelite saw a beautiful woman among captive prisoners of war, he was permitted to take her into his home. She was to be given at least a full month to mourn for her lost family, to shave her head and wear mourning clothes. At the end of that time, the Israelite could then have sexual relations with her—but if he did so, she became his legal wife, not a slave ("you shall be her husband and she shall be your wife," Dt 21:13).

And if the Israelite later decided to divorce her, she left a free woman. "You shall not sell her or enslave her, since she was married to you under compulsion" (Dt 21:14).

Needless to say, ancient Roman aristocrats or Muslim pashas had no such scruples about the sex slaves in their harems.

Finally, the overarching theme that runs throughout the Hebrew Bible—from the Torah through the Deuteronomic History and the prophets—concerns how God ransomed the children of Israel from slavery in Egypt. Over and over again, the Hebrew Bible insists that Israelites must not mistreat their *avadim* (servants/slaves) because "you were once slaves [*avadim*] in the land of Egypt."

Slaves and slavery in the Gospels

"Jesus never even comes close to expressing disapproval of the enslaving of other human beings, and many statements attributed to him reveal a tacit acceptance or even approval of that inhuman institution," says atheist crusader Austin Cline, regional director for the Council for Secular Humanism.

Such sentiments are typical of atheist assaults on the Bible—and have become so common that even many Christian writers parrot them.

But the modern world's attack on the "toleration" of slavery in the Bible, especially when it comes to the New Testament, is a monumental display of historical anachronism.

A Book Atheists Want to Burn

The Victory of Reason: How Christianity Led to Freedom, Capitalism, and Western Success, by Rodney Stark; New York: Random House, 2005. Like living within a civilization that takes reason, freedom, democracy, and capitalism for granted? You can thank Christianity and the Bible.

By the New Testament era, a "slave" (Greek: *doulos*) often should be thought of more as an apprentice or indentured servant. The truth is that, by the first century, slavery in the Roman Empire was such a broad social and legal category it described everything from captured prisoners of war fighting to the death in gladiatorial combat to government bureaucrats who were educated at the state's expense. Slaves could be brutalized quarry workers or famous philosophers (Epictetus), artists, physicians, and administrators (for example, M. A. Felix, the procurator who was Paul's judge in Acts 23:24, was a slave).

It was not uncommon for a first-century urban Roman slave to live apart from his master, to own his own home and have a family. Some slaves even worked for businesses other than those of their masters and received a regular wage (part of which went to the master). Plus, by the first century slavery was no longer for life. Most slaves were set free before their thirtieth birthday and many received Roman citizenship.

Some slaves actually did not *want* manumission (freedom) and would beg their masters to delay their freedom until they had saved more money—and masters, for their part, often wanted to free their slaves sooner because of the expense of feeding and sheltering them. (The high cost of feeding hungry slaves is a common motif in Roman literature.)

This is the context, which modern critics of the Bible predictably ignore, in which St. Paul tells the Corinthians "If you can gain your freedom, avail yourself of the opportunity" (1 Cor 7:21).

But what about Jesus? What did Jesus say about slavery?

The answer is: Very little.

What about Jesus?

From the Gospels, it's clear that Jesus assumed slavery was a fact of life—just as he apparently assumed taxes, the Roman occupation, prostitution, and torture were facts of life because he mentions all of them.

The Gospels do not record Jesus denouncing the Roman occupation—despite what some liberation theologians try to say—but that does not mean that he approved of Roman rule, only that opposing Roman rule wasn't what he was all about. The Gospels never record Jesus publicly condemning torture or the Roman practice of crucifixion, but it is doubtful that he was an enthusiastic advocate for either. This is why the "argument from silence"—which is the mainstay of atheist polemics against the Bible—is such an obvious violation of the rules of logic.

In his parables, Jesus spoke of "slaves" and "masters" very matter-of-factly, but a careful student of the Bible would pay attention to which Greek word was actually being used in any given passage—and would realize that Jesus himself, who likely spoke Aramaic, would not have used any of those words in his actual teaching.

The Gospels actually use four different Greek words that are sometimes all translated as "slave" in English but which actually had different connotations:

Doulos—the most common, comes closest to what modern people think of as "slave." It is the normal Greek word for slave and is used in the parables frequently when Jesus is describing a situation involving a master and a slave.

Diakonos—from which we get the word deacon—means a servant or waiter. In Matthew 20:26, when Jesus says that "whoever would be great among you must be your servant"—the Greek word used is *diakonos* (servant), not *doulos* (slave).

Pais—which means "boy" or "youth." In the synoptic Gospel story of the Centurion's servant, many translations have the Centurion tell Jesus that his "slave" is sick but the word actually means "boy," with the implicit meaning of slave. Later in the story, the Centurion tells Jesus that he is a man under authority, used to getting and giving orders, and says that when he tells his slave (*doulos*) to do something, he expects him to do it.

Oiketes—a word used only once in the Gospels and which means "household servant" or "household slave." The Greek word *oikos* means "house," and *oiketes* means a worker who is part of a household. In Luke 16:13, many English translations say "No one can serve two masters," but the literal Greek means "No household servant can serve two masters."

Many English translations, such as the Revised Standard Version (RSV) and the New International Version (NIV), translate the word *doulos* as servant—because, as we saw above, the historical and social reality of first-century Palestine really does make "servant" a more accurate rendition of what was meant than "slave." However, even in the parables we get a glimpse of the cruelty that even well-treated Roman slaves had to face.

For example, in the parable of the Unmerciful Servant/Slave, Jesus is asked by Peter how often he is to forgive his brother if he sins against him?

Up to seven times? Peter asks. Jesus replies that no, Peter is to forgive his brother seventy-seven times—and then tells the story of the Unmerciful Doulos:

A servant owed his master a great sum of money, but was unable to pay. His master ordered that he, his wife, and his children all be sold to repay the debt. The servant fell on his knees and begged for patience. The master took pity on the servant and cancelled his debt. The servant left and found one of his fellow servants who owed him a day's salary. He began to choke the servant and demanded that he pay back what was owed. The fellow servant fell on his knees and begged for patience. But he refused and had the man thrown into prison. Word traveled quickly and got back to the merciful master. He was not pleased. "You wicked servant (*doulos*)," he said, "I canceled all that debt of yours because you begged me to. Shouldn't you have had mercy on your fellow servant just as I had on you?" In anger his master turned him over to the jailers to be tortured, until he should pay back all he owed.

There are a number of aspects of slavery in New Testament times that we can deduce from this passage. The first is that *douloi*, as Jesus or the evangelists understood them, were in some sense real slaves. They could be bought and sold along with their wives and children. That was just a fact of life in first-century Palestine. Second, the douloi could conduct business transactions themselves.

Of the forty-three instances in the Gospels in which the various noun forms of *doulos* is used in the Gospels, virtually all of them in the Synoptic Gospels (Matthew, Mark, and Luke) are in parables. In the Gospel of John, the evangelist has Jesus using the word *doulos* in ordinary conversation—as when he says that "a slave (*doulos*) is not greater than his master" (13:16) or "no longer do I call you slaves (*doulous*) for the slave (*doulos*) does not know what his master is doing" (15:15). When Jesus speaks of slavery, it is almost invariably in the context of a parable—with the combination of gritty realism and moral idealism that was characteristic of Jesus's stories.

Slavery in the writings of St. Paul

Many "progressive" critics of the Bible hate the apostle Paul because he says things they dislike—for example, that fornicators, adulterers, and homosexuals will not inherit the kingdom of God (1 Cor 6:9) or that women should be silent in church (1 Cor 14:34). Talk about politically incorrect!

Concerning slavery, Paul's attitude seems to be that it doesn't matter much—whether you are slave or free, Greek or Jew, male or female, isn't important.

Writing to the newly founded Christian community in Galatia, in modern-day Turkey, Paul says precisely this:

> Now that faith has come, we are no longer subject to a disciplinarian, for in Christ Jesus you are all children of God through faith. As many of you as were baptized into Christ have clothed yourselves with Christ. There is no longer Jew or Greek, there is no longer slave or free, there is no longer male and female; for all of you are one in Christ Jesus. And if you belong to Christ, then you are Abraham's offspring, heirs according to the promise (Gal 3:23).

In essence, what Paul is saying is that, for the new Christian community, the old distinctions of legal status, race, and sex no longer matter. Later on in his letter to the Galatians, Paul says that "you are no longer a slave but a child, and if a child then also an heir, through God."

It's true that in two instances Paul counsels slaves to "be obedient to your masters" (Eph 6:4 and Rom 13:1). Writing to the Christians in Corinth, for example, he says: "Were you called [to be a follower of Christ] while a slave? Do not worry about it; but if you are able also to become free, do that. For he who was called in the Lord while a slave is the Lord's freedman; likewise he who was called while free is Christ's slave. You were bought with a price; do not become slaves of men" (1 Cor

7: 21–24). Do not become slaves of men? That hardly sounds like an unqualified endorsement of slavery.

That Paul did not approve of slavery as an institution can be seen in his first letter to Timothy (1:10), where he includes "slave traders" (literally "men-stealers," *andrapodistais*) among the "lawless and disobedient," "godless and sinful," "unholy and profane." In this, he was following in the tradition of the Mosaic Law—which, as we saw above, punished "man-stealing" with death.

The slavery that concerns Paul is not social but spiritual: "For freedom Christ has set us free," he wrote to the Galatians (5:1). "Stand firm, therefore, and do not submit again to a yoke of slavery"—by which he means a reliance upon the law for salvation.

In this spirit Paul wrote to Philemon about a "runaway" slave, Onesimus, whom he has met in prison. Paul says that he is sending "my child Onesimus"—whom he calls "my heart"—back to Philemon, who is obviously a fellow Christian.

Paul asks Philemon to accept Onesimus "no longer as a slave but more than a slave, a brother, beloved especially by me." And the apostle urges Philemon to "welcome him as you would me."

In fact, if Onesimus owes Philemon money, Paul says, "charge it to me." Paul's letter to Philemon is often alleged to "prove" that Christians supported slavery. But anyone who actually reads this short letter will see that this is not Paul's point at all: It is that slaves and masters are brothers in Christ.

Prior to the legalization of Christianity by the Emperor Constantine in 313 AD, the early Christian church was powerless to outlaw slavery and was often brutally persecuted itself.

Yet even before Christianity was legalized, and at considerable risk to their own lives, many Christian leaders spoke out forcefully and courageously against the barbarisms of the pagan Empire, including slavery, the gladiatorial games, and the common practices of abortion and infanticide.

For example, we know from St. Clement's Letter to the Corinthians and from the Sherpherd of Hermas, both written about 95 AD, that some of the early Christians used to sell themselves into slavery in order to use the money to ransom others from bondage or to buy them food.[4]

And once Christianity was legalized, St. Gregory of Nyssa, writing in 385 AD, publicly scolded slave-owners: "You condemned a person to slavery whose nature is free and independent, and you make laws opposed to God and contrary to His natural Law," St. Gregory thundered. "For you have subjected one who was made precisely to be lord of the earth, and whom the Creator intended to be a ruler, to the yoke of slavery, in resistance to and rejection of His divine precept. Have you forgotten what limits were given to your authority? Your rulership has been limited to the extent, namely, that you may only have ownership over brute animals."[5]

Unlike pagan Greece and Rome, Christian Europe did not rely on slave labor. So liberal critics have to point to something else. It's true that some church councils and popes supported life imprisonment and hard labor for captured prisoners of war and spies—particularly against Muslim forces threatening to invade Europe.

The Third Lateran Council of 1179, for example, decreed that slavery should be the penalty for those who "provide the Saracens with arms and wood for helmets, and become their equals or even their superiors in wickedness and supply them with arms and necessaries to attack Christians."

But in this, the penalty of slavery differs little from what a U.S. court might impose—life imprisonment in a federal prison—for a spy or someone aiding Muslim terrorists in attacks against Americans. Retired navy warrant officer John A Walker, Jr., for example, was sentenced to life imprisonment in 1985 after he was convicted of spying for the USSR. Jonathan Pollard, an intelligence analyst, was convicted in 1986 of spying for Israel and is still serving his sentence in prison today.

This is the same basic situation that led Pope Nicholas V, on January 8, 1455, to authorize Portuguese military forces, in their battle to the death against Muslim pirates and invaders, to reduce "all Saracens and other enemies of Christ ... to perpetual slavery" (*Dum Diversas*) when captured in battle. These are the two texts cited most commonly by anti-Christian crusaders who claim the Christian church "tolerated" slavery.

But when it comes to slavery as it is usually understood—the kidnapping of innocent persons for sale as personal property—the popes were among the earliest and most forceful of those calling for its complete and total abolition, beginning with Pope Pius II's condemnation of the slave trade as early as October 7, 1462.

Here are just a few statements by the popes against the slave trade:

Eugene IV: Sicut Dudum, 1435:

> They have deprived the natives of their property or turned it
> to their own use, and have subjected some of the inhabitants
> of said islands to perpetual slavery (*subdiderunt perpetuae*

The Bible in American History, Part X

"The fundamental basis of this nation's law was given to Moses on the Mount. The fundamental basis of our Bill of Rights comes from the teaching we get from Exodus and St. Matthew, from Isaiah and St. Paul. I don't think we emphasize that enough these days. If we don't have the proper fundamental moral background, we will finally end up with a totalitarian government which does not believe in the right for anybody except the state."

Harry S. Truman

servituti), sold them to other persons and committed other various illicit and evil deeds against them....Therefore we... exhort...every kind among the Christian faithful of whatever state, grade or condition, that they themselves desist from the aforementioned deeds, cause those subject to them to desist from them, and restrain them rigorously. And no less do *we order and command all and each of the faithful of each sex that, within the space of fifteen days of the publication of these letters in the place where they live, that they restore to their pristine liberty all and each person of either sex who were once residents of said Canary Islands*...who have been made subject to slavery (*servituti subicere*). These people are to be totally and perpetually free and are to be let go without the exaction or reception of any money.

Paul III: Sublimus Deus, 1537:

Therefore, we,...noting that the Indians themselves indeed are true men and are not only capable of the Christian faith, but, as has been made known to us, promptly hasten to the faith and wishing to provide suitable remedies for them, by our Apostolic Authority decree and declare by these present letters that the same Indians and all other peoples—even though they are outside the faith—who shall hereafter come to the knowledge of Christians have not been deprived or should not be deprived of their liberty or of their possessions.

Gregory XVI: In Supremo, 1839:

The slave trade, although it has been somewhat diminished, is still carried on by numerous Christians. Therefore, desiring to remove such a great shame from all Christian peoples...and walking in the footsteps of our predecessors, we, by apostolic authority, warn and strongly exhort in the Lord faithful Christians of every condition that no one in the future dare to bother unjustly, despoil of their possessions, or reduce to slavery (*in servitutem redigere*) Indians, Blacks, or other such peoples. Nor are they to lend aid and favor to those who give themselves up to these practices, or exercise that inhuman traffic by which the Blacks, as if they were not humans but rather mere animals, having been brought into slavery in no matter what way, are, without any distinction and contrary to the rights of justice and humanity, bought, sold and sometimes given over to the hardest labor.

As the social scientist Rodney Stark has written, it is only the profoundly anti-Christian biases of many liberal academics that blind them to the central role that Christianity—and the Bible—held in the abolition of the slave trade and eventually of slavery itself.

"Although it has been fashionable to deny it, antislavery doctrines began to appear in Christian theology soon after the decline of Rome and were accompanied by the eventual disappearance of slavery in all but the fringes of Christian Europe," Stark writes, in his magisterial *For the Glory of God: How Monotheism Led to Reformations, Science, Witch-Hunts, and the End of Slavery* (Princeton University Press, 2003). "When Europeans subsequently instituted slavery in the New World, they did so over strenuous papal opposition, a fact that was conveniently 'lost' from history until recently."[6]

The Bible against slavery

While the French atheist *philosophes* were busily engaged in massacring tens of thousands of innocent people in the Terror that followed the French Revolution, British Quakers, Methodists, and evangelical Anglicans were waging a campaign to purge the evil of slavery from Europe and European colonies.

In the United States, many Christian clergymen and laypeople eventually risked their lives smuggling tens of thousands of runaway slaves to freedom in the Underground Railroad.

When racist southern clergymen attempted to justify slavery with a hodgepodge of biblical proof texts, reputable Christian theologians marshaled the best scholarly tools then in existence to prove that, as the title of the Reverand George B. Cheever's 1857 classic put it, *God Against Slavery.*

Although today virtually unknown, these Christian writers in the early nineteenth century produced literally dozens of scholarly works proving that the Bible as a whole, far from tolerating chattel slavery, in fact denounced it. The Reverend Cheever wrote:

> Undoubtedly, Old Testament truth is a strange thing to many....They are not aware how it burns, how it cuts, how it probes and pierces, as a discerner and reprover of sin, and how the mighty Hebrew prophets, ever living, ever new, seem to hold a grand inquest over our organic iniquities, and to walk among us with the writers ink-horn, and the measuring plumb-lines of the Mosaic Laws. The people, generally, are glad to witness these operations. The people love to hear God's word demonstrating and rebuking the iniquity of slavery... [they] prefer freedom, and are glad to find that God's word not only does not sanction slavery, but is against it, wholly and utterly, from beginning to end.

In a remarkable series of books, such as *The Bible Against Slavery* (1837) by the Reverend Theodore D. Weld, these Christian clergymen set out, with encyclopedic thoroughness, to demolish every biblical argument that Southern slave owners tried to mount in defense of slavery—from the proverbial "curse of Ham" argument from Genesis to the modern critic's claim that the Mosaic Law "tolerated" slavery.

Among the many works produced in these years in addition to *God Against Slavery* and *The Bible Against Slavery*, were:

- The Reverend Beriah Green's *The Chattel Principle: The Abhorrence of Jesus Christ and the Apostles;* or, *No Refuge for American Slavery in the New Testament*
- The Reverend Stephen S. Foster's *The Brotherhood of Thieves,* or, *A True Picture of the American Church and Clergy* (1843)
- The Reverend Parker Pillsbury's *Forlorn Hope* (1847)
- The Reverend William W. Patton's *Slavery, the Bible, Infidelity: Pro-slavery Interpretations of the Bible: Productive of Infidelity* (1846)
- The Reverend John Fee's *Sinfulness of Slavery* (1851) and his *Anti-Slavery Manual*

Adam Hochschild's critically acclaimed history of the early abolitionist movement in England, *Bury the Chains: Prophets and Rebels in the Fight to Free an Empire's Slaves*, singles out two dozen men who in the mid-1700s set out to defy powerful elements in their entire society and begin a systematic campaign to end the slave trade and, if possible, slavery itself. Facing death threats from slave traders, these brave men (primarily Quakers and evangelical Anglicans) succeeded in shaming all of Europe so totally that, one by one, the nations of Europe and North America legally banned the slave trade—first Denmark (1803), then England (1807), then the United States (1808), where however, slavery continued to be practiced.

Yet Hochschild himself tries to ignore the explicitly Christian motivations of these early English abolitionists, because, being a leftist himself,

A Book Atheists Want to Burn

Who Really Cares: The Surprising Truth About Compassionate Conservatism, by Arthur C. Brooks; New York: Basic Books, 2006.

he finds it hard to understand how conservative Christians could strive for, let alone achieve, such a noble "progressive" goal. Similarly, the Nobel Laureate Steven Weinberg implies that it must have been the freethinkers of the Enlightenment—not the Bible—that inspired the Christian abolitionists to launch their crusade to end slavery.

"It is certainly true that the campaign against slavery and the slave trade was greatly strengthened by devout Christians, including the Evangelical layman William Wilberforce in England and the Unitarian minister William Ellery Channing in America," Weinberg concedes. "But Christianity, like other great world religions, lived comfortably with slavery for many centuries, and slavery was endorsed in the New Testament. So what was different for anti-slavery Christians like Wilberforce and Channing? There had been no discovery of new sacred scriptures, and neither Wilberforce nor Channing claimed to have received any supernatural revelations. Rather, the eighteenth century had seen a widespread increase in rationality and humanitarianism that led others . . . also to oppose slavery, on grounds having nothing to do with religion. Although Wilberforce was the instigator of the campaign against the slave trade in the 1790s, this movement had essential support from many in Parliament like Fox and Pitt, who were not known for their piety. As far as I can tell, the moral tone of religion benefited more from the spirit of the times than the spirit of the times benefited from religion."

Wilberforce and his compatriots explicitly credited their Christianity for their conviction that slavery was evil. They spearheaded the abolitionist cause. Yet to atheist academics, slavery could only have been abolished through the moral example of people like themselves.

Chapter Eleven

ENDOWED BY THEIR CREATOR WITH CERTAIN UNALIENABLE RIGHTS

The most secular, rationalistic, and self-consciously non-Christian of all the Founders of the United States—the aristocratic Virginian and slave-owner Thomas Jefferson—ended up writing the most biblically charged words ever enshrined in a political document:

"We hold these truths to be self-evident," he wrote, "that all men are created equal and are endowed by their Creator with certain unalienable rights; that among these are life, liberty, and the pursuit of happiness. That, to secure these rights, governments are instituted among men, deriving their just powers from the consent of the governed; that, whenever any form of government becomes destructive of these ends, it is the right of the people to alter or to abolish it."

Once again, we moderns are so brainwashed and asleep, we fail to appreciate the radical, unprecedented quality of those seventy-nine words—still often denied by totalitarians, judges, and college professors the world over.

As described in the Declaration of Independence, human rights are not *privileges* dispensed or withdrawn at the discretion of the State. Rather, they are *gifts from God* which no prince or potentate, no State or sovereign, may take away.

Guess what?

- The key insight behind the American Revolution is that human rights are not privileges that can be revoked; they are gifts from God which no state or sovereign can take away.

- The concept of "self-evident" truths originated with the Apostle Paul, back in 60 AD.

That is the key insight behind the American revolution, not democracy or majority rule—and it is derived not from secular philosophy, but from biblical religion.

"The sacred rights of mankind are not to be rummaged for among old parchments or musty records," said Alexander Hamilton. "They are written, as with a sunbeam, in the whole volume of human nature, by the hand of Divinity itself, and can never be erased or obscured by mortal power."

This is a sentiment as old as Genesis: God declared that he made the human being (*adam*) in his image (*tselem*) and after his likeness (*damut*), and gave to him authority to rule over all the earth.

This is also what St. Paul was referring to, writing to the Romans, when he said that knowledge of God can be seen through creation and his law, the knowledge of good and evil, is written on the human heart:

"For what can be known about God is evident to them, because God made it evident to them," Paul said. "Ever since the creation of the world, his invisible attributes of eternal power and divinity have been able to be understood and perceived in what he has made. As a result, they have no excuse; for although they knew God they did not accord him glory as God or give him thanks" (Rom 1:19–20).

Thus, the concept of "self-evident" truths did not originate with the French Enlightenment or René Descartes but actually dates back at least to the Apostle Paul, writing in 60 AD.

Paul adds that, even though the Gentiles did not have the benefit of the Torah (instruction), certain basic standards of morality can be known even without special divine revelation.

"For when the Gentiles who do not have the [Torah] law by nature observe the prescriptions of the law, they are a law for themselves even though they do not have the law. They show that the demands of the law are written in their hearts" (Rom 2:14).

Modern secularists believe that the idea of a self-evident human equality that pervades the U.S. Declaration of Independence came primarily from the agnostic intellectuals of the French Enlightenment; and that the theistic sentiments expressed by Jefferson and other Founders were mere rhetoric, designed to curry favor with Christian colonists.

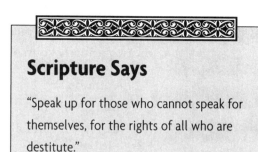

Scripture Says

"Speak up for those who cannot speak for themselves, for the rights of all who are destitute."

Proverbs 31:8

But nothing could be further from the truth.

While some of the Founders (like Jefferson or Ben Franklin) were not orthodox Christians by any stretch of the imagination, neither were they atheists.

They were steeped, from childhood, in the stories and values and ideas of the Bible; and most believed that, as John Adams put it, "the Bible contains the most profound philosophy, the most perfect morality, and the most refined policy, that ever was conceived upon earth. It is the most republican book in the world."[1]

Men like Washington and John Adams, Ben Franklin and James Madison, were warriors and farmers, writers and statesmen, not parsons.

But a raw religious faith was important to them. George Washington, for example, upon taking command of the Continental Army, ordered that each day begin with a formal prayer in every unit.

"The General commands all officers, and soldiers, to pay strict obedience to the Orders of the Continental Congress, and by their unfeigned, and pious observance of their religious duties, incline the Lord, and Giver of Victory, to prosper our arms," the Order went.

As philosopher Michael Novak argues in his remarkable 2002 book, *On Two Wings: Humble Faith and Common Sense at the American Founding*, the revolutionary political philosophy that gave birth to government "of the people, by the people, and for the people" was based on two primary sources:

1) A simple but deeply rooted biblical religiosity that saw human rights as self-evident and "unalienable" gifts of a benevolent and almighty Creator

2) A "plain reason" that grew out of rugged, practical experience in self-government

Revolution based solely on "plain reason," without the moral restraint of religious experience and the fear of God in rulers and legislators, gave birth to the nihilistic atheism, cold calculation, and ultimately bloody massacres of the French Revolution.

The American Founding was different.

It was, as the Great Seal of the United States found on every dollar bill puts it, to be a *novus ordo seclorum*, a new order of the ages. It was a bold, unprecedented attempt to work out a system of self-government and political freedom that recognized the "unalienable rights" endowed by the Creator and bestowed upon "all" men—not just upon a favored class.

Without the fear of God that religion bestowed upon arrogant and powerful men, the Founders knew, tyranny was never far away.

"Can the liberties of a nation be thought secure when we have removed their only firm basis, a conviction in the minds of the people that these liberties are the gift of God?" Thomas Jefferson asked.

George Washington agreed.

"Of all the dispositions and habits which lead to political prosperity, religion and morality are indispensable supports," Washington said in his Farewell Address. "Let us with caution indulge the supposition that morality can be maintained without religion."

The widespread, stubborn, not always orthodox or churchgoing but sincere religious faith of ordinary Americans—that Europeans and media elites find so childish and unsophisticated—has been a hallmark of the American republic since the very beginning.

According to Alexis de Tocqueville, the French aristocrat who penned *Democracy in America* in 1830, "for the Americans, the ideas of Christianity and liberty are so completely mingled that it is almost impossible to get them to conceive of one without the other."

The biblical origins of universal human rights

One of the essential intellectual building blocks of a liberal democracy—the belief in the fundamental equality of human beings and their "unalienable rights"—is not derived from secular philosophy but from the Bible.

More specifically, belief in human equality is derived from the basic theocentric values of the Hebrew scriptures and intensified in the teachings and deeds of the carpenter of Nazareth. Jesus taught the world outside the small circle of Judaism that God hears the cry of the poor, that the widow's mite is worth more than a king's golden treasures in heaven.

No one in the ancient world believed this.

In fact, there was nothing more self-evident in the ancient world than the fact that men—to say nothing of women—are *not* created equal.

In *The Republic*, the Greek philosopher Plato insisted that the gods create *superior* human beings who are fit to rule—he called them the Guardians—and *inferior* human beings who are to *be* ruled.

The inferior classes have few if any rights, and much of *The Republic* is proto-fascist in its advocacy of "strong men," eugenics, and absolute obedience to the State.

The People of Israel rejected this pagan totalitarianism.

More than 2,500 years before Baron de Montesquieu and John Locke, the biblical prophets Jeremiah, Amos, Isaiah, and Hosea proclaimed the equality of all human beings in the eyes of heaven—and the fact that rulers, too, will be held accountable by God.

The prophet Isaiah delivered the Word of God to the people of Israel in the eighth century BC:

> Woe to those who enact evil statutes,
>
> And to those who constantly record unjust decisions,
>
> So as to deprive the needy of justice,
>
> And rob the poor of My people of *their* rights (*mishpat*),
>
> In order that widows may be their spoil,
>
> And that they may plunder the orphans (Is 10:1–2).

The prophet Jeremiah, writing a century later, also had harsh words for those who dare trample upon the rights of the poor:

> For wicked men are found among my people . . . .
>
> They have become great and rich.
>
> They are fat, they are sleek,
>
> They also excel in deeds of wickedness;
>
> They do not plead the cause,
>
> The cause of the orphan, that they may prosper;
>
> They do not defend the rights of the poor.
>
> "Shall I not punish these people?" declares the Lord, "On a nation such as this
>
> Shall I not avenge Myself?" (Jer 5:26, 28–9)

These sentiments were unprecedented in the cultural history of humanity: The creator of the universe will hold unjust rulers accountable for violating the rights of the poor.

But Jesus went further—always further. He took this profound revelation of the biblical prophets and pushed it to extremes.

Not merely are the innocent poor welcomed into God's kingdom, Jesus said, but all the repentant outcasts and abandoned lowlifes of the world—prostitutes and lepers, scammers and ripoff artists and beggars, liars and crooks (tax-collectors), foreigners, heretics, even despised pagan soldiers.

He came, he said, "not to call the righteous, but sinners" (Mt 9:12).

Time and again, in a variety of settings, through word and deed, Jesus emphasized the fundamental equality and innate dignity of all human beings in the eyes of God.

To illustrate what he meant, Jesus told simple but compelling and ultimately subversive stories that continue to reverberate in the human spirit to this very day.

Like this one from the Gospel of Luke:

> A certain man was giving a big banquet, and he invited many people; and at the dinner hour he sent his servant to say to those who had been invited, "Come; for everything is ready now."

> But they all alike began to make excuses. The first one said to him, "I have bought a piece of land and I need to go out and look at it; please consider me excused."

> And another one said, "I have bought five yoke of oxen, and I am going to try them out; please consider me excused."

> And another one said, "I have married a wife, and for that reason I cannot come."

> And the servant came back and reported this to his master.

Then the head of the household became angry and said to his servant, "Go out at once into the streets and lanes of the city and bring in here the poor and crippled, the blind and the lame.'

And the servant said, "Master, what you commanded has been done, and still there is room."

And so the master said to the servant, "Go out into the highways and along the hedges, and compel them to come in, that my house may be filled. For I tell you, none of those men who were invited shall taste of my dinner."

Such stories shocked the pious of Jesus's day, as indeed they shock the pious of our own. By and large, pious people can feel pity for the widow and orphan, and recognize intellectually that God loves them; but Jesus went further, treating everyone as children of God. Jesus's radical egalitarianism, as portrayed in the Gospels, extended to women, criminals, and even to hated occupation (Roman) soldiers.

The Bible in American History, Part XI

"Within the covers of the Bible are all the answers for all the problems men face."

Ronald Reagan

"Of the many influences that have shaped the United States into a distinctive nation and people, none may be said to be more fundamental and enduring than the Bible."

Ronald Reagan

In the first century, a pious Jew did not speak with women, but Jesus spoke openly with many strange women, even, in one case, with a rather disreputable woman from among the hated Samaritan community (Jn 4:7).

That would be almost literally the equivalent of a young Israeli rabbi today stopping to chat with a Palestinian prostitute in Nablus. What would his *haredi* followers think?

As for Jesus's attitude toward the hated Roman occupation authorities, who would in fact put him to death, he not only spoke to them but he even praised their religious faith.

Even if the story of the centurion's servant (Lk 7) was, as some modern critics like to claim, put into Jesus's mouth by the evangelists decades after his execution, it is still congruent with the Gospels' pervasive portrayal of Jesus's friendship with social outcasts.

It's a pretty remarkable story in its own right—especially when you consider that, in all likelihood, it was written just a few years after the Roman Army had massacred up to a million Jews and had leveled the holy Temple to the ground.

As the evangelist Luke tells it, a centurion's slave was sick and about to die. When the Roman officer heard about Jesus and his reputation as a miracle-worker and healer, he sent some Jewish leaders to ask Jesus to come and save the life of his slave.

The Jewish leaders insisted that the Roman was worthy of such a request because "he loves our nation, and it was he who built us our synagogue."

This meant that the man was a *theosobomenos*, a "God-fearer"—a pagan who respected the Jewish religion and sought to live by its precepts without actually converting and undergoing circumcision.

Jesus agreed to help.

But before he could reach the house where the slave was staying, the Centurion sent word that Jesus shouldn't trouble himself to actually visit him—because he knew that a pious Jew would never enter the home of a pagan.

"Lord, do not trouble yourself further, for I am not worthy for you to come under my roof," he said. "But just say the word, and my servant will be healed. For I, too, am a man under authority, with soldiers under me; and I say to this one, 'Go!' and he goes; and to another, 'Come!' and he comes; and to my slave, 'Do this!' and he does it."

When Jesus heard this, Luke relates, he marveled at the Roman officer, turned to the great multitude of pious Jews who was following him and said, "I say to you, not even in Israel have I found such great faith."

Later, Jesus's egalitarian attitude was expressed by Peter in the Acts of the Apostles: "In truth, I see that God shows no partiality. Rather, in every nation whoever fears him and acts uprightly is acceptable to him" (Acts 10:34–35).

Egalitarianism in early Christianity

The political and social implications of Jesus's radical egalitarianism are obvious. If all human beings are equal in the eyes of God—if, as Jesus said, God causes the rain to fall on the just and unjust alike—then that implies that human beings, too, should treat each other equally.

This is precisely how the evangelist Luke, in his Acts of the Apostles, describes the early Christian community. "The community of believers was of one heart and mind, and no one claimed that any of his possessions was his own, but they had everything in common," Luke wrote. "There was no needy person among them, for those who owned property or houses would sell them, bring the proceeds of the sale, and put them at the feet of the apostles, and they were distributed to each according to need."

According to the sociologist and historian, Rodney Stark, this openness to people of all races and social and economic classes explains, at least partly, the phenomenally rapid growth of the Jesus movement in the ancient world.

In his remarkable book *The Rise of Christianity*, Stark attempts to describe and then explain the rapid expansion of Christianity from a tiny, persecuted sect within Judaism to the dominant religion on the planet in just three centuries.

He starts out with the known or suspected end points.

Acts 1:14–15 says that, immediately after the Crucifixion, there were 120 Christians, and by the sixth decade, Acts 21:20 says, there were "many thousands of Jews." After surveying historians on the question, Stark settles on the conservative figure of about 1,000 Christians in the year 40, or ten years after Jesus's execution.

For the ending number, Stark accepts the estimates of historians that set the number of Christians in the age of Constantine as no more than 10 percent of the total Roman population—or about 6 million Christians out of 60 million Romans.

That results in a growth rate of about 40 percent per decade—roughly equal to that of the Mormon church. At that rate, Stark calculates, there would have been:

    1,000 Christians in the year 40
    1,400 in the year 50
    7,530 in the year 100
    40,496 in the year 150
    217,795 in the year 200
    1.1 million in the year 250
    6.3 million in the year 300
    33.8 million in the year 350

That accounts for the *mathematics* of growth . . . but what accounts for Christianity's growth socially and culturally?

One of the reasons Stark gives is the egalitarian ethos of the Christian movement—its openness to people of all social and economic classes, its positive evaluation of women, its strong social concern and interest in the poor and the sick.

Modern enemies of Christianity, from Gibbon and Hobbes to Nietzsche and Friedrich Engels, have insisted that the Jesus movement was made up primarily of slaves and uneducated persons. After all, doesn't Paul say, in his first letter to the Corinthians, that "not many of you were wise by human standards; not many were influential; not many were of noble birth"?

But if Christianity were to meet the mathematics of growth described above, it must have had tremendous appeal among all social and economic classes. The New Testament itself gives tantalizing clues that upper-class persons were attracted to the new movement.

There is little doubt that Jesus had rich and influential followers, such as Nicodemus and Joseph of Arimathaea (Jn 19:38–42) and that he was quite comfortable with the affluent. All four Gospels record an incident in which an apparently rich female follower, whom John names as Mary the sister of Martha, pours an alabaster flask of perfumed ointment on Jesus's feet—which "some" (John says Judas Iscariot) complained cost more than three hundred denarii. And the evangelist Matthew even mentions in passing that Pontius Pilate's wife (not named in the Gospel but called Procula in later tradition) begged Pilate not to harm "that righteous man" because of the nightmares she was having over him (Mt 27:19).

Because of its emphasis on fundamental human equality in the eyes of God, Christianity was open to both slaves and freemen, women and men, pagans and Jews. As the apostle Paul put it, there is no longer "neither Greek nor Jew, circumcised nor uncircumcised, barbarian, Scythian, slave *nor* free, but Christ *is* all and in all."

This meant that Christianity's recruitment universe was vastly larger than those of most ancient religions which tended to restrict membership along ethnic or sexual lines.

The role of women was crucial.

You'd never know it from the shrill talk of "patriarchy" and sexism among today's aging feminists, but Christianity was undoubtedly the most pro-female religion in history.

Not only did Jesus count among his most fervent followers large numbers of women, but the New Testament proves that women were active leaders in the early Christian movement. Writing to the Romans, the apostle Paul commends "Phoebe our sister, who is a minister [deacon] of the church at Cenchreae," and mentions "Mary who has worked hard for you" and "Junia, my relative and my fellow prisoner." He describes the woman Junia and perhaps her husband Andronicus as "prominent among the apostles [who] were in Christ before me."

That Christianity accorded women greater social status, based on its conception of basic human rights, can be seen in the peculiar early Christian rejection of abortion, infanticide, and divorce.

The Christian rejection of divorce tended to give women greater social status, not less, as some modern feminists allege. That's because it conferred upon women a fundamental economic and social security that both Jewish and pagan women lacked. In Judaism, women had no right to divorce at all and could be dismissed by their husbands simply by his putting it in writing (a "bill of divorce" or *ghet*). In Roman law, women had the right to divorce their husbands but, among the lower classes, no way of supporting themselves if they did so.

Another way in which human equality and the concept of fundamental human rights were reinforced was through the Christian ban against infanticide and abortion. Infanticide, which tended to be practiced, then as now, disproportionately against female babies, was forbidden—as was abortion—precisely because life was viewed as a fundamental human right. In the Didache or "Teaching of the Twelve Apostles"—written in 70 AD and one of the earliest Christian documents outside the New Testament—Christians are told that "you shall not procure [an] abortion, nor destroy a newborn child" (2:1–2). Many pagan commentators noticed this strange Christian refusal to kill children (a view also shared by Jews).

The fact that all human infants—including even female infants—possessed, in Christian eyes, a fundamental right to life, naturally reinforced in the Christian community the belief that human beings did possess certain rights that no one could legitimately abrogate.

The development of human rights in Christendom

The ancient world did not have any true conception of human rights. Socrates insisted that he had a right to teach the truth as he understood it; the Athenian assembly disagreed and forced him to commit suicide for his trouble.

For the ancients, with a few exceptions, the state and religion were one and the same thing: What the state decreed to be just was, in fact, what was just.

Aside from the biblical prophets, there were few voices in the ancient world that discerned any distinction between what was legal (in the sense that it was decreed by the state) and what was moral or right.

One of the few exceptions was the Roman Stoic philosopher Marcus Tullius Cicero who did attempt to articulate a theory of natural right over and above the positive law of the state.

In his classic text, *De Res Publica*, Cicero held that "True law is right reason in agreement with Nature . . . it is of universal application, unchanging and everlasting."

He insisted that "there will not be different laws at Rome and at Athens, or different laws now and in the future, but one eternal and unchangeable law will be valid for all nations and for all times, and there will be one master and one rule, that is, God, over us all, for He is the author of this law, its promulgator, and its enforcing judge."

These are noble sentiments. Alas, the reality of Roman society did not allow their application—and Cicero did not follow them himself.

As consul (the highest Roman official) of the senate, Cicero discovered a plot to overthrow the government (the Catiline Conspiracy, 63 BC). He ordered the five ringleaders to be executed without trial.

But he who lives by the sword will die by the sword. When Mark Antony came to power briefly as part of the Second Triumvirate, he ordered the death of Cicero and his entire family. In 43 BC, Cicero was murdered and his head and hands were nailed to the speaker's podium in the Roman Senate.

Such were human rights in the pre-Christian days of the Roman Empire.

It was not until after the legalization of Christianity by Constantine in 313 AD that Christian thinkers developed a theory of human rights separate from and above the power of the state.

The early Christian philosophers, strongly influenced by the teaching of Jesus and the theocentric ideas inherited from Judaism, believed in what is now called natural law. In essence, natural law is simply the idea that there is an objective moral order, established by God and grounded in an essential humanity, which stands above mere human law and against which mere human law must be judged.

There are basically three theories of rights articulated over the last 2,000 years:

Judeo-Christian natural law theory

This is the belief, enshrined in the Magna Carta and the U.S. Declaration of Independence, that human rights are not derived from the whims of the state, but as gifts from the Creator. Man-made laws that violate these fundamental natural rights are not valid and are, in fact, illegal. A government that repeatedly violates God-given natural rights is an illegitimate tyranny and may be overthrown.

Social contract theory

This was a view, gradually evolved in the Middle Ages and then adopted by anti-Christian philosophers such as Thomas Hobbes and Jean-Jacques Rousseau, that sees civil government as primarily an agreement among sovereign individuals to consent to restrictions on their freedoms in order to live better in a group than they can on their own.

Legal positivism and legal realism

These are modern, rather cynical theories of jurisprudence, developed by Jeremy Bentham (c. 1748–1832) and refined by John Austin (c. 1790–1859), that basically hold that law is whatever the state says it is. Law and morality have nothing to do with one another. As described by the U.S. Supreme Court Justice Oliver Wendell Holmes, Jr., legal realism is simply the doctrine that the practice of law is the ability to predict what the Leviathan State, like a large and dangerous animal, might do under certain circumstances—the better to advise clients.

Legal positivism was a highly influential theory of jurisprudence throughout the first half of the twentieth century. But the horrors of World War II and Communist and Nazi totalitarianism made many law professors rethink whether it is a good idea to teach the doctrine that what is legal is whatever the state says is legal.

After all, Adolf Hitler was democratically elected by the people of Germany. The summary executions and brutalities of the Communist regimes were "legal" in the sense that the state authorized them.

Much of what has gone wrong in Western law, over the last 150 years—from the approval of slavery in the *Dred Scott* decision to the legalization of abortion in *Roe v. Wade*—stems from this fundamental, anti-Christian belief that basic human rights do not really exist, that the state may grant, or take away, whatever rights and "privileges" it deems necessary.

In contrast to the "new" theories of rights advocated by Rousseau and his followers, the classic Judeo-Christian view (expressed most succinctly in natural law theory) has always been that governmental elites must answer to a higher law than mere human legislation. When governments repeatedly transgress these fundamental human rights, it is the right of the people—as Jefferson put it in the Declaration of the Independence— "to throw off such government and to provide new guards for their future security."

Governments that fail to respect the "unalienable rights" endowed by God are tyrannies and, therefore, illegitimate.

Once again, these ideas stem, not from atheistic philosophers, but from Christian theologians reflecting upon the truths found in the Bible.

The notion of a Divine Law above mere human law was expressed clearly by Thomas Aquinas in his *Summa Theologica*, ratified by John Calvin in his *Institutes*, and summarized succinctly by Sir William Blackstone in his *Commentaries on the Laws of England* (1765), one of the chief sources used by Jefferson (and all the colonists) in crafting the new American government.

According to Blackstone, civil law is given, not to *create* rights, but to protect already *pre-existing* natural rights.

The primary object of law, he says, is to maintain and regulate those "absolute rights of individuals . . . such as would belong to man in a state of nature, and which every man is entitled to enjoy, whether in society or out of society."

"Those rights then which God and nature have established, and are therefore called natural rights, such as life and liberty, need not the aid of human laws to be more effectually invested in every man than they are; neither do they receive any additional strength when declared by the municipal laws to be inviolable. On the contrary, no human legislature

Who Said It?

"The New Testament is the very best book that ever was or ever will be known in the world."

Charles Dickens

has power to abridge or destroy them, unless the owner shall himself commit some act that amounts to a forfeiture."[2]

This great tradition of classical natural right—which extended from the biblical prophets and the teaching of Christ through the medieval scholastics and Protestant divines up to the U.S. Declaration of Independence—was challenged directly by what is sometimes called "political atheism."

Modern people, indoctrinated as they often are, tend to think of the Renaissance as a great "rebirth" of humanism and enlightenment, but in terms of human rights and of the rights of women it was actually a profound step backwards.

This is because the Renaissance was a return to the ideas of Roman and Greek civilization and a rejection of medieval Christianity—yet it was precisely medieval Christianity which championed what we today call human rights.

A long string of anti-Christian thinkers—first Machiavelli, then Thomas Hobbes, and finally Jeremy Bentham and John Austin—rejected the notion of human rights as nothing more than, as Bentham put it, "anarchical fallacies."

In his revolutionary book *The Prince*, Niccolo Machiavelli (c. 1469–1527) taught that politics must be utterly divorced from moral concerns of any kind. "Men ought either to be indulged or utterly destroyed," he said, "for if you merely offend them they take vengeance, but if you injure them greatly they are unable to retaliate, so that the injury done to a man ought to be such that vengeance cannot be feared."

The English political philosopher Thomas Hobbes (1588–1679) agreed.

In his work *The Leviathan*, he advocated a strong totalitarian government (the "leviathan") as the only way to save human beings from themselves. Famously describing human life as "solitary, poor, nasty, brutish, and short," Hobbes insisted that the reality of human interaction was that of "war of every one against everyone."

From this, he says, it follows that "nothing can be unjust. The notions of right and wrong, justice and injustice have no place [in the state of nature]."

The only hope for a modicum of peace and civilization, Hobbes thought, was for individuals to surrender irrevocably their natural rights to a totalitarian state (such as an absolute monarch). Fear of the "leviathan" would force selfish and violent men to maintain order and limit their crimes. For this reason, Hobbes rejected the Christian notion that individuals could ever disobey immoral laws or criticize the state in any way.

Nevertheless, Hobbes accepted the classic notion, developed in the early Middle Ages, that government derives its powers from the "consent of the governed." This "social contract" idea did influence the American Founders. But for Hobbes, the "consent," once made by a majority, is irrevocable and cannot be changed or transferred without the permission of the original sovereign.

It sometimes happens that a sovereign puts to death an innocent man, he says, but, in essence, this is simply the price people must pay for having a government. "Nothing the sovereign representative can do to a subject, on what pretense soever, can properly be called an injustice or injury, because every subject is author of every act the sovereign does," he says. For this reason, "tyranny" is merely an empty word for a monarchy that someone dislikes...just as "oligarchy" is merely a word used for an aristocracy that someone dislikes.

Needless to say, the American Founders didn't accept Hobbes's notion of absolute, unquestioning obedience to the state. Rather, they worked out an entirely new theory of government that combined the best of both the classic Christian theory of natural rights and the notion, drawn from the early Middle Ages, that the legitimacy of a government was the result of the "consent of the governed." But unlike Hobbes, the Founders believed that, when a government violated a people's natural rights "endowed by their Creator," then it was the "duty" of the people to "alter or abolish it" and to "institute new government."

Not surprisingly, not everyone took to this new theory of government. Totalitarians throughout history, whether monarchists or communists, dislike the idea that the power of government can be constrained in any way.

The English philosopher Jeremy Bentham (1748–1832), who witnessed the American Revolution, rejected entirely the notion of natural rights and the entire natural law tradition. His enemies were both Sir William Blackstone and John Locke. The idea of natural rights, he said, "is simple nonsense: natural and imprescriptible rights, rhetorical nonsense—nonsense upon stilts." The founder of the movement called "legal positivism," which is still influential today, Bentham believed that the only rights that truly exist are rights created by the civil government. If the government hasn't granted the right, he said, it's not a right but a wish. Whereas Aquinas and other Christian thinkers insisted that a civil law that violated the law of God is not a true law and can be justly disobeyed, Bentham and legal positivists insist that this is not the case. According to John Austin, another influential founder of legal positivism, morality and law have nothing to do with one another. The validity of a law lies only in that it is proclaimed by a sovereign. The influence of Thomas Hobbes is evident throughout legal positivism. The power of the state is virtually limitless.

In conclusion, what we can say is this. The ancient world had no concept of what we today call human rights. That concept arose from the assumptions and declarations of the Torah and the biblical prophets, was deepened and radicalized in the deeds and teachings of Jesus Christ, and was further universalized as the early Christian community left the ethnic confines of Judaism and began to evangelize in every language and among diverse groups of people.

As the Christian church began to think through the *political* implications of the belief that every human being is a child of God, created in his image and likeness and possessing an eternal destiny, canon lawyers began to insist that there were God-given *rights* that could not be justly abrogated by government officials. As these ideas developed, in both Catholic and Protestant countries, the Christian tradition of natural rights eventually developed into a theory of self-government that directly influenced the Founders of the American republic.

Those modern philosophers who rejected the truths of biblical Christianity—such as David Hume, Thomas Hobbes, Rousseau, and Karl Marx—not surprisingly also rejected the biblical, Christian theory of human rights.

And as we shall see in the next chapter, once government leaders decided that the only law is man-made law—that human rights are merely "nonsense upon stilts"—then all restraints could be thrown off. At last, ambitious social planners could attempt to remake society in their own image—and the nightmares of twentieth century totalitarianism could begin.

As Dostoevsky said, if there is no God, then all things are permitted.

Chapter Twelve

PUT NOT YOUR TRUST IN PRINCES

One of the most spectacular characteristics of Western societies has been the gradual development of political freedom and the limitation of governmental power.

As usual, the partisans of irreligion take full credit for these social advances—citing the contributions of such anti-Christian or agnostic thinkers as Jean-Jacques Rousseau, David Hume, and Adam Smith.

Indeed, for centuries atheist intellectuals have claimed that the entire world lay in chains until they appeared to break the bonds of slavery, both literal and figurative; but the truth, as we have seen in earlier chapters, is that the intellectual origins of liberty and a belief in limited government lie not in the intemperate ideologies of the French Enlightenment, but in the values and ideas found in the Bible and disseminated far and wide by Christianity.

In the Middle Ages, Christian theologians, reflecting on what the Bible said about a king's duty to obey the moral law and how he should be selected with the consent of the people, developed the beginnings of a social contract theory of government—the notion that a government, in the words of the Declaration of Independence, derives its just powers from the consent of the governed.

Guess what?

- More than 2,500 years before John Locke and James Madison, biblical prophets warned against giving the state too much power.

- The first right set forth in the Magna Carta is freedom of religion.

In fact, it was the explicit *rejection* of Christian natural law theory—first by people like Machiavelli and Thomas Hobbes and then, in the nineteenth and twentieth century, by the early theoreticians of socialism, communism, and fascism—that led to the horrors of twentieth century totalitarianism.

The Old Testament on government

As we have seen, the fundamental belief in the Hebrew Bible is that the One God, creator of heaven and earth, is absolutely sovereign and Lord over all things. "Hear, O Israel, the Lord our God is one."

Thus, it is not surprising that the inspired biblical writers took a dim view of any person or social institution that dared to challenge this divine authority—including the state.

More than 2,500 years before John Locke and James Madison, the biblical prophets warned the people of Israel against giving too much power to the state, in the form of a king. And they insisted that governmental leaders, no less than the common field laborer, must obey a Higher Law—and those who dare to ignore this Higher Law will be held accountable to divine justice.

The early Israelite community appears to have been a quasi-democratic theocracy, a tribal confederation that obeyed the Mosaic Law and were ruled by judges (*shofetim*) selected from among all the people. The judges were strong, prophetic leaders (including women like Deborah) who led the people in moments of crisis and then were replaced.

"Choose wise, intelligent and experienced men from each of your tribes, that I may appoint them as your rulers" (Dt 1:13).

These rulers were not to come merely from an elite aristocracy but from "all" the people.

"You shall also look among all the people [*mi kol ha-am*] for able and God-fearing men, men of truth who hate dishonest gain, and set them as officers over groups of thousands, of hundreds, of fifties and of tens. Let these men render decisions for the people in all ordinary cases" (Ex 18:21–22).

But Israel, anxious to be like the "other nations," asked the last judge and prophet, Samuel, for a king.

God told Samuel, reluctantly, to grant their request—insisting that such a request was ultimately a rejection of God himself.

"It is not you they reject," God tells Samuel. "They are rejecting me as their king."

Samuel warns the Israelites what having a king will mean for them—an apt description of any powerful government.

"He will take your sons and assign them to his chariots and horses.... He will take the best of your fields, vineyards, and olive groves, and give them to his officials. He will tithe your crops and your vineyards, and give the revenue to his eunuchs and his slaves. He will take your male and female servants, as well as your best oxen and your asses, and use them to do his work. He will tithe your flocks and you yourselves will become his slaves" (1 Sm 8:11, 14–17).

But the Israelites insisted upon having a king.

As God predicted, however, the Israelite kings were a rapacious, violent lot—beginning with "wise" king Solomon who overtaxed his people to pay for his palaces, forty thousand horses, seven hundred wives, and three hundred concubines (1 Kgs 11:3). Internecine bickering and palace intrigues led to the country being divided into two kingdoms—the northern kingdom of Israel and the southern kingdom of Judah. The prophets predicted that the violence, lawlessness, and idolatry of the ruling elites would lead to destruction—and both kingdoms were invaded and their populations dragged off into slavery.

Scripture Says

"Put not your trust in princes, nor in a son of man, in whom there is no help."

Psalm 146:3

The northern kingdom (the "lost tribes" of Israel) was scattered, but, after a period of exile in Babylon, the people of the southern kingdom of Judah returned. When they did return, at first they were ruled by governors and the High Priest of the Temple. This continued into the Maccabee period when Israel regained its independence, from the Greek descendents of Alexander the Great, until the region was conquered by Rome in 66 BC.

Rendering unto Caesar what is Caesar's

Numerous texts in the New Testament seem to advocate a passive acceptance of governmental authority—beginning with Jesus's famous maxim to "render unto Caesar the things that are Caesar's, and to God the things that are God's."

It seems certain that Jesus was not a political revolutionary, despite what Roman officials may have thought and modern liberation theologians seem to advocate. His "agenda" appears to have been substantially more ambitious than that—the salvation of the entire world—and, indeed, the movement he launched over a period of just three years ended up conquering, not just Rome, but a large portion of the planet.

In any event, Jesus was quite explicit that he was not a political revolutionary. He came not to rule but to die. "The Son of man," he said, "came not to be served but to serve, and to give his life as a ransom for many" (Mk 10:45).

This does not mean that Jesus's message does not have political consequences—only that his primary purpose does not appear to have been the overthrow of the existing political order.

The early Christian community, too, did not advocate violence or rebellion against Rome. The Pharisee Sha'ul from Tarsus—who became the apostle Paul—was a proud Roman citizen. "Let every person be subordinate to the higher authorities, for there is no authority except from God, and those that exist have been established by God," Paul told the

Roman Christian community in the early 60s AD, when rumblings of rebellion in Judaea were already being heard. "Whoever resists authority opposes what God has appointed, and those who oppose it will bring judgment upon themselves."

Texts such as these have been used, throughout Christian history, to advocate either passivity in the face of governmental abuse or a withdrawal from civic life altogether.

Thus, the early Christians, seeing their mission as primarily the conversion of sinners, and being an oppressed and persecuted minority without any power anyway, did not dwell immediately on the political implications of Jesus's life and teaching. It was only later, once Christians were in positions of power, that they were forced to confront the problem of what to do about abuses of power.

Development of political freedom in the Middle Ages

Once Christianity went from being a tiny persecuted sect within Judaism to the largest religion in Western Europe, during the Middle Ages, Christian leaders faced a new problem: the tendency of political leaders, primarily kings, to assert control over the Church.

It was the so-called Investiture Controversy of the eleventh century that brought to a head the conflict between secular and religious officials—and ultimately forced the Christian church in the West to develop a theory, based on biblical precedents, of the limits of governmental authority.

The Investiture Controversy arose over who had the right to appoint ecclesiastical officials—the Church itself (primarily through the pope) or governmental leaders.

The state (the Holy Roman Empire) wanted the right to appoint bishops and abbots because, as these appointments usually included control over vast properties, it could offer these positions to the highest bidder—a practice the Church considered to be simony (the sale of sacred things).

Due to efforts of a strong pope, the reforming Gregory VII, the secular powers eventually backed down. The dispute forced theologians to work out principles by which secular powers legitimately govern and set out a theory that limited that power.

According to Manegold of Lautenbach (c. 1030–1106):

> No man can make himself king or emperor. The people raise a man above them in this way in order that he may govern them in accordance with right reason, give to each one his own, protect the good, destroy the wicked, and administer justice to every man. But if he violates the contract (*pactum*) under which he was elected, disturbing and confounding that which he was established to set in order, then the people is justly and reasonably released from its obligation to obey him. For he was the first to break the faith that bound them together.[1]

Manegold insisted the king's power is strictly limited and arises, not from conquest or divine right, but from the consent of the people. It was precisely this idea that would be enshrined in the *Magna Carta Libertatum*—the "Great Charter of Freedoms" that was adopted in 1215 and which established that the king, too, is bound by law.

The Magna Carta had an enormous influence on the development of English common law and on the development of the U.S. Constitution. The first of all the rights, in order of precedence, is freedom of religion:

> First, We have granted to God, and by this our present Charter have confirmed, for us and our Heirs for ever, That the Church of England shall be free, and shall have her whole rights and liberties inviolable. We have granted also, and given to all the freemen of our realm, for us and our Heirs for ever, these liberties underwritten, to have and to hold to them and their Heirs, of us and our Heirs for ever.

But what happens if a king or government does *not* obey the law, of man or of God, and exercises power in a tyrannical way? Does the Bible require that citizens merely suffer such wrongs in silence?

Not at all, said medieval theologians. The English bishop John of Salisbury (c. 1115–1180), in his book *Policraticus* ("Statesman's Book"), insisted that resistance to tyranny, including if necessary tyrannicide, is not merely permitted but is an actual *duty*.

"He who receives power from God serves the laws and is the slave of justice and right," John said. "He who usurps power suppresses justice and places the laws beneath his will. Therefore, justice is deservedly armed against those who disarm the law.... Tyranny is, therefore, not only a public crime, but, if this can happen, it is more than public ... and whoever does not prosecute [a tyrant] transgresses against himself and against the whole body of the early republic."

This was a question that was taken up by numerous medieval theologians, most notably and systematically by Thomas Aquinas.

In his magisterial compendium of Christian doctrine, the *Summa Theologica*, Aquinas addressed the issue of tyranny systematically—and drew upon the Biblical texts.

In Question 105, Aquinas asks "Whether the Old Law enjoined fitting precepts concerning rulers?"

He notes that the Mosaic Law has no provision for the selection of a king and that, when God allowed the Israelites to appoint a king, in 1 Samuel, they established a tyrant. He also notes that the primitive Israelite government was a "democratic government in so far as the rulers were chosen from all the people."

Aquinas concludes that the best form of government combines features of a kingdom, an aristocracy, and a democracy—prefiguring, in an astonishing way, the division of powers established in the U.S. Constitution among an executive branch, a judicial branch, and an elected assembly.

"Accordingly, the best form of government is in a state or kingdom, where one is given the power to preside over all; while under him are others having governing powers: and yet a government of this kind is shared by all, both because all are eligible to govern, and because the rulers are chosen by all. For this is the best form of polity, being partly kingdom, since there is one at the head of all; partly aristocracy, in so far as a number of persons are set in authority; partly democracy, i.e., government by the people, in so far as the rulers can be chosen from the people, and the people have the right to choose their rulers. Such was the form of government established by the Divine Law."[2]

"All the people should take some share in the government," Aquinas says, "for this form of constitution ensures peace among the people, commends itself to all, and is most enduring." The problem with a kingdom, Aquinas adds, is that "the power of a king easily degenerates into tyranny."

But what should Christians do when faced with tyranny?

After all, doesn't Romans 13 seem to insist that Christians are obligated to obey governmental authority—which, Paul says, is "from God"?

In his *Commentary on the Sentences of Peter Lombard* (book 2, dist. 44, quest. 2, art. 2), Aquinas addressed just this issue. The first thing to note, he said, is that Paul is not talking about *anyone* who happens to have coercive power but only about authorities who meet certain conditions and therefore derive their authority legitimately from God. For example, if a leader acquires power through violence or an illegal coup he or she is not a legitimate authority and can be justly disobeyed. He also insists that if a legitimate authority commands an immoral act "not only is there no obligation to obey the authority, but one is obliged to disobey it, as did the holy martyrs who suffered death rather than obey the impious commands of tyrants."

Strong words, indeed.

Centuries later, this radical teaching was encapsulated in the phrase "rebellion to tyrants is obedience to God"—first coined by John Bradshaw (1602–1659), the lawyer who served as president on the parliamentary commission which sentenced British king Charles I to death. Thomas Jefferson and Benjamin Franklin (both alleged secularists) proposed that it become the motto for the Great Seal of the United States.

The medieval and later Reformation theologians were not, of course, opposed to all civil government. They accepted the biblical teaching that civil government is "from God," part of Divine Providence, but they also understood that, in the hands of sinful human beings, government power could be abused and therefore should be strictly limited.

As a result, they worked out a theory called "interposition," which means that private individuals should not oppose tyranny directly but that lesser officials, operating in a governmental capacity, should be the normal means for opposing abuses of governmental power.

In his book *Vindiciae Contra Tyrannos* (A Defense of Liberty Against Tyrants, 1579), a French Huguenot author, writing under the pseudonym of Stephen Brutus, insisted that governmental leaders are bound by the same laws of God as anyone else. "The Holy Scripture does teach that God reigns by his own proper authority, and kings by derivation, God from himself, kings from God, that God has a jurisdiction proper, kings are his delegates," Brutus wrote. "It follows, then, that the jurisdiction of God has no limits, that of kings bounded, that the power of God is infinite, that of kings confined, that the kingdom of God extends itself to all places, that of kings is restrained within the confines of certain countries."

Thus, it was in Christian natural law theory, developed in the Middle Ages and drawing upon biblical teaching, that the first principles of ordered liberty and self-government can be found.

Later theologians would work out in more detail the obligations of subjects when faced with tyrants. For example, just as in Christian Just War theory, a person must consider whether the evil that would be remedied by war is worse than the evil caused by war, so, too, citizens or subjects suffering under an unjust government must weigh carefully whether resistance to tyranny—through the overthrow of the existing government—will create more social unrest (and greater harm) than temporary obedience.

This is precisely what the U.S. Declaration of Independence says: "Prudence, indeed, will dictate that governments long established should not be changed for light and transient causes; and accordingly all experience hath shown that mankind are more disposed to suffer, while evils are sufferable, than to right themselves by abolishing the forms to which they are accustomed. But when a long train of abuses and usurpations, pursuing invariably the same object evinces a design to reduce them under absolute despotism, it is their right, it is their duty, to throw off such government, and to provide new guards for their future security."

Liberal democracy: The legacy of Christendom

The historical evidence clearly shows that the enemy of political liberty is not Christianity or Judaism, as false liberals like Robert Reich and Sam Harris like to claim, but the dangerous idea that there is no Higher Authority to which politicians must be accountable and that, therefore, the ends always justify the means.

Societies that have actually done what atheist polemicists now advocate and deliberately rejected "bourgeois" Christianity in favor of a more "rational," more "modern," more "scientific" approach to politics—such as revolutionary France, Communist Russia, and fascist Germany—ended up, not in the utopia of their dreams, but in a bloody tyranny.

That liberal democracy owes its origins to Christian and Jewish civilization can easily be seen just by consulting a map.

Each year, the international democracy watchdog organization Freedom House publishes its annual survey which attempts to measure the degree of democracy and freedom in every nation of the world, producing "scores" that represent the levels of political rights and civil liberties in each state and territory—from 1 (most free) to 7 (least free). It then groups scores together as "Free" (1 to 2.5), "Partly Free" (3 to 5) and "Not Free" (3.5 to 7). Countries such as New Zealand, Canada, and Japan are "free," while Russia, China, and Saudi Arabia are rated "not free."

Out of 194 countries and territories surveyed for 2006, 73 countries (38 percent) were rated Free, 54 (28 percent) were rated Partly Free, and 67 (34 percent) were rated Not Free. This is a marked improvement over 1980, when only 23.9 percent of nations were rated Free, 24.8 percent were rated Partly Free, and 51.3 percent were Not Free.

A quick glance at the organization's annual "freedom map" demonstrates that freedom and human rights are almost exclusively the product of Western Christian civilization.

Those nations and territories that are rated "free" exist largely in areas once dominated by Christian culture—Europe, North and South America, Australia and New Zealand, and in those parts of Asia where colonial powers ruled for centuries (such as India) or where, as in the case of Japan, the U.S. imposed a Western-style democracy as part of the settlement of the Second World War.

In dramatic contrast, those nations rated "not free" are found overwhelmingly in non-Christian areas of the world, including parts of Africa, the entire Middle East with the exception of Israel, most of Asia and Central Asia (with the interesting exception of Mongolia), and the areas once dominated by the communist regime of the Soviet Union.

You can quantify this striking correlation between Christian culture and political freedom by comparing the "freedom" rankings produced by Freedom House with the percentage of the population in each country ranked as Christian by the CIA. (The CIA designation refers more to "nominal" rather than "practicing" Christians—Denmark, for example, is rated 98 percent Christian even though most Danes do not cross a church threshold more than once a year—but nevertheless is illuminating when it comes to the cultural context that produces civil liberties.)

Almost all of the countries with a Christian population above 50 percent are rated either 1 (the highest) or 2 for civil liberties and political freedom by Freedom House—with a few notable exceptions.

Percentage of Christian Population in a Country Compared to Its Rating for Political Rights and Civil Liberties by Freedom House

Among the countries ranked as the most free and with the highest respect for civil liberties are Australia (66 percent Christian), Austria (78.3 percent), the United States (79 percent), Canada (66 percent), Costa Rica (92 percent), Belgium (100 percent), Chile (100 percent), Denmark (98 percent), France (90 percent), Finland (86 percent), Germany (68 percent), Great Britain (71.6 percent), Ireland (93 percent), Iceland (93 percent), Norway (90.1 percent), Portugal (98 percent), Spain (94 percent), Switzerland (78.9 percent), Sweden (87 percent), Italy (90 percent), and New Zealand (79.5 percent).

Among the countries ranked as not free are Algeria (1 percent Christian), Azerbaijan (4.8 percent), Bhutan (0 percent), Burma (4 percent), Cambodia (0 percent), China (4 percent), Egypt (10 percent), Iran (1 percent), Iraq (3 percent), Libya (3 percent), North Korea (0 percent), Pakistan (1 percent), Qatar (1 percent), Russia (15 percent), Saudi Arabia (0 percent), Somalia (0 percent), Sudan (5 percent), Syria (10 percent), United Arab Emirates (2 percent), Vietnam (7.2 percent), and Zimbabwe (25 percent).

Interestingly enough, as the percentage of Christians in a country declines below 50 percent, so does its rating for political freedom and human rights. For example, those countries rated only "partly free" also tend to have smaller Christian populations. For example, Albania, with only 33 percent of its population Christian, rates a 3 for both political freedom and civil liberties; Nigeria, with a 40 percent Christian population, rates a 4 for both political freedom and civil liberties; Lebanon, 39 percent Christian, rates a 5 for political freedom and a 4 for civil rights; Liberia, which is 40 percent Christian, rates a 4 for both political freedom and civil rights; and so on.

These are not fixed absolutes, of course. There are exceptions.

Haiti, for example, is listed as 96 percent Christian by the CIA yet has among the very worst record for human rights and political freedoms. The same is true of Rwanda: Rated 93.6 percent Christian by the CIA, it scores a 6 out of 7 for political freedom and a 5 for civil liberties. Swaziland, rated 50 percent Christian, is nevertheless "not free" and ranked a 7 for political freedom (the worst). Some Latin American countries, just emerging from years of civil war or military dictatorship, have higher Christian populations but somewhat restricted freedom. For example, El Salvador, which is 83 percent Roman Catholic, is rated "free" but only scores a 3 for civil liberties. Mexico, which is 95 percent Christian despite its historically anti-Christian government, is rated 2 for political freedom and civil liberties. The Philippines, which is 89 percent Christian, is rated "partly free" with a rating of 3 for both political freedom and civil liberties.

But at the opposite end of the spectrum, those countries with the smallest percentage of Christians are rated overwhelming "not free" by Freedom House and are among those with the worst ratings for civil liberties by far—but again, with a few interesting exceptions.

Almost all of the Islamic countries have very small Christian populations and rank near the bottom when it comes to political freedom and civil rights—including Saudi Arabia (0 percent Christian and no political freedom), Sudan (5 percent Christian and no political freedom), Libya (3 percent Christian and no political freedom), Iran (1 percent Christian and no political freedom), and so on.

Current communist regimes, such as China (4 percent Christian), Burma (4 percent Christian), Cambodia (0 percent), North Korea (0 percent), Laos (1.5 percent) and Vietnam (7.2 percent), also have very low Christian populations and virtually no freedom whatsoever.

Interestingly enough, some of the former Communist states are still ranked as "not free" or "partly free," including Russia (only 15 percent Christian) and Albania (30 percent); but a number of former Communist countries with sizable Christian populations are now ranked near the top in terms of civil liberties and political liberty.

Once these countries were freed of Soviet military domination, they quickly adopted laws protecting political liberty and basic human rights. These include Bulgaria (83.8 percent Christian), which scores in the top rank for political freedom and a 2 for civil liberties; Poland (91.2 percent Christian), which now scores 1 for both civil liberties and political freedom; Hungary (74 percent Christian), which now scores 1s as well; Lithuania (85 percent), which now scores 1s; Romania (99 percent), which scores 2s.

There are also some countries that are neither Christian nor communist but which nevertheless score badly in terms of civil rights and political freedom, including Bhutan (0 percent Christian), rated 6 for civil liberties and 5 for political freedom; Nepal (0.2 percent Christian), rated 6 for political freedom and 5 for civil liberties; the Maldives (0 percent Christian), rated 6 for political freedom and 5 for civil liberties; Guinea (8 percent), rated 6 for political freedom and 5 for civil liberties; and Malaysia (7 percent), which scores 4s.

There are also a handful of countries with extremely low Christian populations but nevertheless score high in terms of political freedom and civil liberties. These are Israel (2 percent), which scores 1 for both political freedom and civil liberties; Japan (0.7 percent), which also scores 1s; Taiwan (4 percent), which scores 1s; South Korea (26 percent), which scores 1s; and India (2.3 percent), which scores 2s.

Clearly, therefore, a sizable Christian population is not a *requirement* for civil liberty and political freedom, but you could still make the case that those non-Christian societies that have a solid record on human rights and political liberty benefited from prolonged contact with, and influence by, Christian nations.

Israel is a special case because, as we have seen, respect for fundamental human rights and political freedom is a preeminently Jewish cultural legacy, one that is implicit in the Torah and which Israel bequeathed to Christianity; but you could say that many of the founders of the State of Israel, a large percentage of them refugees from Europe, learned some of the practical details of parliamentary-style democracy in their former counties.

Japan, of course, had its Western-style democratic government imposed by U.S. Occupation Forces after World War II—but what was imposed by force has now taken root and grown into a distinctly Japanese style of liberal democracy. South Korea was occupied by U.S. forces after World War II and the U.S. established a military government until the creation of the First Republic in 1948. South Korea, only 26 percent Christian, struggled for decades with autocratic leaders, military coups, and political assassinations, but today has achieved a high level of political freedom and civil liberties. Finally, India, which was a colony of Great Britain's for more than 175 years—and still prides itself on its membership in the Commonwealth and its record as preeminent cricket champions—is a federal republic with a president, a prime minister, and a bicameral Parliament, and a legal system based on English common law. While only 2.3 percent Christian, India has adopted many of the cultural values of liberal democracy and retains, like other members of the Commonwealth, remarkably strong ties to Britain.

In conclusion, therefore, we can say that the enemies of Christianity and Judaism have it exactly backwards: Far from being a threat to liberal democracy and political freedom, biblical religion is, in fact, the intellectual matrix out of which both arose. The values and beliefs that permeate the Bible—the notion that all human beings are equal in the eyes of God and that no king or ruler may claim unquestioned obedience—were the proximate cause for the development of a religious theory of liberty. For more than a thousand years, the most brilliant minds in Christendom meditated on Biblical texts that emphasized God's absolute sovereignty in the face of human arrogance and concluded, as did Thomas Aquinas, that unjust governments lose their right to rule and may be overthrown.

The political legacy of biblical religion, in short, is nothing less than liberal democracy itself—which can be empirically verified by the fact that those nations that embrace political freedom and civil liberties are either predominantly Christian or were aided, in the establishment of their governmental institutions, by predominantly Christian nations. This is another example of how the ideas contained in the Bible have shaped the world we now live in—even for those who mistakenly believe the Bible is irrelevant to their lives.

Chapter Thirteen

WHO DO YOU SAY THAT I AM?

In just three years or less, the mysterious figure we now know (or think we know) as Jesus of Nazareth somehow changed the face of the world.

His real name was almost certainly Yeshu'a bar Yosef. From all the available evidence, he was a semi-skilled Jewish journeyman from a tiny village in northern Palestine who became, very briefly, an itinerant prophet, miracle-worker, and social revolutionary, one who challenged the religious and social institutions of his day so radically that he was put to death for it.

Of course, for two billion people on the planet today, he is also something much more: The Word of God, the wisdom and mercy and justice of God incarnate.

What is undeniable to the honest historian is that this one man's life, teaching, and symbolic acts eventually created a social and cultural revolution that reverberated far beyond Palestine and altered almost every institution on earth—and is still felt today.

In short, Jesus changed everything: politics, art, science, law, the rules of warfare, philosophy, sexual life, the family. Even Napoleon was amazed: "Alexander, Caesar, Charlemagne, and myself founded empires; but upon what foundation did we rest the creations of our genius? Upon

Guess what?

◈ Without armies or force, Jesus founded one of the largest empires in history. (Even Napoleon gives him credit for such a feat!)

◈ To the chagrin of Gnostic fans everywhere, the New Testament is the earliest and most authentic historical record we have of the real Jesus.

force. Jesus Christ founded an empire upon love; and at this hour millions of men would die for Him." But the question is: *how*?

Beyond the piety of believers and the doubts of modern skeptics lies an enduring mystery: what did Jesus do and say, in as little as one year and a maximum of three years, that could possibly have had such an impact? How could his ragtag band of illiterate fishermen, reformed prostitutes, and tax collectors create the philosophical and social revolution that we have described in this book—one that made possible such diverse realities as experimental science, the abolition of slavery, and the recognition of universal human rights?

In short: How do we explain the *fact* of Christianity?

Jesus Christ Superstar

One answer, given by scholars from a wide variety of perspectives—including that of so-called liberation theology—is that Jesus's movement was neither small nor ragtag.

Instead, it was just as portions of the New Testament describe it as being: a *massive* popular outpouring of messianic enthusiasm, especially among the poor and marginalized, that alarmed the Jewish religious leaders of the time and made Roman military officials very nervous.

Many modern people think of Jesus as something like the befuddled hippie Christ in the 1970 play and 1973 film *Godspell*, teaching his message of peace and love to small groups of dazed flower children.

But what if Jesus was actually more like the Jesus portrayed in the film *Jesus Christ Superstar*: A fiery, charismatic, rugged populist who drew crowds by the thousands, even tens of thousands—and whose caustic, subversive, often very funny parables about the "reign of God" and the arrogant elites who try to stand in its way electrified an entire country already seething with rebellion?

What if Jesus wasn't the meek and mild pacifist of Christian iconography but actually something far more dangerous—a genuinely courageous iconoclast who had the sheer guts to stare down a crowd about to stone a woman to death and who stormed right into the holiest place on earth and began attacking the sales people and money-changers *with a whip?*

Scripture Says

"I have come to bring fire on the earth, and how I wish it were already blazing! ... Do you think I came to bring peace? No, I tell you, but division."

Luke 12:49, 51

Such a man could very well have put the fear of God (quite literally) into almost everyone in power—the moneyed aristocracy who controlled the Jerusalem Temple (the Sadducees); the pious frauds who lay unjust burdens upon people's shoulders; certainly the small band of Roman military officials charged with keeping the peace.

The truth that both religious believers and modern skeptics have forgotten is this: Jesus proclaimed his message of divine reconciliation and universal peace in a time of ferocious violence and red-hot religious hatred. It was a time eerily like our own: an age of empire and brutal terrorism, of ethnic hatred and spiritual yearning.

The reign of God that Jesus inaugurated and proclaimed with his own blood was born in fire, in the social tumult preceding one of the most violent civil and religious wars in the history of mankind. It was a war that would turn out to be a thousand times more deadly than the current Israeli-Palestinian standoff and at least two to four times more deadly than the "ethnic cleansing" in Kosovo in the late 1990s. Historians estimate that fully forty percent of the Jewish population in Judea may have been wiped out in the Jewish War of 66–70 AD, when the Roman army besieged Jerusalem, tore the famous Temple down and slaughtered hundreds of thousands.

Jesus and the Zealots

One of the few attempts to look seriously at the military context out of which the Jesus Movement arose is S. G. F. Brandon's classic, albeit controversial work, *Jesus and the Zealots: A Study of the Political Factor in Primitive Christianity* (New York: Charles Scribner's Sons, 1967).

Brandon was a professor of comparative religion at the University of Manchester from 1951 until his death and not a professional biblical scholar as such; nevertheless, his work was enormously influential. He was a spokesman for the traditional view that saw the Zealots as an organized movement, founded perhaps by the Jewish robber-baron Hezekiah but hearkening back to the Maccabees, that existed throughout the New Testament period and had many important ties to, and affinities and minor disagreements with, the movement inaugurated by Jesus.

Brandon's work is 384 pages of dense, detailed, extensively quoted arguments that, in essence, make the claim that the evangelists radically misrepresented who Jesus was and what he was all about. For Brandon, Jesus was a radical Jewish nationalist fully in harmony with the primary goals and attitudes of the Zealots—including with the use of violence to achieve his means. Unlike the Zealots, however, the object of Jesus's reformist zeal was not the Roman occupiers but rather the corrupt sarcedotal aristocracy in Jerusalem which controlled the Temple. Jesus, like the Zealots, sought to establish the reign of God on earth, but Jesus believed the way to do that was through a radical reform of Jewish religion, particularly in the Temple.

For Brandon, Jesus's brazenly messianic and triumphal entry into Jerusalem on Palm Sunday was immediately followed, if not on

A Book Atheists Want to Burn

Jesus of Nazareth by Joseph Ratzinger (Pope Benedict XVI); New York: Doubleday, 2007. The pope takes the tools of modern, critical biblical scholarship and uses them to affirm the authenticity of traditional interpretations of the New Testament.

the very day, by a virtual assault on the Temple precincts—not merely by himself alone, but by thousands of his followers, all clamoring that he be made king of Israel. This violent, albeit primarily religious mission might have occurred simultaneously with a far more violent uprising by Zealot forces against the Romans or Roman sympathizers, and two of these men, possibly led by Barabbas, were executed side by side with Jesus on Calvary.

For Brandon, in other words, the Gospels are a complete whitewash of what really happened—an attempt to make Jesus and his movement palatable to a Roman world after the Jewish Revolt of 66 to 70 AD had been crushed. His critical reading of Mark points out a number of apparent inconsistencies in the narrative that are not, for Brandon, easily reconciled. For one thing, Mark portrays Jesus as an innocent victim of scheming on the part of Jewish leaders, falsely accused of sedition and executed by the Romans. Yet the evangelist also admits that Jesus's popularity with the crowds was so great that Jewish leaders "feared to arrest him publicly" and had to send an armed party to do so, and at night. The fears of the Jewish leaders were apparently somewhat justified, Brandon says, because their attempts to arrest Jesus were met, at first, by armed resistance (when one of the "bystanders" cut off the ear of the High Priest's servant).

Yet there are important differences between the Zealots, as Brandon describes them, and Jesus and his followers. For one thing, the Zealots, like the Pharisees, were *shomrei ha-mitzvot*, Torah rigorists. Josephus describes them as being unwilling to even touch a coin that bears the image of a pagan king. Indeed, the paying of tribute to a foreign king was a *casus belli* for the entire Zealot movement. That is the politically charged context, then, of the question posed to Jesus about paying tribute: Is it lawful to pay the census tax to Caesar? Jesus's brilliant answer, "Repay to Caesar what belongs to Caesar, and to God what belongs to God," upholds the principle of divine sovereignty without conceding the Zealot ideal of tax resistance. For Brandon, however, this authentic saying of Jesus was meant to say, and was taken by his audience to mean, that pious Jews should *not* pay the Roman tribute: In other words, that Jesus agreed with the Zealots! Indeed, says Brandon, had Jesus taught anything other than that—given the universal hatred of the Romans by ordinary Jews—he could not have had any support whatsoever among the people, and the historical evidence indicates that he had a substantial following.

However, as much as Brandon wishes to make Jesus and James out to be conservative, traditional Jews, and thus in sympathy with the Zealot cause—as opposed to Paul, the Gentile-loving innovator—it is difficult to build that case from what the Synoptic Gospels say about Jesus's many run-ins with the Pharisees. Throughout the Synoptics, Jesus is shown to be at odds with conservative Jewish (Pharisaical and Zealot) ideas of what it means to serve God. Jesus's somewhat defiant attitude towards Sabbath-keeping, his willingness to openly challenge accepted Jewish practice in the Temple, his table fellowship with tax-collectors (considered nothing less than collaborators with the hated Romans), his own willingness to speak with Roman officials and even Samaritan women, his sayings about ritual hand-washing and unclean food—all of these things in the Gospels present a Jesus who would not have been in sympathy with the violent xenophobia of the Zealots.

The quest for the historical Jesus

Brandon is typical of much of the scholarly work done on Jesus over the last two centuries. This work can raise fascinating, tantalizing questions, but it usually operates out of one overriding, often unquestioned assumption: that the "real" Jesus was something quite other than what his followers, and the New Testament, said that he was.

This modern quest for the "real" or the "historical" Jesus began with a German Deist named Hermann Samuel Reimarus (c. 1694–1798), wound its way through works by the German theologian David Strauss (1808–1874), the French philosopher Ernest Renan (1823–1892) and the Alsatian physician and humanitarian Albert Schweitzer (1875–1965), and then hit a dead-end with the radical historical skepticism of the Lutheran New Testament scholars Martin Dibelius (1883–1947) and Rudolf Bultmann (1884–1976).

In recent decades, however, there have been a second and then a third "quest" to identify who the "real" Jesus was—with the portraits as varied as the scholars who fashioned them. Recent efforts have sought, often successfully, to more fully recover the "Jewishness" of Jesus and his first followers. These respected, often quite "conservative" historical Jesus scholars include Joachim Jeremias (1900–1979); the Jewish scholars Hyam Maccoby (1924–2004), Jacob Neusner (1934–), and Geza Vermes; E. P. Sanders; the Catholic priests Raymond Brown and John P. Meier; the Anglican bishop N. T. Wright; and the evangelical scholar Ben Witherington III.

However, the most notorious and controversial of "historical Jesus" scholars are those associated with what was called the Jesus Seminar— an ad hoc committee of liberal intellectuals and writers, organized under the auspices of the Westar Institute in 1985, by Robert Funk and the former Irish priest and bestselling author John Dominic Crossan. The seminar included dozens of liberal scholars and just ordinary liberals, including the Dutch film maker Paul Verhoeven (who has a Ph.D. in mathematics but is best known for directing such epic religious films as *RoboCop*, *Total Recall*, *Basic Instinct*, and, of course, *Showgirls*), Episcopal bishop John Shelby Strong, and ex-nun and author Karen Armstrong.

The Jesus Seminar was best known for its practice of meeting in groups and voting, according to a predetermined system of colored beads, on which words and deeds of Jesus were "authentic" and what were likely invented by the early Church. Unfortunately, the seminar participants found most of the New Testament to fall into the latter category. They

A Book Atheists Want to Burn

The Resurrection of the Son of God, by N. T. Wright; Minneapolis: Augsburg Fortress Publishers, 2003. Think the Resurrection is not a historical fact? Try this 817-page tome by an Anglican priest and scholar, part of a multivolume study. He nails it.

voted only 11 percent of the words of Jesus in Mark to be authentic, 17 percent in Matthew, 20 percent in Luke and pretty much none in the Gospel of John. Jesus's deeds didn't fare much better: The seminar participants found that only 16 percent of 176 distinct "acts" recorded in 387 "reports" to be authentic or probably authentic (meaning they actually occurred). The Jesus Seminar liberals were pretty sure that there was a Jesus from Galilee who was born of Mary with the "assistance" of Joseph, that he was baptized by and was a disciple of John the Baptist, that he cured sick people, that he was crucified by the Romans, that his body decayed as all corpses do, and that the Resurrection didn't literally happen. Beyond that, they can't say much.

Although the Jesus Seminar participants tried to present themselves as cutting-edge scholars in the "mainstream" of New Testament research, they immediately had many critics from within the scholarly community. One common criticism was that very few members of the seminar were actually professional Bible scholars; the majority were, instead, public intellectuals and educated persons but without any formal training in biblical studies. One critic, the Catholic New Testament scholar Luke Timothy Johnson of Emory University in Atlanta, even went so far as to call the seminar a "self-indulgent charade." That's because the seminar's conclusions were pre-determined before a single vote was cast by the selection of the seminar participants and the methodology they used to evaluate the biblical evidence. Whatever else they may have been, co-founders Funk and Crossan were certainly not what you would call orthodox believers. "The plot early Christians invented for a divine redeemer figure is as archaic as the mythology in which it is framed," Funk explained on the

Jesus Seminar Web site. "A Jesus who drops down out of heaven, performs some magical act that frees human beings from the power of sin, rises from the dead, and returns to heaven is simply no longer credible. The notion that he will return at the end of time and sit in cosmic judgment is equally incredible. We must find a new plot for a more credible Jesus."

Other critics pointed out that at least some of the criteria that the Jesus Seminar used to judge whether the New Testament passage was "authentic" or not were logically consistent. These criteria included:

The criterion of dissimilarity

This is the notion, common outside of the seminar, that if a saying or act of Jesus is unlike something the early Church would say or do, it is probably authentic. But this is a crazy notion, when you think about it: It requires you to believe that Jesus's early followers had nothing in common with the Teacher whose memory and message they were risking their lives to preach to the entire world.

The criterion of embarrassment

This is the belief that if something is inherently embarrassing, such as the apostles being a bit cowardly or stupid, it is probably authentic because people don't usually make up stories that make them look bad.

The criterion of self-reference

This is the assumption that Jesus would never refer to himself in grandiose terms or to his having an important mission. This is why the Seminar rejects most of the sayings in the Gospel of John, such as "I am the way, the truth, and the life" (Jn 14:1).

The criterion of diverse settings

As we'll discuss below, the Synoptic Gospels often quote the same saying of Jesus but have it in varying contexts. As a result, the seminar participants believed most of the "framing" material around a saying was made up by the evangelists.

The criterion of community needs

If a saying of Jesus has anything to do with the early Christian community, such as instructions for missionaries or references to Peter as "the rock" upon which the church is built, it is almost certainly inauthentic.

The criterion of theological agendas

The seminar participants believed that any saying that is in harmony with the identified theological "agenda" of a given evangelist is almost certainly inauthentic. For example, the prophecy of the sheep and the goats was voted inauthentic because it allegedly fits in with Matthew's intent to distinguish between true and false followers of Christ.

Of course, some of these criteria are used by mainstream biblical scholars, although in different ways. As we will see below, it is widely accepted by virtually all reputable New Testament scholars that the evangelists, in writing their own Gospels, arranged their material and selected from their sources those parts of the story that emphasized the points they, the evangelists, were trying to make. But mainstream scholars don't draw from this commonsense observation the radical skepticism exhibited by the Jesus Seminar. For example, the fact that a given evangelist includes a saying of Jesus that makes one of the evangelist's key theological points, or puts it into a particular place in his narrative, doesn't *necessarily* mean that he made it up. We know, because we can see for ourselves in the Gospel texts, that one evangelist will use a saying of Jesus and another one won't. All this means is that the evangelists, like modern journalists choosing which quotations to use in an article, *selected* those sayings of Jesus, and arranged them in a particular way, to support the points they were trying to make—and not that they made them up.

Contemporary biblical scholarship

It goes without saying that the Jesus Seminar at least engaged biblical scholarship. Some of its leaders were real scholars trained in some of the best universities in the world. To that degree, it's possible to debate the Jesus Seminar's conclusions.

But there is a whole other "school" of New Testament bashing that is beyond the reach of reason or of critical comment. That would include those who, like Christopher Hitchens, still insist that Jesus Christ was likely a mythical figure who never even existed in the first place.[1] It also includes the millions of people who believe *The Da Vinci Code* was based on real events—that Jesus survived the crucifixion, married Mary Magdalene (the real "holy grail"), and fathered descendants who became the kings and queens of France. In a similar way, most faithful Christians and Jews don't really have ready answers for those who insist that the Old Testament was based on aliens docking the Mother Ship on Mt. Sinai (after all, Exodus describes a mountain of "fire and smoke")—a view popularized by a series of books (e.g., *Chariots of the Gods*) in the 1960s by Swiss author Erich von Däniken.

The truth is, recent attacks on the New Testament by atheist crusaders, such as Harris, Dawkins, and Hitchens, are closer to the *Chariots of the Gods* or *The Da Vinci Code* school of biblical scholarship than to that of the Jesus Seminar.

Christopher Hitchens, for example, in *God Is Not Great,* titles his chapter on Jesus "The 'New' Testament Exceeds the Evil of

A Book Atheists Want to Burn

Real Jesus, by Luke Timothy Johnson; New York: HarperOne, 1997. Johnson, a Bible scholar at Emory University, tears into the New Testament skeptics and shows them for the shallow headline chasers that they are—while affirming that the evidence confirms the traditional Christian understanding of the gospels. Want another? Try: *The New Testament Documents: Are They Reliable*, by F. F. Bruce; Grand Rapids, MI: Wm. B. Eerdmans, 2003. Bruce, a great classical scholar, comes at the question as an Evangelical, Johnson as a Catholic.

the 'Old' One." He asserts that the Gospels' "multiple authors—none of whom published anything until many decades after the Crucifixion—cannot agree on anything of importance." He finds any differences at all in the Gospels to be *ipso facto* proof that they are all complete frauds and contain nothing worth thinking about.

He says: "They flatly contradict each other on the 'Flight into Egypt,' Matthew saying that Joseph was 'warned in a dream' to make an immediate escape and Luke saying that all three stayed in Bethlehem until Mary's 'purification according to the laws of Moses,' which would make it forty days, and then went back to Nazareth via Jerusalem."[2] Elsewhere, Hitchens explains that the "contradictions and illiteracies of the New Testament have filled up many books by eminent scholars, and have never been explained by any Christian authority except in the feeblest terms of 'metaphor' and 'a Christ of faith.'"

But the reality is that the discrepancies and "inconsistences" in the four canonical Gospels, far from being an argument against their authenticity, are actually arguments for their genuine testimony. In the earliest days of the Church, the Christian community had the opportunity to publish a harmonized "one volume" account of Jesus's life and teaching with all the inconsistencies and disagreements of fact ironed out. In fact, many of these harmonizations were actually written and were quite popular. The most famous and influential was called *The Diatessaron*, probably written in Syriac around 175 AD by an Assyrian (Syriac) Christian named Tatian and used in the Syriac church for two centuries.

But when it came time for the Christian Church to officially approve those books that most accurately portray the Christian faith as it has been handed down, from teacher to disciple, over the generations, the early Christian leaders deliberately chose the four canonical Gospels (with all their "inconsistencies") rather than a neatly harmonized account. They did so because they believed the truth of who Jesus was and what he taught and did was better served by these varying accounts, with all their discrepancies, than by any attempt to try to fit them all together in a neat package.

As Brandon and others have argued, thousands, perhaps tens of thousands of people heard Jesus teach and saw his deeds. Decades after his death, there were undoubtedly thousands of "hearers of the Lord" still living. They naturally traded stories about things Jesus had done and said. Eventually, these sayings of Jesus were translated from their original Aramaic into koine Greek and gathered together into a collection or collections which modern scholars call "Q" (from the German word Quelle for source). Later, when the evangelists began their task of writing about Jesus's life and teaching, they almost certainly had access to this basic "sayings source" as well as to other, independent sources and to the various eye-witness testimonies of apostles and disciples still alive. The evangelist Luke says this explicitly, "Since many have undertaken to compile a narrative of the events that have been fulfilled among us," he says in the opening words of the Gospel—and note the words "many" and "compile"—"just as those who were eyewitnesses from the beginning and ministers of the word have handed them down to us, I, too, have decided, after investigating everything accurately anew, to write it down in an orderly sequence for you, most excellent Theophilus, so that you may realize the certainty of the teachings that you have received" (Lk 1:1–4).

In other words: Luke, at least, claims that he investigated "everything accurately anew" and drew upon the testimony of "those who were eyewitnesses from the beginning."

Most (but not all) modern scholars believe that the Gospel of Mark was likely written first, in Rome in the late 60s AD, followed by Luke in the early 70s and Matthew in the late 70s AD, and then by John sometime in the 80s AD. Liberal scholars often argue for later dates, and some conservatives argue for earlier dates. But the scholarly consensus is that Mark comes first because Luke and Matthew follow the basic order of events

The Bible in American History, Part XII

"I have just repeated word for word the oath taken by George Washington two hundred years ago, and the Bible on which I placed my hand is the Bible on which he placed his."

George H. W. Bush, on his inauguration in 1989

in Mark almost exactly, with a few minor changes (such as cleaning up poor Greek grammar), and because there are big chunks of texts that are not in Mark but are found, word for word, in both Matthew and Luke.

In piecing together the facts of Jesus's life, and drawing upon the same or similiar "sayings source" (Q), the evangelists sometimes differed as to where a particular "saying" should be put in the narrative (its setting) and sometimes modified the saying itself. The evangelists were each individuals, writing from different locations for different communities, perhaps in different languages, and each had his own "agenda" or particular points he wanted to make. Of course, Christian apologists have long pointed out that Jesus traveled from town to town all over Palestine, preaching his message and telling his parables, and it is likely that he would have repeated himself often. Thus, it's natural that some eyewitnesses would remember his saying something in one context and other witnesses might remember him saying it in another.

Anyone interested in the details of all this can see for themselves by consulting what's called a "synopsis" of the Gospels (such as the one published by the United Bible Societies and edited by Kurt Aland) that shows the accounts of Jesus's words and deeds arranged in parallel columns by Gospel. A humorous example of how the concerns of the individual evangelists can determine what they do and do not put into their version of events—and which demonstrates how so-called "critical" scholarship often strengthens the case for the authenticity of the Gospels—is the account of the woman with a hemorrhage.

According to all three of the Synoptic Gospels, when Jesus was on his way to cure the daughter of a synagogue official named Jarius, a woman who suffered from hemorrhages for years came up to him and touched him, seeking to be cured. Keeping in mind the idea that Mark probably wrote his gospel first, notice how the three versions differ slightly—and remember that, according to tradition, the evangelist Luke was a physician by trade:

Mark 5:25	Matthew 9:20	Luke 8:43
And there was a woman who had had a flow of blood for twelve years, **and who had suffered much under many physicians, and had spent all that she had, and was no better but rather grew worse.** She had heard the reports about Jesus, and came up behind him in the crowd and touched his garment.	And behold, a woman who had suffered from a hemorrhage for twelve years came up behind him and touched **the fringe of** his garment.	And a woman who had had a flow of blood for twelve years **And could not be healed by any one,** Came up behind him, and touched **the fringe of** his garment.

Minor differences, of course. But notice that the version by the alleged physician Luke removes the biting comments about how the woman had suffered under "many physicians" and had spent all she had on them but only grew worse. Also, notice how Mark, probably writing from Rome for at least some Gentiles, refers merely to Jesus's "garment" while Matthew, whose concern above all else is to show how Jesus is the fulfillment of Jewish prophecies and teaching, adds the detail about the "fringe" (Hebrew: *tzitzit*) of his garment, a reference to the traditional *tallit* or "prayer shawl" commanded in Numbers 15. It is through this kind of careful, "critical" reading of the New Testament that scholars attempt to discern the theological assumptions and emphases of the biblical writers and, through them, to discover more about who Jesus really was and what he did. In other words, we learn more looking through the eyes of four evangelists—each with his own agenda and purposes—than we would from a "harmonized" account that tried to remove the apparent contradictions and inconsistencies that skeptics so dislike.

Interestingly enough, modern scholarship is not as original, or as shocking, as modern skeptics would have people believe. Faithful Christians have always known the basic facts of how the New Testament came to be written. We have numerous (again, conflicting) accounts of how the New Testament was fashioned in the writings of early Christian theologians, such as Papias (c. 120) and Eusebius (c. 270–339). Papias, a bishop in what is now central Turkey, wrote a lost book called *Interpretations of the Sayings of the Lord* that obliquely testifies to the existence of a Q source. We no longer have his works, but the Church historian Eusebius quotes Papias's account of how the New Testament books came to be written:

> Mark having become the interpreter of Peter, wrote down accurately whatsoever he remembered. It was not, however, in exact order that he related the sayings or deeds of Christ. For he neither heard the Lord nor accompanied Him. But afterwards, as I said, he accompanied Peter, who accommodated his instructions to the necessities [of his hearers], but with no intention of giving a regular narrative of the Lord's sayings. Wherefore Mark made no mistake in thus writing some things as he remembered them. For of one thing he took especial care, not to omit anything he had heard, and not to put anything fictitious into the statements. Matthew put together the oracles

[of the Lord] in the Hebrew language, and each one interpreted them as best he could.[3]

This account actually jibes quite neatly with what many modern scholars believe. Due to the many semiticisms and Aramaic words in the Greek text of Matthew, for example, many scholars believe it was originally written in Aramaic and later translated into Greek.

The lost Gospels

A final issue when it comes to New Testament studies: The so-called "lost" Gospels. As skeptics tell it, reflecting the worldview captured in *The Da Vinci Code*, the Christian church systematically suppressed the truth about Jesus and his early disciples, "censoring" alternative accounts of Jesus's life and teaching because these texts didn't reflect the "dogma" (primarily the alleged "sexism" and "homophobia") of the institutional church. Examples of these "alternative" Gospels include the Gospel of Thomas and the Gospel of James. More recently, a Gospel of Judas was discovered and published.

The Da Vinci Code was hardly original in taking this line: In 1972, novelist Irving Wallace wrote a thriller called *The Word* that described, interspersed with lots of sex, the alleged discovery of an alternative Gospel (the Gospel of James) that would "blow the lid" off of institutional Christianity and reveal the truth that the evil church had kept hidden for millennia. In *The Word*, as in *The Da Vinci Code*, there is even a secret society that has suppressed the truth that Jesus survived the crucifixion—and a man who, "if he can survive long enough," struggles to tell the whole world what really happened.

So, is there truth to the charge? Did the Christian church "suppress" lost facts about and sayings of Jesus?

The answer of mainstream biblical scholars would be: *If only!* That's because, for two centuries now, scholars have been poring over every word of every "apocryphal" (non-canonical) Gospel available, desperately searching for a lost saying or an authentic new fact. Far from being "lost," every single apocryphal Gospel extant can be easily read in translation in such collections as *The Nag Hammadi Library* (edited by James Robinson), or in more popular anthologies such as *The Complete Gospels* (edited by Robert J. Miller) or *The Other Gospels: Non-Canonical Gospel Texts* (edited by Ron Cameron).

Alas, the results have been disappointing.

The research of such scholars as Elaine Pagels and Bart Ehrman have taught us a lot about early Gnosticism but precious little new about Jesus. The primary reason for this is because these lost, "apocryphal" Gospels were written, by and large, decades, sometimes even centuries after the canonical Gospels. They were the creation of Gnostic sects (sort of second- and third-century New Agers) that usually just followed the outlines of the canonical Gospels and simply put into the mouth of Jesus various philosophical ramblings of a particular Gnostic sect. Most of them strike modern readers as deadly dull and quite bizarre—and nothing like the canonical Gospels in vivid, real-life detail.

Here is a typical passage from the Gospel of Mary (Magdalene), a favorite with New Agers and conspiracy theorists:

> The Savior said, "All natures, all formations, all creatures exist in and with one another, and they will be resolved again into their own roots. For the nature of matter is resolved into the [roots] of its nature alone. He who has ears to hear, let him hear."

As you might guess, if the church "suppressed" these texts it was probably more for bad writing than for heresy. The simple truth is that, when the early Christian leaders looked over these various works purporting to be about the life and teaching of Jesus, they found that most had little if anything to do with the Jesus proclaimed by the Church and instead were full of bizarre Greek philosophical ideas that were alien to Jesus. That's why the church historian Eusebius, writing around 324 AD, spoke of the books that are "adduced by the heretics under the name of the apostles, such as the Gospels of Peter, Thomas, Matthew, and others beside them or such as the Acts of the Apostles by Andrew, John, and others." He

Did Jesus Really Say What the Gospels Say He Said?

What Skeptics Say: The Gospels were written between thirty and forty years after Jesus was executed on the Cross by authors who were not eyewitnesses to the events they describe. Clearly they just made things up and put words into Jesus's mouth that he didn't say. The Jesus Seminar scholars insist that less than 10 percent of the sayings of Jesus in the Gospels are authentic.

Reply: The evidence is overwhelming that the Gospel writers made use of a collection of Jesus's sayings as well as eyewitness reports of his life (Lk 1:3). The Gospels describe Jesus attracting vast crowds and there were certainly hundreds, perhaps even thousands of people still alive when the Gospels were written who had personally seen and heard Jesus. The very fact that the Gospels do not agree on all the details is further proof of multiple eyewitness reports. What's more, we've seen numerous examples in the past two centuries of important religious figures—from the Hindu saint Ramakrishna to St. Thérèse of Lisieux—whose sayings were written down by close disciples and then used later for biographies of their lives. As for the Jesus Seminar, it was a serious but somewhat sensationalistic group of liberal scholars whose methodology has been widely challenged by experts. Some of their criteria for evaluating the authenticity of Jesus's sayings are questionable to say the least. For example, they claim that if a saying of Jesus is in harmony with the beliefs of the early church, then it is probably *not* authentic—a bizarre notion that assumes that Jesus's followers quickly repudiated everything he taught. While this idea appeals to the *Da Vinci Code* school of New Testament studies, it is not taken seriously by many mainstream scholars.

added the common sense observation that "indeed the character of the style itself is very different from that of the apostles, and the sentiment and purport of those things that are advanced in them, deviating as far as possible from sound orthodoxy, evidently proves they are fictions of heretical men." These "other" Gospels, Eusebius concludes, are "spurious writings [that] are to be rejected as altogether absurd and impious."[4]

What do the earliest texts say?

So, if the "real" Jesus can't be found in the New Age ramblings of third-century Gnostic Gospels, or in the radical revisionism of Jesus Seminar intellectuals and pundits, or in the violent revolution planned by the forerunners of the Zealots, where can he be found? Perhaps in the last place many people appear to want to look: the New Testament itself.

Modern New Testament scholars have actually done a pretty good job of identifying which parts of the New Testament were written first—by correlating passages with known historical events. When they did this, however, they made a discovery that undermined two centuries worth of "certainties" about Jesus and Christianity. In the nineteenth and early twentieth centuries, liberal theologians (such as Adolf von Harnack) believed that the first followers of Jesus were pious Jews for whom Jesus was a rabbi, perhaps a prophet, but nothing more, and it was only *after* the Jesus Movement spread out into the Gentile world that his followers began using grandiose language that described Jesus as having divine or quasi-divine status. The idea was that the early Greek followers of Jesus (pagans all!) simply adapted Greek "divine man" myths to speak about Jesus. These liberal theologians believed, therefore, that the earliest Christian tradition would speak of Jesus as a simple teacher, the later writings as an exalted quasi-divine figure.

But after scholars successfully identified the lowest "strata" in the New Testament, the earliest pieces of tradition, they made a shocking discovery: The very *earliest* traditions, not just the latest, speak of Jesus as sharing in God's unique sovereignty over all things. In fact, a fairly "high" christology of Jesus permeates virtually the entire New Testament.

The British New Testament scholar Richard Bauckham names this strange, unexpected phenomenon "Christological monotheism," meaning the earliest traditions about Jesus see him sharing in the very life and wisdom and even the power of God.[5] This can be seen, Bauckham says, in a number of ways.

First, the earliest New Testament texts speak of Jesus's lordship over "all things," which is a status in Jewish thought previously allocated to God alone. Writing to the Corinthians in 55 AD or thereabouts, Paul says that Christ will destroy death itself (1 Cor 15:26).

Second, Bauckham says, Jesus shares God's exaltation above the angels. In Ephesians 1:21–22, perhaps written in 62 AD, Paul (or his scribes) say that "[God] raised [Jesus] from the dead and seated him at his right hand in the heavenly places, far above all rule and authority and power and dominion, and above every name that is named, not only in this age but also in the age to come. And he has put all things under his feet. . . ."

Third, Jesus is given the Divine Name, the Tetragrammaton (YHWH)—the name, says Bauckham, "which names the unique identity of the one God, the name which is exclusive to the one God. . . ." According to Philippians 2:9:

Christ Jesus . . . Who, though he was in the form of God

Did not regard equality with God

Something to be grasped.

Rather, he emptied himself

Taking the form of a slave. . . .

Because of this,

God greatly exalted him

And bestowed on him the name

That is above every name,

That at the name of Jesus

Every knee should bend,

Of those in heaven and on earth and under the earth

Fourth, Jesus's participation in the divine sovereignty extends even to worship. The central, unalterable truth of Israelite religion is the Shema: Hear, O Israel, the Lord our God, the Lord is One. Or as the First Commandment puts it: "You shall have no other gods beside me." Yet in the Gospel of Mark, Jesus is asked by the High Priest, "Are you the Messiah, the son of the Blessed One?" And Jesus answers:

I am, and you will see the Son of Man

Seated at the right hand of the Power

And coming with the clouds of heaven.

At this, Mark says, the high priest "tore his garments" and said, "Have we further need of witnesses? You have heard the blasphemy."

The word that the New Testament uses to express this unique incorporation of the man Jesus into the very life of God is "sonship." The way the New Testament scholar Burton Mack describes what this means is:

In Paul's mind, the Christ was now a historic person, now a son of God, a "corporate personality" representing a collective humanity, a cosmic king, a spiritual power pervading the cosmos, the hidden meaning behind the significant events of Israel's history, and the incarnation of the very mind, promise, and intention of God for humankind.... The Christ had become an overwhelming, all-encompassing symbol of the agency of a Jewish God in a Greek world.[6]

The important point to remember, however, is that these unusual, mind-boggling modifications to traditional Jewish monotheism were made, not by Greek-speaking Gentiles in far away Rome or Athens, but by the *earliest Jewish followers* of the very Jewish Jesus.

The same man who quotes the early Christological hymn in Phillipians (quoted above), the Pharisee convert Paul, brags in the very same letter that he was "circumcised on the eighth day, of the race of Israel, of the tribe of Benjamin, a Hebrew of Hebrews, in observance of the law a Pharisee" and claims he was a Jewish Zealot who studied under the great Torah scholar Gamaliel and persecuted the early followers of Jesus.

Some scholars have pointed to Semitic characteristics behind the Greek text and argue that this hymn originated from the early Jewish-Christian community at Jerusalem. This means that perhaps the earliest extant *stratum* in the New Testament, from a distinctly Jewish provenance, perhaps learned by Paul within the first five or ten years after Jesus's death in 30 AD, displays the same elevated understanding of Christ that liberal theologians used to believe came only very late, in the second century, among pagans.

The bottom line for faith

You don't have to go as far as evangelical apologists like C. S. Lewis or Josh McDowell and say that either Jesus was a madman or the Son of God because that begs the question as to whether the Gospels accurately report what Jesus *really* said or merely put words into his mouth, as modern skeptics claim and as later Gnostic writers actually did.

Are the Gospels a Cover-Up?

When Mel Gibson's film *The Passion of the Christ* was released in 2004, critics complained about the film's (and the New Testament's) potrayal of Pontius Pilate as being opposed to the Temple elite who wanted Jesus put to death. On the contrary, said the critics, the Romans completely dominated the Temple elite and told them what to do. Thus, both the Gospels themselves, and Gibson's film, are a fabrication.

Newsweek magazine, in its 2004 cover story on "Who Killed Jesus?" was typical: "To take the film's account of the Passion literally will give most audiences a misleading picture of what probably happened in those epochal hours so long ago," the magazine's editor and resident biblical scholar, Jon Meacham, wrote, with the typical certitude of the media. "Jewish priests and their followers are the villains, demanding the death of Jesus again and again; Pilate is a malleable governor forced into handing down the death sentence. In fact, in the age of Roman domination, only Rome crucified. The crime was sedition, not blasphemy—a civil crime, not a religious one. The two men who were killed along with Jesus are identified in some translations as 'thieves,' but the word can also mean 'insurgents,' supporting the idea that crucifixion was a political weapon used to send a message to those still living: beware of revolution or riot, or Rome will do this to you, too. The two earliest and most reliable extra-biblical references to Jesus—those of the historians Josephus and Tacitus—say Jesus was executed by Pilate."

But what Meacham and *Newsweek* neglect to mention is that Josephus, the first-century Jewish historian cited, actually *corroborates* the Gospel accounts of events. The actual text that Meacham refers to but does not quote says: "When Pilate, *at the suggestion of the principal men among us*, had condemned [Jesus] to the cross, those that loved him at the first did not forsake him..." (*Antiquities of the Jews*, 18.63).

While it's possible that the phrase "at the suggestion of the principal men among us" is an interpolation of later Christian scribes, it's unlikely. The Talmud also says that someone named "Yeshu" was executed, not merely as a political criminal against Rome, but for religious offenses,

although scholars don't agree if this Yeshu and Jesus (Yeshu'a in Aramaic) were one and the same: "On the eve of Passover, they hung Yeshu and the crier went forth for forty days beforehand declaring that '[Yeshu] is going to be stoned for practicing witchcraft, for enticing and leading Israel astray. Anyone who knows something to clear him should come forth and exonerate him.' But no one had anything exonerating for him and they hung him on the eve of Passover" (Sanhedrin 43a).

What's more, it is by no means clear that modern biblical scholarship refutes the Gospel version concerning Pilate. For one thing, most experts believe that the Roman garrison stationed in Caesarea was probably no more than 3,500 Greek mercenaries, the remnants of King Herod's old army. These "Sebastenians"—renamed the Ala I Sevastenorum and Cohortes I-V Sebastenorum—were supervised by a small number of Roman (Italian) legionaries. According to the Acts of the Apostles, by 40AD there was an Italian Cohort (Cohors II Italia) stationed in Caesarea which would have been at least half Italian. That would have been approximately 480 men.

The Romans depended upon the fear of their main army, of perhaps 40,000 troops, stationed a three-days' march away in Antioch, to prevent an uprising. That army had defeated Jewish rebellions in the past and would in the future. Contrary to what *Newsweek* and other instant Bible scholars assert, Pilate had good reason to be fearful of an enormous crowd of fervent, anti-Roman pilgrims. The proof of that is that thirty-six years later, when the Jews finally did rebel against Rome, they easily and quickly wiped out the entire Roman garrison!

But was it plausible, as the Gospels state and Gibson's film portrayed, that a Jewish "mob" opposed to Jesus and his movement would have dared to harangue Pilate? Is that even within the realm of possibility? Wasn't this clearly an anti-Semitic fiction made up by the early Church?

The answer is: Possibly but not necessarily. It is not only possible that crowds could have dared to importune Pilate, we know for a fact that they did, numerous times. The Jewish historian Josephus describes at least *three* incidents in which large crowds demonstrated angrily and courageously at Pilate's doorstep, sometimes successfully and others unsuccessfully.

For example, almost immediately upon taking office in 27 AD, Pilate displayed his contempt for Jewish sensibilities through a deliberately hostile and provocative act: Under cover of darkness, he ordered his auxiliary troops to bring into Jerusalem the Roman standards that carried images of the emperor, Tiberius. Previous prefects, out of deference to the Jewish religious ban on images, had kept these standards out of the holy city to avoid creating a disturbance.

But Pilate appears to have been singularly anti-Semitic and was intent on teaching the Jews who was in charge. A great multitude of Jews poured into Caesarea, demanding that the Roman standards be removed. Pilate refused. When more and more Jews streamed into the seaside city, demonstrating against Pilate's action, he signaled that he would hear the Jews' complaint in the open market. When he did, he had the crowd of Jews surrounded by soldiers and announced that, if they did not accept the Roman standards, he would have the soldiers slaughter them all to a man. Much to his surprise and consternation, however, the demonstrators merely dropped to their knees and exposed their necks to the drawn swords of the soldiers. Pilate knew that such a rampant slaughter of unarmed men, during his first year on the job, would not sit well with the emperor. As a result, despite the loss of face that it invited, he ordered the standards removed. The courage and faith of the Jewish people prevailed.

We do not know, but can perhaps surmise, that such a humiliating "defeat" at the hands of a large Jewish crowd, so early in his appointment, did not sit well with the proud Roman official. He might, in fact, be quite disinclined to do whatever a Jewish crowd might demand—if only to reassert who was "in charge."

That is why one Jewish New Testament scholar, Paula Fredriksen, insists that the Gospel account of Pilate resisting an attempt by Jewish officials to have Jesus executed—not out of compassion, as in Gibson's film, but out of orneriness—was, in fact, historically quite plausible.

The *last* thing that the proud Roman Pilate would want to do would be to instantly accede to the demands of Jewish leaders. That part of the Gospel story, in fact, makes particular sense given what we know of Pilate from Josephus.

But any fair evaluation of the historical evidence has to admit this at least: the earliest, most authentic documents we have—which are, to the chagrin of Gnostic fans everywhere, the canonical books of the New Testament—clearly claim that Jesus was something *much more* than merely a prophet or even the long-awaited Jewish messiah.

Of course, many faithful Jews then and since could not accept that, and many modern people can no longer accept it as well. But that is *precisely* what the New Testament says, at the very earliest strata of the tradition: The man Jesus of Nazareth, the carpenter of Nazareth who electrified all of Galilee and Judea with his fiery denunciations of religious hypocrisy and calls for true repentance, somehow shares in the very mind and mercy and even power of God himself.

Far from refuting that fact, the best biblical scholarship of the past century actually confirms it.

Of course, that doesn't answer the most important question of all: Whether it's true. In this, the great New Testament scholar and theologian Rudolph Bultmann was correct: from a strictly historical perspective, we can never really know what Jesus *actually* did and said but only what the Gospels *say* he did and said. The New Testament is virtually the only historical document we have. As a result, whether Jesus really is the Son of God is not a question that can be answered by "critical" biblical scholarship or archaeology. It can be *illuminated* through such scholarship, explored and debated and expanded, but not, ultimately, answered.

That is why people rarely come to faith in Christ based on a critical study of textual variants in the Gospel of Luke. Instead, they come to faith in Christ as the ultimate revelation of God primarily because they are born into, or encounter, communities of faith (which we call "churches" or "assemblies") that have preserved his memory for nearly 2,000 years.

For two millennia, the tribe that calls itself Christians has gathered together in groups—some large, some small—to hear Jesus's words,

Who Said It?

"If there is anything in my thoughts or style to commend, the credit is due to my parents for instilling in me an early love of the Scriptures."

Daniel Webster

meditate upon his deeds, and obey his last request that he be remembered in the breaking of the bread.

Across the ages, this international community has continued to pass on the memory and the testimony of who Jesus Christ was and is—from father to son, mother to daughter, catechist to student, in an unbroken chain of "apostolic succession," for generations. This faith is often communicated orally and visually, depicted in the stain glass windows of Gothic cathedrals and celebrated in songs in "rock operas." That's why you don't have to be a historian or a biblical scholar to believe in Jesus—and why the great saints and mystics of Christendom, from St. Francis of Assisi to John Wesley, Corrie ten Boom to Mother Teresa of Calcutta, knew more about who Jesus was than the hundreds of supposed experts in the Jesus Seminar.

Thus, on a practical level, deciding whether to believe the Christian testimony is less about history, archaeology, and Greek paleography than it is about our own understanding of people, the world, and our eternal destinies.

People usually decide to remain or become Christians because the story of who Jesus was, what he did, and the words he said, seem to "fit" their experience of the world. Put simply, it rings true. The Gospel stories of Jesus's encounters with sinners and sycophants, the powerful and the impoverished, seem believable—far more believable than the elaborate conspiracies and dubious reconstructions postulated by scholarly skeptics. Jesus's words of mercy and forgiveness, his challenge to live a life of integrity far beyond the minimum required by religious law, his humor and courage and simple decency, strike ordinary believers as too authentic and "real" to have been made up. That is not, as undergraduate philosophizers like Sam Harris like to say, blind faith, but rather a judgment that attends to data other than those produced by scientific instruments or the random facts we can cull from archaeology.

The simple truth is that the New Testament claims that Jesus of Nazareth is Lord of heaven and earth, the ultimate revelation of who God is and what he wants from his creation—and about one-third of the planet's population finds this credible. The snide put-downs, sophomoric arguments, and thinly veiled threats of people like Richard Dawkins, Sam Harris, Christopher Hitchens, and Penn and Teller do not impress them. Forced to choose between what the cynical media say is plausible and "scientific," and what the Bible says about Jesus, hundreds of millions of people prefer the Bible. They know Jesus, and trust him—more than all the scholars in the Jesus Seminar.

ACKNOWLEDGMENTS

y interest in the Bible was intensified by the time I lived in Israel in the late 1970s and early 1980s, when I studied Hebrew in two *ulpanim* (intensive Hebrew language schools for new immigrants). As I struggled to learn the ancient Hebrew words for such modern realities as "electricity" or "computer," I spent many months traveling all over the country on my motorcycle and got to see what Israelis call simply The Land (*ha-aretz*) up close and personal. There is nothing like going to a rock concert in the biblical Ashkelon (with the lyrics in Hebrew), or spending an afternoon lounging in seaside cafés on the Sea of Galilee, to make the ancient stories of the Bible really come alive. To this day, I will always be grateful to my wise and patient Hebrew teachers (one a German refugee from the Holocaust) who casually shared their vast erudition, and their lives, with me. I am also grateful to my wife and children who, years later, patiently endured my absences when I attended a graduate program in biblical studies and spent many hours away from home, in seminars or dusty libraries. Finally, I would like to thank Harry Crocker of Regnery who, out of the blue, asked me if I would like to write this book, as well as Miriam Moore, my patient editor.

Robert Hutchinson

September 2007

NOTES

Chapter One:

Why Do the Heathens Rage?

1. Aaron Christensen, "Celsus and Modern Anti-Mormonism," The Foundation for Apologetic Information and Research. Http://www.fairlds.org.

2. Porphyry, "Against the Christians" (fragments), Internet Medieval Sourcebook, Fordham University Center for Medieval Studies. Http://www.fordham.edu/halsall/sbook.html.

3. Christopher Hitchens, *God Is Not Great* (New York: Twelve Books, 2007), 104.

4. Robert Reich, "Bush's God," *The American Prospect*, July 1, 2004. Available online at: http://www.prospect.org/web/page.ww?section=root&name= ViewPrint&articleId=7858.

5. "U.S. and World Population Clocks," U.S. Census Bureau, http://www.census.gov/main/www/popclock.html.

6. "World," The World Fact Book, Central Intelligence Agency, updated July 19, 2007. Https://www.cia.gov/library/publications/the-world-fact-book/eos/xx.htm/#people.

7. Published online at: http://www.anti-naturals.org/15cst/no19/p1.htm.

8. Gordy Slack, "The Atheist," Salon.com. Http://dir.salon.com/story/news/feature/2005/04/30/dawkins/index.html.

9. Michael Weisskopf, *Washington Post*, February 1, 1993.

10. Sam Harris, *Letter to a Christian Nation* (New York: Knopf, 2006), 23.

11. R. J. Rummel, "Power Kills," University of Hawaii, http://www.hawaii.edu/powerkills/20TH.HTM.

12. "World War II: In Depth," United States Holocaust Memorial Museum. Http://www.ushmm.org/wlc/article.php?lang=en&ModuleId=10007314.

13. Richard Dawkins, *The God Delusion* (New York: Houghton Mifflin, 2006), 278.

Chapter Two:

The Stones Cry Out

1. Ammiel Hirsch, "Bible Criticism," SimpleToRemember.com. Http://www.simpletoremember.com/vitals/Bible_criticism.htm.

2. George A. Barton, *Archaeology and the Bible*, Seventh Edition, 460–461.

3. *Time*, December 18, 1995 Volume 146, No. 25.

4. David Perlman, "A Judgment About Soloman," *San Francisco Chronicle*, April 11, 2003. Http://www.sfgate.com/cgi-bin/article.cgi?f=/chronicle/a/2003/04/11/MN24970.DTL.

5. Shanks, Hershel. "Fingerprint of Jeremiah's Scribe," *Biblical Archeology Review* 2 (1996): 36–38.

6. "Jerusalem Tunnel Dates to King Hezekiah," *Christian Century*, October 4, 2003. Http://www.findarticles.com/p/articles/mi_m1058/is_20_120/ai_109132342.

7. Daniel Lazare, "False Testament," *Harper's*, March 2002. Http://www.worldagesarchive.com/Reference_Links/False_Testament_(Harpers).htm.

8. Teresa Watanabe, "Doubting the Story of Exodus," *Los Angeles Times*, April 13, 2001. Http://www.raceandhistory.com/historicalviews/doubtingexodus.htm.

9. "Amarna Letters*,*" *The Anchor Bible Dictionary* (New York: Doubleday, 1992), Vol. 1, 174 ff.

10. K. A. Kitchen, *On the Reliability of the Old Testament* (Grand Rapids, MI: Wm. B. Eerdmans Publishing, 2006), 311.

Chapter Three:
All Scripture Is God-Breathed

1. Mircea Eliade, *A History of Religious Ideas: From the Stone Age to the Eleusinian Mysteries*, Vol. 1 (Chicago: University of Chicago Press, 1978), 205.

2. Yehezkel Kaufmann, *The Religion of Israel: From its Beginnings to the Babylonian Exile* (New York: Schocken Books, 1960), 60. This is a translation and abridgement of Kaufmann's eight-volume masterpiece, *Toledot ha-Emunah ha-Israelit* (Tel Aviv: Bialik Institute-Dvir, 1937–56).

Chapter Five:
Be Fruitful and Multiply

1. John Shelby Spong, *The Sins of Scripture: Exposing the Bible's Texts of Hate to Reveal the God of Love* (San Francisco: HarperSanFrancisco, 2005), 75.

2. The Talmudic sages, debating in the first centuries after Christ, knew all about various birth control methods and forbade most of them, including the use of a contraceptive sponge, except in cases involving girls under the age of twelve, pregnant women, and nursing mothers (Nedarim 35b).

3. Quoted by Phillip Longman in "The Return of Patriarchy," *Foreign Policy*, March 2006.

4. Naphtali Lewis, *Life in Egypt Under Roman Rule* (Oakville, CT: David Brown Book Company, 1999), 54.

5. Moralia 2.17.

6. Histories, 5.5. Link to: http://classics.mit.edu/Tacitus/histories.5.v.html.

7. Lectures on Genesis, quoted by Alan Carlson, Ph.D., "The Protestant Sellout on Contraception," June 1999, http://www.profam.org/docs/acc/thc_acc_sellout.htm.

8. Ibid.

9. *Birth Control Review* (October 1921), 5. Quoted in Robert Marshall and Charles Donovan, *Blessed Are the Barren: The Social Policy of Planned Parenthood* (San Francisco: Ignatius Press, 1991), 9.

10. Margaret Sanger, *The Woman Rebel*, reprinted in *Woman and the New Race 1* (1922). Cited by Michael J. Smith, "The Public Policy of Casey v. Planned Parenthood," http://www.leaderu.com/humanities/casey/ch4.html.

Chapter Six:

In the Image and Likeness of God

1. R. A. Torrey, *The Fundamentals: The Famous Sourcebook of Foundational Biblical Truths* (Grand Rapids: Kregel Publications, 1958), 613.

2. Richard Dawkins, *The Blind Watchmaker: Why the Evidence of Evolution Reveals a Universe Without Design* (New York: W.W. Norton & Company, 1987), 287.

3. "Statistics and Trends," Generous Giving, http://www.generousgiving.org/page.asp?sec=4&page=161#300.

4. Arthur C. Brooks, "Religious Faith and Charitable Giving," *Policy Review*, The Hoover Institution. Http://www.policyreview.org/oct03/ brooks.html.

Chapter Seven:

Keep My Commandments

1. Ronald L. Eisenberg, *The 613 Mitzvat* (Rockville, MD: Schreiber Publishing, 2005), 195.

2. William Blackstone, *Commentaries*, http://www.constitution.org/tb/tb-1102.htm.

Chapter Eight:

Sodom and Gomorrah

1. Peter J. Gomes, *The Good Book: Reading the Bible with Mind and Heart* (New York: William Morrow & Company, 1996), 158.

2. John U. McNeill, S.J., *The Church and the Homosexual* (Mission, KS: Sheed Andrews and McMeel, 1976), 55.

3. David F. Greenberg, *The Construction of Homosexuality* (Chicago: University of Chicago Press, 1990)

4. Dennis Prager, "Judaism's Sexual Revolution: Why Judaism (and Then Christianity) Rejected Homosexuality," *Crisis* 11, no. 8 (September 1993), 25–32.

5. Against Apion 2.199.

6. William F. Arndt and F. Wilbur Gingrich, translators and editors, *A Greek-English Lexicon of the New Testament and Other Early Christian Literature*, 2nd Edition (Chicago: University of Chicago Press, 1952), 489.

7. John Boswell, *Christianity, Social Tolerance, and Homosexuality* (Chicago: University of Chicago Press, 1981), 106.

8. Ibid., 341.

9. Joseph Fitzmyer, S. J., *Romans* (New York: Doubleday, 1992), 288.

10. Robert A. J. Gagnon, *The Bible and Homosexual Practice* (Nashville: Abingdon Press, 2001), 194.

Chapter Nine:
The Heavens Declare the Glory of God

1. Bertrand Russell, *The Faith of a Rationalist* (Girard, KS: Haldeman-Julius Publications, 1947), 208.

2. *Confessions*, Book 7, Chapter 5.

3. Lao Tsu, *Tao Te Ching*, translated by Gia-Fu Feng and Jane English (New York: Random House, 1972), No. 32.

4. Sir Isaac Newton, *Mathematical Principles of Natural Philosophy* (Chicago: Encyclopaedia Britannica, 1952), Great Books Volume 34, 370.

5. Rodney Stark, *For the Glory of God: How Monotheism Led to Reformations, Science, Witch-Hunts, and the End of Slavery* (Princeton: Princeton University Press, 2003), 170–172.

6. G. S. Viereck, *Glimpses of the Great* (New York: Macauley, 1930), 186. Http://www.einsteinandreligion.com/spinoza.html.

Chapter Ten:
You Were Called to Freedom

1. *Histories*, Book IX, 10.

2. Taken *from Essays, Moral and Political* (1742), quoted in Isaac Kramnick, editor, *The Portable Enlightenment Reader* (New York: Penguin Books, 1995), 629.

3. Ibid., 637.

4. "We know many among ourselves who have given themselves up to bonds, in order that they might ransom others. Many, too, have surrendered themselves to slavery, that with the price which they received for themselves, they might provide food for others."

5. Http://guweb2.gonzaga.edu/againsthate/Journal2/GHS109.PDF.

6. Rodney Stark, *For the Glory of God: How Monotheism Led to Reformations, Science, Witch-Hunts, and the End of Slavery* (Princeton, NJ: Princeton University Press, 2003), 291.

Chapter Eleven:
Endowed by Their Creator with Certain Unalienable Rights

1. Quoted in Michael Novak, *On Two Wings: Humble Faith and Common Sense at the American Founding* (San Francisco: Encounter Books, 2002), 37.

2. Commentaries on the Laws of England, Section 2. Http://www.constitution.org/tb/tb-1102.htm.

Chapter Twelve:
Put Not Your Trust in Princes

1. Quoted in Gary T. Amos, *Defending the Declaration: How the Bible and Christianity Influenced the Writing of the Declaration of Independence* (Brentwood, TN: Wolgemuth & Hyatt, 1989).

2. *Summa Theologica.*

Chapter Thirteen:
Who Do You Say That I Am?

1. "The best argument I know for *the highly questionable existence of Jesus* is this," he writes in *God Is Not Great* (emphasis added). "His illiterate living disciples left us no record and in any event could not have been 'Christians.' Since they were never to read those later books in which Christians must affirm belief, and in any case had no idea that anyone would ever found a church on their master's announcements" (114). At other places, however, Hitchens concedes that there are "oblique reason[s] for thinking that some such personality may at some time have lived" (118).

2. Ibid., 111.

3. Eusebius, *Ecclesiastical History*, Book 3, Chapter 39. This translation comes from http://www.seanmultimedia.com/Pie_Fragments_of_Papias.html. Another translation is available in Eusebius' *Ecclesiastical History*, translated by C. F. Cruse (Peabody, MA: Hendrickson Publishers, 1998), 105.

4. *Ecclesiastical History*, Book 3, Chapter 25.

5. Richard Bauckham, *God Crucified: Monotheism & Christology in the New Testament* (Grand Rapids, MI: Eerdmans, 1998), 25.

6. Burton Mack, *Who Wrote the New Testament?* (New York: Harper One, 1996), 144–145.

INDEX